EXPERT SYSTEMS IN BUSINESS:
A Practical Approach

ELLIS HORWOOD BOOKS IN INFORMATION TECHNOLOGY
General Editor: Dr. JOHN M. M. PINKERTON, Principal, McLean Pinkerton Associates, Surrey (formerly Manager of Strategic Requirements, ICL)

EXPERT SYSTEMS IN BUSINESS: A Practical Approach
M. BARRETT, Expertech Limited, Slough, and A. C. BEEREL, Lysia Limited, London
ELECTRONIC DATA PROCESSING, Vols. 1 and 2*
M. BECKER, R. HABERFELLNER and G. LIEBETRAU, Zurich, Switzerland
EXPERT SYSTEMS: Strategic Implications and Applications
A. C. BEEREL, Lysia Limited, London
SOFTWARE ENGINEERING ENVIRONMENTS
P. BRERETON, Department of Computer Science, University of Keele
SMART CARDS: Their Principles, Practice and Applications*
R. BRIGHT, Information Technology Strategies International Limited, Orpington, Kent
PRACTICAL MACHINE TRANSLATION*
D. CLARKE and U. MAGNUSSON-MURRAY, Department of Applied Computing and Mathematics, Cranfield Institute of Technology, Bedford
KNOWLEDGE-BASED SYSTEMS: Implications for Human–Computer Interfaces
D. CLEAL, PA Computers and Telecommunications, London, and N. HEATON, Central Computer and Telecommunications Agency, London
KNOWLEDGE-BASED MANAGEMENT SUPPORT SYSTEMS
G. I. DOUKIDIS, F. LAND and G. MILLER, Information Management Department, London Business School
KNOWLEDGE ENGINEERING FOR EXPERT SYSTEMS
M. GREENWELL, Expert Systems International, Oxford
KNOWLEDGE-BASED EXPERT SYSTEMS IN INDUSTRY
J. KRIZ, Head of AI Group, Brown Boveri Research Systems, Switzerland
ARTIFICIAL INTELLIGENCE: Current Applications*
A. MATTHEWS and J. RODDY, Aregon International Ltd., London
INFORMATION TECHNOLOGY: An Overview*
J. M. M. PINKERTON, McLean Pinkerton Associates, Esher, Surrey
EXPERT SYSTEMS IN THE ORGANISATION: An Introduction for Decision-Makers*
S. SAVORY, Nixdorf Computers AG, FRG
BUILDING EXPERT SYSTEMS: Cognitive Emulation
P. E. SLATTER, Telecomputing plc, Oxford
SPEECH AND LANGUAGE-BASED COMMUNICATION WITH MACHINES: Towards the Conversational Computer
J. A. WATERWORTH and M. TALBOT, Human Factors Division, British Telecom Research Laboratories, Ipswich

* In preparation

EXPERT SYSTEMS IN BUSINESS:
A Practical Approach

MICHAEL L. BARRETT
Consultant Knowledge Engineer
Expertech Limited, Slough

and

ANNABEL C. BEEREL
Director, Lysia Limited, London

ELLIS HORWOOD LIMITED
Publishers · Chichester

Halsted Press: a division of
JOHN WILEY & SONS
New York · Chichester · Brisbane · Toronto

First published in 1988 by
ELLIS HORWOOD LIMITED
Market Cross House, Cooper Street,
Chichester, West Sussex, PO19 1EB, England
The publisher's colophon is reproduced from James Gillison's drawing of the ancient Market Cross, Chichester.

Distributors:

Australia and New Zealand:
JACARANDA WILEY LIMITED
GPO Box 859, Brisbane, Queensland 4001, Australia

Canada:
JOHN WILEY & SONS CANADA LIMITED
22 Worcester Road, Rexdale, Ontario, Canada

Europe and Africa:
JOHN WILEY & SONS LIMITED
Baffins Lane, Chichester, West Sussex, England

North and South America and the rest of the world:
Halsted Press: a division of
JOHN WILEY & SONS
605 Third Avenue, New York, NY 10158, USA

South-East Asia
JOHN WILEY & SONS (SEA) PTE LIMITED
37 Jalan Pemimpin # 05–04
Block B, Union Industrial Building, Singapore 2057

Indian Subcontinent
WILEY EASTERN LIMITED
4835/24 Ansari Road
Daryaganj, New Delhi 110002, India

© **1988 M. L. Barrett and A. C. Beerel/Ellis Horwood Limited**

British Library Cataloguing in Publication Data
Barrett, Michael L. (Michael Leslie), *1958–*
Expert systems in business.
1. Business firms. Applications of expert systems
I. Title   II. Beerel, Annabel C. (Annabel Constance), *1953–*
658'.05633

Library of Congress Card No. 88–3218

ISBN 0–7458–0269–9 (Ellis Horwood Limited)
ISBN 0–470–21083–4 (Halsted Press)

Phototypeset in Times by Ellis Horwood Limited
Printed in Great Britain by Unwin Bros., Woking

Table of contents .

Preface

Expert systems are a phenomenon in computing. For the first time, computers are being used to assist a person's thinking rather than merely providing information to think about. Expert systems provide the chance to be a little wiser, not just better informed.

Despite the widespread interest in expert systems, the pool of people who have successfully built even one expert system is still small. This book aims to help those who would make use of expert systems, but as yet have little experience of their own.

The book is firmly rooted in practical experience. Both the authors are actively involved in building and using expert systems in their daily lives. One is involved mainly as a domain expert in the area of finance, and the other as a knowledge engineer who has built a wide range of expert systems over the past five years.

The authors have attempted to distil the lessons of their own experience and that of their colleagues, and to convey these lessons in a form which will be useful to others. Therefore the work is clearly based on an empirical knowledge of building expert systems, and not on any claimed theoretical advances. In the same spirit, we make no apology for concentrating on expert systems which are practical to build now, and which can provide deliverable benefits for business. We have recommended definite actions wherever possible, and have avoided debating those issues which are still the subject of research.

The principal aims are as follows:

— to provide a broad understanding of what expert systems are and how they can be applied, in terms which are relevant to business;
— to identify the business benefits that can be obtained, and where the limitations are; we regard this as an essential part of a practical expert systems book;
— to show how expert systems differ from conventional computer systems, and also where they can work together; there are messages here for data processing and expert systems professionals as well as business managers;
— to provide a step-by-step strategy for identifying potential expert system applications and deciding if they are likely to be profitable;
— to explain the technology in a clear but technically sound manner,

bringing out the practical implications for managers and system developers;

— to show how to identify the right experts and knowledge engineers to build the system; this is critical to the success of a project but has been neglected before;

— to give a detailed account of knowledge engineering in practice, including how to overcome many common problems; whereas most accounts describe procedures, this focuses on what the knowledge engineer actually does and how he must behave;

— to provide an insight into how experts participate in an expert system project, and how they can accomplish their tasks; we believe the presentation of these views to be unique;

— to give specific guidance on how to manage projects successfully, showing the important differences from conventional software methods;

— to show how an organisation can get started in expert systems and achieve early returns.

The book is divided into six parts. Part I provides a brief background to expert systems, concentrating on those aspects which are relevant to business. Part II shows where the business benefits of expert systems lie, and how they can be obtained. This includes specific guidance on identifying potential applications and deciding if they will be profitable. Part III gives a concise introduction to the technology, and Part IV covers computer hardware and software tools. Part V is a unique guide to building expert systems, including details of how a system builder carries out his task and the role of the expert who provides the knowledge. Finally, Part VI summarises the key points for business and indicates the way forward.

We have aimed to provide a handbook for those who will be directly involved with expert systems projects — be they management or users, technical people or subject experts — which will guide them to successfully building, using, and exploiting expert systems.

Note. For reasons of fluency we have referred to individuals as 'he' or 'him' throughout the book. This does not mean that expert systems is a purely male preserve! 'She' or 'her' can be freely substituted.

ACKNOWLEDGEMENTS

This book would have been much the poorer without the help of friends and colleagues who were willing to discuss their experiences, and to help us clarify our ideas. However, responsibility for the views expressed and any errors therein must remain our own.

Alex d'Agapeyeff has been a partiuclar source of inspiration. He was the first to identify the enormous potential of sharing expertise via expert systems, a concept which has only recently been accepted by many professionals in the field. He continues to be valued source of insight and provocative ideas.

We are also grateful to the knowledge engineers at Expertech Ltd, and those customers who press forward with delivering practical expert systems. We have benefited greatly from their collective experience. Special thanks are due to Mike Keen, a senior knowledge engineer with Expertech, for his detailed comments on the knowledge engineering sections. His questioning, cajoling, and irrepressible enthusiasm have led to many half-formed ideas being crystallised and new ones being generated.

Lastly, Mike Barrett would like to thank his wife, Philippa, for tolerating more than the usual neglect whilst this book was being prepared.

Part I
Setting the context

1

Introduction

1.1 WHAT THIS BOOK IS ABOUT

This book provides a self-contained guide to designing, building, and applying expert systems which exploit the accumulated experience of experts. The aim of these expert systems is not to produce an 'intelligent' computer, but rather to provide an assistant which will help the human user to perform that much better.

Expert systems represent a major step forward in terms of what a computer can do to assist human performance. For the first time, computers can now contribute directly to man's thinking and decision making efforts, rather than just handling the data which provide input to those decisions. In terms of their utility, expert systems have been likened to the coming of the automobile — 'wheels for the mind' (Feigenbaum and McCorduck, 1984). Since 1982 we have seen the emergence of expert systems out of the era when they had to be hand-built by craftsman. Mass production is on its way. Low cost expert system products are already selling in some quantity, even if mass popularity equivalent to the Ford Model T has yet to be achieved. Cars gave us physical mobility, whereas expert systems give an intellectual mobility, and we can expect corresponding changes in our working lives.

The purpose of this book is to equip business people with the knowledge to be able to exploit expert systems for themselves. This begins with the priorities of top management, and goes through to practical details of the building process. The focus is on using expert systems in industry and commerce, not on distant promises being pursued by research. The key questions being answered here are:

- Are expert systems of use to me?
- How can I identify profitable applications of expert systems?
- How should I go about designing, building, and using such systems?

Throughout the book, the emphasis is on systems which can give real benefits to the solving of business problems. It will be shown that these are systems which aim to help people to perform better, not to replace one or more of their functions. The day when a computer can completely replace a human is as far off as ever.

The book is based on experiences which have been gained on expert systems projects, both by the authors and by others kind enough to contribute their insights. Like most human activities, building an expert system is not amenable to a fixed procedure which will guarantee success every time. If that were so, then building an expert system would be little more than a clerical task. In reality, building successful expert systems is demanding, and requires skill. However, there are practical guidelines derived from experience. These correspond to the sort of advice that a skilled expert systems builder would give when faced with a real-life situation. It is the aim of this book to convey these guidelines along with sufficient background knowledge for them to be successfully applied.

1.2 AN HISTORICAL INTRODUCTION

The prospect of making something with an intelligence of its own is fascinating. In her book *Machines who think*, McCorduck (1979) suggests that the concept was described as long ago as 850 BC. In Homer's *Iliad*, Hephaestus, the God of fire and the divine smith, was said to be able to animate the objects he made. Among other occupations he forged the android Talos, a bronze warrior who defended the beaches of Crete by hurling boulders at would-be raiders. More recently, the irksome products of the Sirius Cybernetics Corporation are familiar to millions, for example the lift controller which would discuss with you which floor would be best, rather than taking you to the one you selected. It is also possible that the obvious fascination of home computers for young children lies in the computer's apparent ability to do something of its own accord.

However, there is also a more dignified side: the scientific effort to build machines which in some way could be called intelligent. This is the discipline of 'artificial intelligence', and it is the parent of expert systems. The 'child' has proved to be wilful, and has carved out a commercial presence far greater than the parent. A summary of relevant history serves to illustrate some of its special strengths and weaknesses.

In the 1950s it was accepted fact in scientific circles that humans were effective at making decisions because they were clever. In other words, they had a basic ability to solve problems which could be applied to whatever task was urgent at the time. It seemed obvious that if we were to build an intelligent machine, then it had to perform in some way like the human mind. Therefore the path to an artificial intelligence was to build a device which reproduced the general-purpose problem solving ability which humans were supposed to have.

The idea of a generalised problem solver was very attractive to computer scientists, and attempts were made to build one starting in the late 1950s. An outstanding team (Newell, Shaw and Simon) built a system called the General Problem Solver, known as GPS. Although it was able to solve some elegant problems in mathematics and logic, GPS became completely bogged down even in simple real-life problems. With hindsight, the difficulty is obvious. General-purpose problem solving methods have no way of deciding which avenues of investigation are promising for the particular task in hand, and which are not. Since there are an enormous number of ways of approaching even simple, everyday problems, GPS had an impossible task.

Problem-solving computer programs made little headway until there was a change of approach. The revised view can be summarised by the saying 'in the knowledge lies the power' — the problem solving power at least. In the 1970s a group of workers from the Heuristic Programming Project at Stanford University, California, led by Professor Ed Feigenbaum, set out to build high performance decision making programs. They took as their basis that high performance came from applying large quantities of relevant knowledge. And they were very successful. For the first time, they were able to produce computer programs which were comparable with human experts, i.e. the expert system reached a correct answer about as often as the human expert. The developers chose highly specialised subjects such as chemical analysis and treating particular medical conditions. With sufficient development, they were even able to show that the programs could out-perform the world's best experts on a one-to-one comparison. As will become clear, this level of performance is not at all typical of business expert systems, but Dendral (chemistry) and Mycin (medicine) are still among the most quoted expert systems in the world (see Appendix B).

Rather like the 4-minute mile, once one group had shown it could be done then many others would follow. Thus the basis of modern expert systems was laid. The very term 'expert system' was coined to describe these programs which performed as expert consultants. The key ingredients for success were:

— clear limits on the problem area to be tackled,
— reasoning methods which worked well for that area (irrespective of how general they were), and
— plenty of high-class knowledge.

Expert systems derive their power from applying relevant, practical knowledge. The niceties of the reasoning process are secondary. It is still the case that the reasoning used by expert systems is hopelessly primitive compared with that of human beings.

The rise of expert systems in the late 1970s was also fuelled by technology. Computer processing power and memory sizes were soaring, and improved programming methods enabled large and complex systems to be built. In fact, the push from artificial intelligence workers provided several developments in software which we now take for granted on business computers. Expert systems were also entering the commercial arena, for example another famous system called Prospector which helped with mineral prospecting.

Most of this work took place in the USA. The Lighthill report of 1969 effectively stopped all UK Government funding for artificial intelligence work throughout the 1970s. Only isolated groups survived, notably the robotics work at Edinburgh University under Professor Donald Michie.

Then in 1982 the Japanese government made its announcement. They unveiled a bold plan to build a so-called 'Fifth Generation' computer (Fig. 1.1). This would be a giant stride forward, not only in technology, but also in its capabilities. A Fifth Generation computer would be able to hold a conversation, 'see' objects, and adapt itself to new tasks (Moto-oka, 1982). It would also have memory and reasoning capabilities way beyond any computer in existence then or now. The Japanese also laid out a project plan, and set up an agency called ICOT to recruit staff and begin the work. They appeared to mean it.

Naturally, an intense research effort would be called for. Fundamental advances would be needed in several basic technologies. The Japanese government invited international collaboration.

The world refused.

Both the US and European governments reacted defensively, setting up their own programmes to develop advanced computer systems. Critics suggested that the Japanese were intent on dominating the information industries of the 1990s and beyond, in the way that they already dominated industries such as automobiles, cameras and consumer electronics. Artificial intelligence and expert systems became a national concern. In the UK, the Alvey programme (1982 to 1987) sponsored some 250 projects. Seven major projects were funded which were intended to force the technological pace. It appears that none of these produced deliverable products, but they did provide a major stimulus for collaboration between industry and academia. In the USA, the defence agency DARPA continues to invest large sums in expert systems and machine intelligence, usually of the most advanced kind. A group of US industrial companies has also established the Microelectronics and Computer Center (MCC) to develop new technologies. The European Community has an ongoing programme on a broader front known as Esprit, to be followed by Framework.

The other effect of the Japanese Fifth Generation plan was to stimulate much broader commercial interest in expert systems. In the rush to gain an advantage, corporations invested millions of dollars in research and development projects in the early 1980s. All too often these did not yield a usable computer system: the tasks selected were too ambitious and/or the sponsor's expectations had been built too high. Even today, expert systems suppliers are not always sufficiently careful to clarify the difference between research goals and that which can be achieved with existing technology. Predictably, the euphoria could not last. During 1986 there was a clear downturn in the fortunes of specialist artificial intelligence companies in the USA.

However, there has always been a more realistic (less ambitious) body of work on expert systems, particularly in the UK. In summary, this less ambitious approach seeks to capitalise on what can be done relatively easily rather than to pursue the holy grail of 'intelligent' computers. The distinction is obviously important. Business problems require solutions which can be used within the constraints of running a business. By contrast, research is concerned with developing the theory without much regard for constraints.

Generation	Built from	Programmed using
1st	Vacuum tubes	Soldering iron
2nd	Transistors	Machine-level instructions
3rd	Integrated circuits ('silicon chips')	'High level' languages, still using machine concepts
4th	Large/very large scale integrated circuits (LSI/VLSI)	Improved high-level languages
5th	Even larger scale integrated circuits? New materials?	Human oriented languages?

Computers are now being built using 4th generation technology, although 3rd generation machines will be in use for many years.

Fig. 1.1 — Computer generations.

Our purpose here is to bring out the business-oriented approach rather than the theoretical one.

1.3 ARTIFICAL INTELLIGENCE AND EXPERT SYSTEMS

The phrase 'artificial intelligence' is often associated with work on expert systems, without clarifying the distinction between the two ideas. Perhaps the greatest harm is done by implying that computer programs actually have 'intelligence' at all! For business, the key point is that artificial intelligence is a research discipline, whereas expert systems are a commercial reality, and can produce benefits today. Business managers need to be aware of the gulf between the goals of artificial intelligence and the practicality of what expert systems can deliver. We can define the two disciplines in everyday terms as follows:

Artificial intelligence:
'The attempt to build machines which carry out tasks that would be considered to require intelligence if performed by a human.'

Expert systems:
'The construction of computer programs which can solve problems that would otherwise require a human expert.'

It can be seen that artificial intelligence is the broader description. It encompasses all aspects of human behaviour, whereas expert systems focus on the intellectual task of problem solving.

Artificial intelligence research includes efforts to emulate a wide range of human activities. For example:

— speech understanding, e.g. extracting meaning from a phrase or sentence spoken into a microphone;
— machine vision, e.g. recognising objects which are in the view of a video camera or in a photograph;
— robotics, e.g. developing mechanical arms with human-like dexterity;
— planning, e.g. enabling a vehicle such as a Mars rover to choose its own route.

Considerable progress is required before any of these become a commercial reality. There are isolated successes, for example a vision-guided welding machine, but there is still a vast gulf between these systems and human capabilities. It is ironic that physical activities such as grasping an object can be done by humans without conscious thought, but are among the hardest problems for artificial intelligence.

Expert systems are a commercial spin-off from artificial intelligence work. They are usually thought of as being applied to *difficult* or *complex* problems. The complexity lies in the vast number of possible solutions, and in the subtlety of the reasoning required to reach a good solution. The contribution of an expert system is that expert knowledge is encapsulated in a computerised 'reasoning' system which allows users to solve complex problems without the personal benefit of the expert's experience or hindsight.

Expert systems have the following key features:

• they contain practical knowledge from a human expert,
• the knowledge is explicit and has not been encoded into a non-human form,
• they are natural in operation, i.e. comprehensible to people, and
• they are able to explain their reasoning on demand.

The knowledge in an expert system comes from human experts. It reflects the practical problem-solving methods which the expert has found to be effective. It is important that this is not a theoretical knowledge, since the computer has no understanding and will not be able to apply it. An analogy is with teaching a child how to cross the road. You tell them what to do when they want to cross. You do not instruct them in vehicle dynamics, lines of sight, acoustics, etc. and expect them to work it out for themselves. Expert systems are the same.

To say that the knowledge is explicit means that both the developers and the users should be able to read it, to understand it, and to modify it without difficulty. Indeed, if a system being examined does not display these qualities, then it is likely that it is not an expert system at all. This is in stark contrast to a conventional computer program where the knowledge being used is converted into a form suitable only for computers, not for people.

Having the knowledge explicit frees an expert system from many of the constraints of normal computer programming.

Because an expert system applies the knowledge of a human expert, it should emulate the reasoning of the expert if faced with the same task. The reasoning used on the computer is primitive compared with that of the human, but at least the steps taken by the expert system should be understandable.

Lastly, all expert systems are able to explain what they are attempting to do, and how they have reached their conclusions. Since the expert system is applying expert knowledge, the reasoning can be explained in terms of that knowledge. For example, if the user asks 'Why are you asking that question?', then the expert system can reply with a message to the effect 'Because I am trying to establish a particular conclusion using this piece of knowledge.'

1.4   THE RELEVANCE FOR BUSINESS

Man's ability to solve complex problems is his most important asset. Over a sustained period, scientists have attempted to emulate some part of this ability using computers. However, the goal of an artificial intelligence remains as elusive as ever.

Expert systems are a practical spin-off from this research, a response to the business world which demands profitable applications and deliverable solutions. The key to success lies in exploiting the knowledge of human experts within the computer system, rather than depending on special abilities within the system itself. Despite primitive reasoning (by human standards) these systems are able to solve problems which are beyond the reach of scientific methods, such is the power of human expert knowledge.

Partly because of their exotic heritage, expert systems might be accused of being a 'solution looking for a problem', a view which can generate opposition to any form of change. Expert systems undoubtedly represent a change in the way that computers can be used in problem-solving, and it is a stride forward. Instead of just transforming data from one form to another, they can now assist with its interpretation and the resulting choice of action. Expert systems can be adopted as powerful problem-solving tools for everyday use, and indeed this is already happening in major organisations around the world.

The most important assets in any organisation are the people who are dedicated to furthering its objectives. The success of the whole enterprise depends on how effectively these individuals carry out their tasks. Herein lies the great contribution that expert systems can make. Expert systems can harness the knowledge of skilled people within the organisation, and enable the rest of the organisation to gain by making more skilful decisions themselves. The business benefits are obtained by combining the understanding of a human user with the knowledge and speed of an 'expert' computer assistant. This book explores how that can be achieved.

2

Expert systems

2.1 THE ROLE OF EXPERT SYSTEMS IN BUSINESS

Expert systems are computer programs which aim to replicate the reasoning of an expert in solving fairly complex real-world problems, where lessons learnt from experience play an important part.

Expert systems are concerned with the problem-solving aspects of human expertise. They aim to reproduce the reasoning and analytical abilities of a human expert, in such a way that the users of the expert system can apply that expertise themselves. The system takes the role of a coach or an assistant, providing guidance and suggestions about the problem in hand.

It is important to stress that the expert system cannot be expected to replace an expert. Firstly, there is great difficulty in equalling the quality of reasoning leading up to an expert's decision. Secondly, humans have powers of analogy, intuition and creativity, plus a broad knowledge of the world and a sense of what is reasonable as a decision. All of these are completely lacking in computers.

What the expert system does provide is access to the lessons of experience concerning a specific topic. It is a reservoir of lessons already learnt, possibly by several people, which can be brought to the aid of inexperienced staff. What the user receives is:

— guidance on how an expert would approach the task,
— access to the knowledge that the expert would be using, and possibly
— specific suggestions as to what to do.

It may be thought that a written document could achieve these aims without the inconvenience of using a computer. This is not so. Firstly it is well known that reading a manual is a course of last resort, as witnessed by the adage:

> when all else fails
> then read the instructions

This is no accident — real expertise is rarely written down (see section 3.2). Manuals do not help the user with 'experience on tap': expert systems do. Additionally, people respond much more strongly to the interactive nature of an expert system — ideally it should be as if they can watch the expert at work. The expert system will also submit to endless cross-examination, experimentation and repeated sessions. Furthermore, the developing expert system is itself the best means of clarifying the expert's own knowledge (see section 11.4). Since experts cannot completely describe what they do, there may be no other practicable way of obtaining the expertise.

Expert systems obviously bring the attributes of computerisation. They are objective, they will work tirelessly, they never ignore or overlook an issue, they provide consistent and impartial guidance, and they are easy to replicate. On the other hand they are constrained by the fact that they are inanimate. They have no common sense, they cannot 'put things into context', they have no access to emotional or non-verbal signals from the user, they do not learn from experience, and have no knowledge of 'self' and their environment.

	Human quality	Computer quality
Advantages of the computer		
Knowledge	Perishable	Permanent
Consistency	Variable	Total
Cost	Expensive	Affordable
Processing	Slow	Fast
Stamina	Limited	Endless
Reproduction	Slow	Easily replicated
Advantages of the human		
Knowledge	Evolves	Static
Adaptability	Remarkable	Nil
Empathy	Perceptive	Obtuse
Processing	Multiple	Singular
Expertise	Creative	Uninspired
Common sense	Some	None

Fig. 2.1 — Experts vs. expert systems.

Another important feature is learning — or lack of it. If we take learning to mean acquiring new concepts by information or experience, then expert systems do not learn at all. Identifying interesting new concepts can only be done by humans. However, if learning means adjusting future behaviour in the light of past experience then the position is more hopeful. There are tantalising glimpses of achieving this in practice, albeit only in ways which have been built in by the system developers. (Whether this is learning or not we leave to the reader.) Here we have the prospect of expert systems being 'self-adjusting' in response to their particular environment. At present, business expert systems do not learn from experience — everything has to be taught.

Let us consider how an expert system might be used in an organisation:

To replace an expert

Expert systems have been developed which have been shown to equal the performance of the best human specialist, albeit at considerable cost. There is then the tantalising prospect that the expert system might out-perform the expert one day. However, these comparisons are made in very constrained circumstances, e.g. for medical cases where the patient has an infection of the blood. If presented with a case of a broken leg, the expert system would still do its best to diagnose a blood infection and to recommend appropriate treatment. The computer has no understanding of what it is doing.

It is quite impossible to replace an expert completely. Even if it were feasible to achieve expert level performance, the human expert's creativity, generality, and ability to adapt to new situations would all be lost. Continuing access to an expert is also required to keep the system up-to-date.

In business, aiming to match the decision making performance of the expert is likely to be wishful thinking. Expert systems are usually best applied to the 80% or more of problems which could be tackled by non-experts if only they knew what to do.

As an additional expert

The difficulty of achieving expert level performance has already been stressed. However, an expert system may be an adequate substitute for very specific purposes when no human expert is available. This may be literally true, for example in remote locations, or effectively so, such as when junior staff only have limited call on an expert's time. In the latter case an expert system might handle those jobs which were well understood, freeing the expert to concentrate on tasks which demanded his unique abilities.

As an adviser

Here the expert system provides answers and the user is expected to act on them. The level of the task can be high (as in substituting for an expert) or low (as in completing a form). The user's only contribution is to answer the questions posed by the expert system. A number of expert systems have been constructed in this mould, failing to recognise that the decision making involved is qualitatively different from (say) adding up a column of numbers. If the task is a responsible one, this approach will lead above average staff to rebel and below average staff to deny their responsibilities. Additionally, the system's mistakes will be faithfully carried out — maliciously or otherwise.

As an assistant

An expert 'job assistant' is treated as a useful source of suggestions, and perhaps even advice in commonly occurring situations. Compared with advice giving (above), this is both more practical to achieve and more acceptable to users. The critical difference here is that the user is fully involved, and takes the final responsibility for any decision made.

As a source of know-how

The fact that a well-developed expert system contains a body of high-class knowledge can be exploited for its own sake. The principal aim is to make that expert knowledge more widely available to users. This means that in addition to having access to the system's suggestions, they can also access the expert know-how which was applied. As a result the users are better equipped to make skilful decisions, and will gradually become a little more expert themselves. Too seldom do we take advantage of learning from other people's experience.

As a knowledgeable servant
In any business there are information-handling tasks which call for a degree of expertise and judgement but which are highly repetitive. These usually fall to the least qualified, since more skilled staff will not tolerate the boredom. A typical example would be screening application forms, processing management reports to identify exceptions, or checking the details of sales quotations. Expert systems can be very effective here, especially as the relevant expertise may be quite small. The expert system will be endlessly vigilant, and can take over many such 'first pass' reviews.

It will be clear from the above that the expert system does not have an independent role. The system can only act as a support to, and never as a substitute for, the decision maker. An appropriate rule would be:

> if the computer proposes decisions
>   and a wrong decision can be harmful
> then do not use an expert system
>   unless there is a human responsible for
>   the ultimate decision

The practical expert systems discussed in this book take the role of assistants and sources of know-how. The typical users are people who are broadly familiar with the problem area but lack specific experience. Not only can they obtain useful advice, but they can also make good use of the expertise because they have the necessary concepts and jargon. Some expert systems are also intended for outsiders — those who are not familiar with the problem area. These expert systems require a considerable effort from the developers to make them understandable to their intended audience.

It is unlikely that an expert system will improve on the performance of other experts, except in consistency and an absence of subjective bias. This is because of the extent and detail of an expert's skill, and the expert's ability to overcome gaps in his specific knowledge by referring to similar cases. However, an expert system is often welcomed as a useful aide-mémoire, and as a means of reinforcing their own confidence and understanding. There are also clear benefits for the experts who participate in building the expert system, as described later.

At the other extreme, incompetent and unmotivated staff are unlikely to benefit at all. Their difficulties lie elsewhere.

2.2 AN EXPERT SYSTEM IN ACTION

A session with an expert system (a 'consultation') is usually structured as a question and answer session via a computer terminal. The user begins by making an enquiry, and the expert system asks a series of questions as it attempts to reach its conclusions. When presented with a question, the user might choose to:

— enquire why the question is being asked,
— request further explanation of the question,
— reply that he does not know, or
— reply with an answer.

In addition to questions, the expert system will also respond with its conclusions either during the consultation or at the end. Therefore the user may also enquire how a particular conclusion was reached.

The following dialogue is taken from a session with 'Corporate Evaluation', an expert system developed by the authors. The purpose of Corporate Evaluation is to investigate the creditworthiness of a business requesting a loan, from a banker's point of view. The system can also be used for investigating inward investments, for example when a large corporation invests in one of its business units. The underlying philosophy is that profitable lending decisions can only be made on the basis of a sound understanding of the business itself, and whether it is likely to prosper. Therefore Corporate Evaluation builds up a picture of the business environment and the business itself, and uses this to interpret the current and projected financial performance. The comments made and conclusions reached are gathered up and used in making the decision.

What follows is a typical fragment from a session which might involve a hundred or more questions, plus accounting information and financial forecasts. The consultation is under the control of the Business Economics module which examines how the business generates revenue and where the costs are incurred. Previous modules examine the industry at large, the past performance of the business, and the quality of the management. Subsequent modules perform the calculations and the financial analysis, and guide the user to a decision. Note that all of the data from previous modules is still available to the expert system (ES). In the case being run, the user has already said that the loan is required to fund R&D.

ES:	(Question)
	Does the business's past success and company image warrant such an investment in R&D?
User:	why? (i.e. why ask this question)
ES:	(Justification)
	Trying to determine 'past performance justifies further R&D' using rule 92:

if the purpose of the loan is to finance R&D
and high technology is important in the products
and past performance justifies further R&D
then the loan will be used effectively

(Question repeated)
Does the business's past success and company image warrant this investment in R&D?

User: yes

ES: (Question)
You have said that the security offered is existing contracts and order book. Is that asset fairly valued in the accounts?

User: yes, fairly valued

ES: (Question)
Is it possible that the valuation of the security might drop radically during the course of the loan (3 to 5 years in this case)?

User: explain (i.e. explain the question)

ES: (Explanation)
In the event of the business going bankrupt, the assets will be sold to pay the creditors. Items such as stock may have a greatly reduced value in a forced sale — 10% is not unknown. Alternatively, stock may deteriorate or become obsolete.

If the security is likely to drop in value during the period of the loan then you may want to increase the cover.

(Question repeated)
Is it possible that the valuation of the security might drop radically during the course of the loan (3 to 5 years in this case)?

User: possible

ES: (Conclusion)
Since the security may decrease in value, this will be an issue for the negotiating terms. You may wish to down-grade the valuation or ask for further guarantees.

(Question)
You have said that technological changes cause a drain on the business's resources.
Does the business have a sufficient capital base to support the technological developments which will be needed to remain competitive?

User: no

ES: (Conclusion)
Extra capital from shareholders (equity) is needed to provide long-term funding. This should take priority over any new loans.

User: how? (i.e. how did the system reach this conclusion about the need for further equity?)

ES: (Justification of the conclusion)
'further equity is needed as a priority' was obtained from rule 100:

if technological changes cause a drain on resources
and the business does not have a sufficient capital base
then further equity is needed as a priority

This dialogue illustrates the simplest use of an expert system. The expert system leads the user through a series of questions, and should arrive at one or more conclusions. More sophisticated uses might include the user making specific enquiries, the user volunteering information before being asked, acquiring data from other computer programs (rather than solely from the user), or using 'what if?' to investigate sensitivities.

2.3   WHAT IS AN EXPERT?

The existence of a human expert is a prerequisite for building an expert system. Expert systems are about capitalising on hindsight, or past experience. If that experience does not exist, or is not willingly available to the development team, then an expert system cannot be built. It is also true that if the 'expert' does not perform well, then the expert system will not perform well either. This means that expert systems are not substitutes for having expertise in the first place. They are a means of exploiting what already exists in at least one person.

For the purposes of an expert system, an expert is someone who is effective at solving the given problem or making the required decision on a day-to-day basis. Finding suitable experts and identifying true expertise is covered in detail in chapters 13 and 14. Suffice it for now to say that practical experts are not necessarily recognised as being the authority within an organisation. The most senior man may be highly skilled, but might only be familiar with solving the devious and unexpected cases. He might be well removed from the kinds of problems which potential users of the expert system actually wish to solve.

Human experts have three particular qualities which are a part of their being recognised as experts:

— they make good decisions,
— they make those decisions quickly, and
— they are able to cope with a wide range of problems.

Expert systems can make good decisions too: this is probably the least difficult aspect to achieve. However, human experts apply highly flexible strategies to getting a solution quickly. These include jumping to solutions, recognising familiar situations, and taking all manner of short cuts. This skilful behaviour is harder to achieve in an expert system, and the developers have to make a particular effort to include such knowledge in the system. Lastly, practical experts have breadth: they are not restricted to a sharply defined type of problem. This means that they are still able to perform well on a task which is a little outside their speciality. They are able to apply what they know to novel circumstances, and respond to the different constraints. Expert systems have no such breadth, and their ability to give correct advice usually drops off very sharply when applied outside their context. This is a result of the expert system having no appreciation of what it is doing. It follows that the scope of an expert system must be clearly defined, because it will take no account of being used outside the region in which it is valid. This is one of the major reasons for wanting users to benefit from the expertise in the expert system, not just its advice. Human users are able to adjust to new situations, and can compensate for the expert system's rigidity.

2.4   EXPERT SYSTEMS CONCEPTS

The idea of using a computer as an assistant is very different from their normal use. With a conventional computer program, the computer is an obedient moron. For the purpose of making a decision, the data may be in a more convenient form but the decision itself still has to be made. However, an expert system attempts to guide the user's decision making process itself. It does this by reasoning with ideas, expressed in words — and almost any idea can be expressed in words. The expert system aims to reproduce the way that an expert would apply his knowledge and skill to reach a decision. As illustrated in section 2.2, this usually involves a 'conversation' between the user and the expert system via a computer terminal. The expert system will ask the user a series of questions, and will eventually reach one or more conclusions and possibly generate some advice. During the session the user is able to enquire about what is being done and why, and to obtain detailed explanations when necessary. The process should be similar to that of discussing a problem with a knowledgeable assistant.

Naturally, the computer has no understanding of the words which are being used during the consultation. It simply handles them as rows of characters, and reproduces them on demand. The computer has no more understanding of its message than a sign outside a theatre understands that it is advertising the current production. However, the content of the words can be very potent for the user, since he is able to attach meaning to them. 'Look behind you!' is only a row of 16 characters to a computer, but has a clear message for any reader. Therefore the expert system is simply a means to an end, that end being delivering relevant expertise to the user for him to interpret and to act on or reject.

One last point is important — the fact that expertise is a commodity and can be engineered. Many experts seem to feel that they operate according to 'intuition' or 'gut feel', and that this *know-how* which they have acquired can never be trapped in a computer. This is not the case. Their know-how may be complex, and it may take effort to define, but if an expert can describe what he does then at least some fraction of his expertise can be recorded in an expert system. This point is discussed further in chapter 3.

The process of clarifying, recording and refining expertise has become known as 'knowledge engineering', and the professionals involved as 'knowledge engineers'.

> Knowledge engineering is the discipline of working with subject experts to encapsulate the lessons of experience in a computer-based expert system.

2.5 EXPERT AND CONVENTIONAL SYSTEMS

It may seem that there is much similarity between conventional computing — whether used for data processing or decision support — and expert systems. Both of these do involve processing information on a computer, but their uses are quite different.

Conventional computing is concerned with handling data which might subsequently be used in a decision making process. Data processing takes the first step by organising data and transforming it from one form into another. Decision support builds on this by allowing the manager to view his data at a level which is convenient to him (e.g. as a summary, as a trend, or as a 'what if' report), rather than at the basic level presented by data processing. However, the user still has to make a decision using his own expertise, even though the data is presented in a much more useful form.

Expert systems take the next step. They build on the results of data processing and decision support by assisting the user with the interpretation of the data and forming a response. They do this in the same way that a human would, by applying human knowledge. Rather than resulting in more data, an expert system will often generate suggestions for action. Therefore expert systems provide a lever on the decision making process itself. They are a fundamental change from the way that computers are used in conventional systems.

It will be apparent that tasks which are handled well by expert systems are generally handled poorly by data processing, and vice versa.

2.6 DISPELLING THE MYTHS

These points are gathered here because they are frequent concerns for managers and/or put about as facts by the less informed. Many of them are covered in detail elsewhere.

Expert systems are better than humans: FALSE
After prolonged development (millions of pounds investment), expert systems have been built which could out-perform a single, human expert in a narrow, technical discipline (e.g. specialist medicine, configuring complex equipment). However, an expert system will never have the human's generality, creativity or ability to deal with the unexpected. Most expert systems do not approach expert performance — but are still very useful for the less expert.

Expert systems learn from experience: FALSE
'Learning' in the everyday sense means identifying new concepts or relationships by reviewing experience. This simply does not exist for machines. Expert systems must be 'taught' by having knowledge added to them by hand. (A degree of adaptability, which may have the appearance of learning, seems feasible but has yet to become commercially available. See also section 7.7 on induction.)

Expert systems can replace people: FALSE
Replacing a person with an expert system is like replacing a waiter with a coffee machine. Both will provide coffee, but the machine can do nothing else. The unique contribution of expert systems is not to replace people but to help people do better. For example, an expert system might allow a greater proportion of tasks to be handled by junior staff. Since no computer has common sense, its results must still be monitored by a human.

However, expert systems certainly can make people more efficient as well as more effective. Like any productivity boost, this means that those people can handle more work, or a given amount of work can be done by fewer people. Coffee machines mean fewer tea ladies.

Expert systems can make mistakes: TRUE
An expert system is only as good as the expert's knowledge which it uses. Even experts can make mistakes sometimes. At least an expert system does not get tired or forgetful.

Expert systems can solve some problems which mathematical or scientific techniques cannot: TRUE
The vast majority of practical problems cannot be solved by formal methods. Real world problems are far too complex. However, humans solve such problems using what they know — their 'know-how'. Expert systems can use this know-how to the same effect.

You must have specialist 'knowledge engineers' to build the system: DEPENDS
Many small expert systems have been built by amateur teams or by the experts themselves. However, as projects grow in size and complexity then professional knowledge engineers become more important. For example:

> if the target audience is large
> then professional knowledge engineers are advisable

Knowledge engineers need a university degree in Artificial Intelligence: FALSE
Unless you are running a research project.

You must use a special-purpose computer to run the expert system: FALSE
There are hundreds of expert systems running on conventional business computers — often personal computers at that.

Experts will not cooperate: usually FALSE
The experience is quite the reverse. Properly informed experts soon realise that an expert system can only offer to take on their repetitive tasks. They may even enjoy the activity!

Experts cannot describe what they do: almost always FALSE
This is part of the folklore, but is rarely found in practice. If an expert is truly inarticulate, then find another expert. Detailed techniques for handling experts are given in chapters 13 and 14.

Expert systems are expensive: DEPENDS
Research type systems can be very expensive, i.e. where the aim is to put a degree of intelligence into the computer. The down payment can be upwards of £200,000. Business expert systems aim to produce useful tools to help their users. A modest system running on a personal computer might be built for as little as £20,000 including the cost of the participants' time. In both cases, a more typical cost might be twice these figures. (See section 4.6 for more information.)

Expert systems should be specified in advance: FALSE
Building an expert system is an exploration in uncharted territory. The builders have to *discover* the knowledge, so they cannot hope to know the full implications at the start. Therefore all projects should be tackled as many, short steps.

Expert systems cannot be managed: FALSE
There is now ample experience of managing expert systems projects. However, managers may have to accept that their usual measures may not be entirely appropriate. In compensation, results come quickly, progress can be assessed directly, and the financial exposure can be monitored and contained.

3

Knowledge

3.1 WHY EXPERT SYSTEMS WORK

Expert systems are effective because of the quality of the knowledge they contain. What that knowledge is and how it is expressed are described in the following sections. The point to make here is that expert systems can sometimes solve problems which formal or logical methods cannot.

Imagine that you are just waking up one morning. In your half-comatose state you are grappling with a serious problem — whether to have breakfast. What will affect your decision to have breakfast, not to mention what you might have to eat? It could depend on:

> what is in the cupboard,
> what you ate last night,
> whether you are going out for lunch,
> whether you have time to walk the dog before you leave, or
> who is going to make the breakfast.

Even if each of these questions were restricted to a yes/no response, the half-awake brain would still have thirty-two possible combinations to work through — or would it? Most of us are able to decide on breakfast before reaching the kitchen — even though in reality there are more possible breakfasts than stars in the sky.

Typical business problems are vastly more complex. They have countless possible solutions. Mathematicians know this as the 'combinatorial explosion'. As the number of available choices increases, the total number of possible solutions goes up at an ever-increasing rate.

Humans overcome such complexity with unconscious ease. The brain is superbly equipped to recall relevant knowledge and to apply it to the problem in hand. The function is so natural that we are unaware of it. It is almost impossible to stop one's thoughts leaping ahead, focusing on those possible solutions which are relevant, and not even considering the rest. The process is entirely dependent on the quality of the knowledge in order to reach a good solution. This is not a logical process, precisely because a logical process would fail. However, it is characteristic of a skilled expert. This then is the power of practical, expert knowledge: the ability to focus on key issues, to identify known situations, to take short cuts, and to recognise good solutions. Together, these amount to a problem solving power way beyond the reach of formal methods. Expert systems are a means of exploiting this problem solving power using a computer.

3.2 KNOWLEDGE AS KNOW-HOW

There is a vital distinction between a theoretical knowledge of a subject and a practical knowledge of how to solve the problems which occur in business. For expert systems we must have the latter, the empirical knowledge of what skilled experts actually do in practice.

When one talks of 'knowledge' in everyday conversation, it usually refers to something abstract like Mathematics or Biochemistry. It is the stuff of Universities and textbooks. However, consider what an expert system builder might find if he had studied a relevant and comprehensive manual, and then went to check his new 'knowledge' with a time-served expert. Replies have included:

> 'That's what we say, not what we do.'
> 'The book is for the suckers.'

and even:

> 'That's only there in case the inspector calls!'

The point is that practical expertise is very rarely written down. The convention is so powerful that experts will often write a description of what they do, or what others should do, which is quite different from what they actually do. The same is true of justifications given after the event. In all probability the explanation will consist of a logical, step-by-step progression from problem to solution. Each step will be a little closer to the solution, and there will be no effort wasted on 'blind alleys'. Our culture seems to expect written descriptions to be presented in this idealised way. However, in reality the expert may have gone wrong on occasion and had to backtrack, or proposed solutions which were later discarded. He will also have used familiar patterns, analogies, a knowledge of what to do next, and all manner of ad hoc methods. These are all things that one learns by experience of successfully solving problems.

Such practical expertise is commonplace in spoken explanations, but exceedingly rare in writing. This means that it is essential for expert system builders to heed what experts say they do, not what they put in writing. The basic method of obtaining know-how from an expert is to provide a prompt such as an example case, and to ask him how he would go about dealing with it. This process is fully described in Part V.

The cultural aspects are interesting. In Japan, the man who acts intuitively and without apparent thought is highly esteemed. Contrast this with the Western view that the peak of learning is demonstrated by the deepest analysis, such as that expected from University professors and learned scientists. However, in Western culture there are instances of great respect for practical, everyday knowledge which are not always recognised as such. It has been observed that society uses up its specialists for peripheral tasks such as designing machines, identifying diseases and examining theories. However, for really serious matters — like depriving someone of their freedom — society turns to 'twelve good men and true', a jury chosen from among the general population.

The following example, taken from a real case, is just one instance of the contrast between written and spoken expertise. A computer software company was exploring the feasibility of building an expert system to help answer telephone queries. Several skilled technicians were being kept fully occupied responding to calls from customers, even though the majority of the calls were highly repetitive. This was expensive, and was diverting essential skills away from productive work. The intention was that with the aid of the expert system, telephone clerks would be able to resolve at least half of the enquiries, and would only pass on those which actually required technical input. The software company sought advice from an expert systems supplier, who arranged an initial meeting with a knowledge engineer. Two experts came to the meeting, rather sceptical as to why they were needed at all. It was 'all in the book', a manual of procedures and flow diagrams. The clear implication was that all necessary knowledge was recorded in the manual.

Following a quick scan of this manual, the knowledge engineer (KE) opened with a well tried line of questioning:

KE: 'Suppose I were to call your enquiries number, say who I was, and that I had a problem with my spreadsheet†. What would you do?'
Expert: 'I would check that you had a maintenance contract!'
KE: 'OK, let's suppose I have. I also have an error message which I don't understand — Memory Full.'
Expert: 'Well, find the bottom right-hand corner of your spreadsheet. Is it where you expected it?'
KE: '!'

This was totally unexpected. There had been nothing at all about the company's software, nor any reference to the procedures listed in the manual. Instead, the expert had recognised a familiar situation and was attempting to apply the following rule of thumb:

        if your spreadsheet says 'Memory Full'
           and the bottom right-hand corner is not where you expected
        then it may be that your spreadsheet is far too big
           because a simple typing error can easily do this

† For those unfamiliar with personal computers, a spreadsheet is the electronic equivalent of a ledger sheet, and is extensively used for financial analysis.

In fact, the great majority of the know-how needed for this application was all about identifying common errors and misunderstandings, not about software faults at all. Only about one-third of the expertise came from the manual (standard procedures). Another third came from handwritten notes on loose pages inside the front cover (recognising common problems, recently found 'bugs', what to ask for if the problem is not clear, etc.). The rest came from the experts themselves (how to tackle the task under different circumstances). The manual, whilst correct, did not reflect the know-how which people were actually using.

The incident just quoted illustrates the empirical knowledge which an expert acquires by experience of doing the job successfully. This is what is meant by 'know-how'. Know-how is what distinguishes an expert from a novice. If there can be any doubt about the value of know-how, consider in whom you would place your trust at a time of great need. Suppose you were to have an operation which was necessary to save your eyesight, but the operation carried a risk of losing your eyesight altogether. Eyesight is very precious. Would you go to a brilliant student, or a consultant with a sound track record? The consultant's practical experience is too important to ignore, despite the fact that the student may well have the better theoretical knowledge. The difference lies in the consultant's practical knowledge of how to do the job successfully — his know-how.

The very term 'know-how' is indicative of practical skill. It has connotations of everyday good sense, the kind of advice that you would get if you spoke directly to an expert. Know-how can be defined as 'the verbal expression of practical expertise'.

A person's know-how need not be acquired purely by doing the job. It can also be acquired secondhand by listening to the experiences of others and watching their skills demonstrated. This is the basis of apprenticeship. Expert systems now bring a third way: by exercising a computer system which itself contains know-how. Hence expertise can be transferred from an expert (or several experts) to many users via an expert system. The expertise can be applied by the expert system on behalf of the users, or still better it can enable the users to apply the expertise themselves.

No one knows how knowledge or know-how is stored in the brain, and we are not going to speculate here. However, people are able to communicate their know-how in terms of rules of thumb. This simple fact makes it practical to build expert systems.

> Whatever the internal form of know-how,
> people are able to discuss their decision making expertise
> in terms of rules of thumb.

A rule of thumb is simply a statement of the form 'if these conditions occur, then these actions or consequences follow'. Provided that they share the same jargon, experts and non-experts alike can discuss a task in terms of rules of thumb. Well expressed rules of thumb have a fascination in themselves, for example:

> if you are taking antibiotics
> then try to avoid painkillers
> because painkillers tend to reduce the effect

which is not widely known, but is believed to be correct.

Another memorable rule is included in an expert system to help a company overcome a loss of petrol supplies to run their vehicles. (This is an example of an expert system operating as a 'Rare event guide', i.e. what to do in the event of an unusual happening.) This piece of know-how was recorded after bitter experience during a strike of petrol-tanker drivers. The company had found great difficulty locating service engineers to go to customer sites towards the end of the day. With the benefit of hindsight, they identified a rule to the effect:

> if one parent has company petrol
> and the other does not
> then guess who will be collecting the children from school

This is a splendid example of know-how, and will be available to those future managers who will deal with the next such shortage. (The company took an enlightened policy decision. In future, provide the spouse with enough petrol to collect the children!) Note that if this rule were just employed in a 'black box' computer system to give advice, then it would only apply to petrol supply crises. However, it is relevant to any situation which affects parents caring for children, whether widespread or just applying to an individual. See the value of the expert system providing know-how, not just advice.

Rules of thumb are an integral part of human society. We speak of 'the verbal tradition', a means of passing on experiences and values from one generation to the next. This reaches its peak in the form of aphorisms, wise sayings which have been refined to a form which is relevant, concise and rythmic. Once heard, they are hard to forget. If the rules of thumb used in an expert system can achieve even a fraction of this appeal, they will readily be taken up by the users.

Researchers have coined the term 'heuristics' to denote the rules which an expert uses in his or her specialist area (referred to as the 'domain'). A heuristic is essentially a rule of thumb, based on experience. Lenat's slick definition is 'compiled hindsight'.

Rules of thumb, or heuristics, form an empirical body of knowledge. They rely on experience for their authority. There is not necessarily any proof, and a heuristic may only be valid over a certain range. Indeed, the more specific the context, the more powerful the heuristic tends to be. The authority for a rule in an expert system can often be simply that the expert says it is so, and it appears to work in practice. There are two consequences which all users of expert systems should bear in mind:

(1) Expert systems can make mistakes.

By their very nature, heuristics cannot be guaranteed to work in every case. They may be uncertain in themselves, and all heuristics have a context. It follows that expert systems can make mistakes. In this they are no different from human experts. However, unlike a human expert, an expert system has no common sense and cannot judge when a result is unreasonable. Therefore users must always regard the output from an expert system as a useful guide, and not as definitive advice.

The expectation that an expert system might ever be perfect is a major pitfall for the unwary. Expert systems vendors have not always been forward in pointing it out.

The possibility of mistakes might provoke the question 'How can you possibly trust a computer system which can make mistakes?' The answer is simple. Most human activities are not done perfectly — expert systems help to do them a little better.

(2) Good decisions can follow from imperfect knowledge.

If they are honest with themselves, most people will admit that some of their own rules of thumb are doubtful, or even wrong. But this does not prevent them from making good decisions day in and day out. The reason is that people have a surplus of know-how, a huge surplus, and it can be used at many levels of abstraction. This means that there are many checks and balances, even to the extent of knowing what we do *not* know. Over-provision of know-how is a valuable feature in expert systems too, and can give the expert system a robustness which is completely lacking in conventional computing.

The major points about knowledge as know-how are these:

- Practical expertise, or know-how, is different from book knowledge.
- Know-how is what makes an expert, and an expert system.
- Know-how can be discussed in terms of rules of thumb, whatever its internal form in the brain.

3.3 RULES

Rules of thumb, or heuristics, can be expressed directly in rules for use in an expert system. A rule is simply a statement of the form:

>   if (these conditions are true)
>   then (these consequences or actions follow)

where the brackets are simply to emphasise the if–then form. Section 8.2 gives details of how rules are written in different software systems.

Everyone is familiar with if–then statements, and this is a cardinal strength. The intelligibility of the know-how in an expert system is all important, and the if–then form can be understood by any literate user.

Using an if–then form is not special in itself. It is shared with nearly all computer programming languages. The significance lies in the way that the rules are used rather than the way in which they are written.

In an expert system, each rule is a 'nugget' of know-how which is valid in itself. When an expert system is running, the expert system software will select which rules to apply, and when, in order to solve the current problem. (See section 6.3 for details of how this is done.) The system builder only has to specify what the rules are, leaving it to the expert system to organise how they will be used. Such a statement of 'what' rather than 'how' is said to be a 'declarative' statement of the know-how. Compare this with conventional computer programming where the programmer must specify 'how' in every detail.

Therefore, in an expert system:

— rules can be added, modified, or deleted independently of one another,
— rules can be input in any order, and
— people with no computer skills can understand the 'program'.

In practice things are far from perfect. For example, the order of entering rules often has some effect on the order in which rules are processed. The level of readability also varies greatly between different software tools, and perhaps most important of all are the attitude and skills of the knowledge engineer. It is quite possible to build a totally opaque expert system using even the best of software tools.

However, rule-based expert systems are quick to build and easy to modify. The ability to add rules at any point and to make changes without generating hidden side-effects (the curse of conventional programming) are a boon to the developer. Development can be 100 times faster (yes, one hundred times faster) than would be achieved in a conventional programming language such as Cobol. Additionally, it becomes practical to develop systems incrementally, i.e. to begin with a prototype of the key know-how, and progressively to refine and extend it. Users can also have access to the prototypes for comment. This greatly increases the chance of providing a system which they will actually like, and will choose to use.

Maintenance is also a major issue. Conventional computer systems fall into disrepair because they cannot be maintained. The ease of modification offered by expert systems makes it possible not only to maintain them, but to follow changes in the expertise and the system's objectives. This is vitally important, as a successful system will be maintained and developed over many years.

3.4   OTHER INTERPRETATIONS OF KNOWLEDGE

Know-how has already been described as the accumulated lessons of experience. However, there are at least two other interpretations of the word 'knowledge' which are used in connection with expert systems. We have called these other interpretations 'formal knowledge' and 'process knowledge'. This section explains these approaches, and shows how they have different purposes. Note that software systems using any of these three types of knowledge are all freely described as expert systems. The norm is for builders to behave as if their interpretation was the only one possible.

3.4.1   Formal knowledge

The notion of computerised systems as being possible replacements for human experts has led to the pursuit of maximum problem-solving performance. This idea is founded in the US work of the 1970s, and is well entrenched in the academic literature. The objective is to equal, or even to out-perform human expert levels of skill. Such systems attempt to go beyond the problems which an expert knows how to solve, or at least beyond those which he handles well. The usual approach has been to aim for a generalised model of the problem area, and to reason about it in generalised ways. Such models must work from general principles, hence we refer to the knowledge they contain as 'formal' knowledge; it is akin to textbook knowledge rather than spoken advice (which is the expression of know-how).

The justification for using formal knowledge (sometimes called 'deep knowledge') is that the system might be able to solve new problems as well as those which have been seen before, or that it might solve problems more effectively. The expert system aims to be cleverer than the expert. The supposition is that the computer's thorough, logical methods might be better at solving problems than the expert's methods. There is an obvious contrast with the know-how approach (as described above), which focuses on exploiting past experience.

An actual example may serve to illustrate the contrast. At least two automobile manufacturers are building expert systems to diagnose gearbox problems. Using a know-how approach, the expert system would pool the expertise of the company's best gearbox diagnosticians. It would include generally applicable rules plus highly specific experience such as 'old Joe' knowing that Mk 5 gearboxes rumble in 3rd gear, and it is not important. The system would gain its power from the quantity and quality of the rules of thumb it contained. Its use would be to equip those staff needing to diagnose a gearbox fault with the accumulated experience about that gearbox. Note that it would always be an assistant: 'old Joe' near at hand when needed. By contrast, a formal knowledge approach would attempt to build a general model of how a gearbox diagnostician performed his task, and to apply that to a description of the gearbox concerned. This is equivalent to asking a designer to diagnose faults in a gearbox which has yet to be built. It assumes that there is an underlying gearbox diagnosis method which can be identi-

	know-how	formal knowledge	process knowledge
source of the knowledge	spoken	model	programming requirements
relationship with practical expertise	direct	theoretical	none intended
intelligibility to experts	high	low	high (for programmers)
intelligibility to users	high	low	nil
usual expression	rules	rules, nets, frames, etc	any

Fig. 3.1 — Forms of knowledge used in expert systems.

fied, generalised, and applied to a design description of a gearbox. The attraction of this latter approach is that if the system could be built then faults could be diagnosed in *any* gearbox design — not just ones which 'old Joe' knows about.

System builders using formal knowledge have been led to devise programs which attempt to reproduce the expert's thinking. The source of the 'knowledge' enshrined in the system is not what the expert says, but is a model of what the builders believe the expert would do if he were to tackle a completely unfamiliar problem, i.e. starting from first principles. It is a formal description designed to reproduce the expert's behaviour. The software often makes use of sophisticated structures such as frames and networks which lend themselves to sophisticated reasoning methods (see chapter 9).

It is not clear if the implementors of such systems are really trying to emulate knowledge as it is used in the human brain. We suspect that they would deny it, but that is what the method implies. It is important to recognise that formal knowledge does not necessarily relate *in any way* to the knowledge that an expert actually uses in solving the problem. Furthermore, there is no reason to suppose that the expert will recognise or understand the 'knowledge', which is claimed to be his, being used in the expert system. This means that the system has lost its intelligibility — a crucial drawback. A sure sign is when the implementation team have to construct a translation of the formal knowledge for the expert to work with (a so-called 'paper model'). Building a theoretical model of the expert's reasoning carries the risk that there may not be a deliverable system at the end of the project.

So here we have two approaches to using human expertise in an expert system: formal knowledge and know-how. Formal knowledge is a model of reasoning which attempts to reproduce what the expert does. Know-how is an explicit statement of what the expert actually does on real problems. Know-how captures spoken expertise, whereas the formal approach aims to build an underlying model.

3.4.2 Process knowledge

For completeness, there is also a third school of thought about knowledge in expert systems. Here, the aim is simply to achieve a given piece of data processing. The 'knowledge' bears no relation to practical expertise, and is not intended to. Its sole purpose is to make the computer program perform the desired process, and accordingly we refer to it as 'process knowledge'.

This use of expert systems is a natural view for some data processing professionals. They recognise that expert systems tools can provide high productivity, ease of maintenance, and the possibility of incremental development. All of these qualities are in a different class to those available with conventional programming methods, even if the resulting systems are much less efficient at carrying out repetitive processing.

Effectively, expert systems methods are being used as another form of software tool for data processing. The implementors are not always willing to declare that such methods are being used: they fear that their clients may be wary of this 'new-fangled technology'. As a result, several such systems are being embedded in larger, conventional applications without being declared as expert systems.

Using process knowledge in an expert system has no relation with exploiting human expertise, and will not be considered further.

3.5 IMPLICATIONS FOR BUSINESS

The significance of using know-how or formal knowledge in an expert system is that the risks and the returns are quite different. For brevity, expert systems using know-how are referred to here as 'know-how systems'. Compared with the formal knowledge approach, know-how systems:

— are less ambitious, in that they aim to help the user rather than replace him (or one of his functions);
— are much more likely to succeed, because their objectives are more realistic;
— are better able to assist with unfamiliar or loosely related problems because the user can make use of the know-how, not just accept or reject the advice;
— can be valuable even when only partly complete;
— are considerably quicker and more economical to implement, perhaps by a factor of 10.

In essence, the distinction is between trying to amplify the abilities of the computer (formal knowledge systems), and trying to amplify the abilities of the user (know-how systems). Recent reports have shown that by emphasising the less ambitious path, commercial organisations in Europe have been achieving earlier payback on their expert systems than their counterparts in the USA (Hewitt and Sasson, 1985, Hewitt *et al.*, 1986).

	systems using know-how	systems using formal knowledge
role	assistant	adviser
method	the system guides the user to solve the problem	the system solves the problem itself
scope	limited to known problems	claimed to tackle new problems as well
expertise	transferred to the user	used internally
cost	low to medium (e.g. 0.5 man years)	high (e.g. 5 man years)
principal skill required	subject know-how	AI programming
systems in use	hundreds	a few

Fig. 3.2 — Implications for business of different forms of knowledge.

There is a distinct difference in the methods of use. In a formal knowledge system, the expert system is there to give top-class advice, and is expected to make better judgements than the user. Effectively, that part of the user's decision making responsibility is being replaced. This role is described as being an 'adviser'. By contrast, a know-how system is an 'assistant'. Its function is to guide users to making decisions for themselves. The principal means of doing so is to show how the expertise would be applied to the current problem. Obviously a know-how system can also give advice within the limits of its stored experience, but that is not the sole aim. The main benefit is that the users will acquire some of the know-how, and thereby become a little more expert themselves.

It follows that know-how systems are useful even when they are only partly complete. Even a little guidance is better than none. This is excellent for management, since the benefits begin to accrue even when only part of the system has been developed. (Obviously there needs to be sufficient substance to avoid the system seeming trivial because of being too narrow in scope.) Anyone who has developed a know-how system will have experienced the eagerness with which prototype versions are carried off for potential users to explore. Even when incomplete, transferring know-how to a user makes that user more effective.

The motivation for using formal knowledge may simply be that of following the precedents set out by theoretical studies. If the project sets out to do research then the sponsoring organisation should be prepared for the investment to be completely written off. A different motivation might be the lure of solving novel problems, i.e. those which have not been previously solved by humans. This is appealing, but ambitious. Since the system is being used as an adviser, there is a heavy responsibility to produce correct answers under all circumstances. It is difficult enough to achieve good answers on a well-known class of problem, let alone problems which have yet to arise. There is a real risk that even when a formal knowledge system can be made to work, it will conduct its analysis on a theoretical basis. It will lose out by not having practical experience. This is like the naivety of a clever student before he acquires experience on the job.

In the limit, no computer has common sense. This single fact means that any advisory system can only be effective in the context assumed by the builders. For a new problem, the computer system has no means of recognising if the task is within its scope. Even 'obvious' exceptions will be not be recognised. In such cases, know-how systems are actually more effective, since the user can interpret the know-how in the light of the special circumstances. The combination of the user and his expert system assistant (using know-how) is more effective than the expert system adviser alone (using formal knowledge).

Expert systems built using formal knowledge are usually expensive. 'Expensive' means perhaps ten times the cost of the alternative approach using know-how. There are still international consultancies whose representatives will advise their clients not to get involved in expert systems unless they have a first year budget of at least £200,000, and several times that if they wish to tackle 'serious' applications. They assume that an expert system can only use formal knowledge.

Fig. 3.3 indicates how project costs can grow as the expectation of what the computer will do for itself is increased. The least costly approach is that of sharing expertise, which is the essence of an effective know-how system. Replacing some human function, the usual objective of using formal knowledge, may increase costs ten-fold. This is because of the high level of technical skill required, and the protracted development time. As yet, machine intelligence cannot be bought at any price.

The relative risks and rewards are reflected in the population of expert systems which have reached service. Many know-how systems are already in use in industry — perhaps a hundred in the UK. The corresponding number of operational systems based on formal knowledge is only a handful. Even some of the best-known suppliers in the latter field have yet to deliver a live system.

The use of know-how systems in industry was first documented in a survey carried out for the UK government's Alvey Directorate in 1984. It concluded that:

> It is necessary to correct the impression (from the literature) that expert systems are inherently complex, risky and demanding. (d'Agapeyeff 1984)

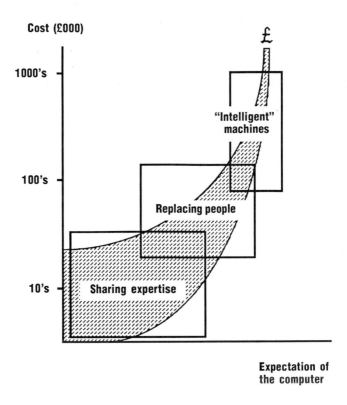

Fig. 3.3 — The cost rocket.

The report identified a class of 'simpler' expert systems. These were being built in industry, by the people who had the expert knowledge, working in small teams, on ordinary business computers. Each of these features reversed the approach which had become institutionalised in the research literature.

The archetypal 'simpler' system was Tracker, built by British Telecom to help engineers diagnose faults with particular power supplies. The aim was a modest one: to help the majority of engineers to repair these power supplies a little faster. This may seem of marginal benefit, until it is realised that the loss of the power supply disabled a telephone exchange. Even a small improvement in the availability of telephone exchanges is of considerable economic benefit to an organisation as large as British Telecom.

It should be clear that, in the authors' view, expert systems using formal knowledge lean towards artificial intelligence research. Their stated or implied aim to equal, or even to out-perform, human expert levels of skill can lead business managers to expect intelligence, learning, and a better-than-human level of ability. Experience shows that these hopes will be disappointed.

The advantages of expert systems using know-how compared with a formal knowledge approach are:

— users supported by the expert system will be able to solve a wider range of problems than the system or the user could if working alone;
— users will themselves become more proficient by using the system;
— users will be able to interpret any advice in their own particular context, rather than having to accept the result at face value;
— the quality of the knowledge in the system will be higher because the expert can relate to it;
— systems can usually be built in weeks rather than months or years.

Part II

Expert systems in business

4

The commercial view

In business, few things are undertaken for enjoyment or for the experience value. Both people and organisations have limited time and funds, so all investments have to be judged on the basis of relative risks and relative rewards. Expert systems are subject to the same commercial appraisal. See Beerel (1987) for an extended account of the strategic implications and applications of expert systems.

4.1   ARE EXPERT SYSTEMS FOR ME?

The first challenge for business management is to decide on the appropriate criteria for their own investments in expert systems. For most business investments the criteria used are reasonably standard, the main variation being the weighting given to each. The same is true for expert systems, although there are extra complexities.

Firstly, expert systems are a new type of system and as yet there is little history to refer to. This makes it difficult to predict the ultimate cost of the investment to establish an effective system. Secondly, establishing and quantifying the benefits of a proposed system is often extremely difficult. The benefits may only be measurable when the system has been in use for some time. Thirdly, expert systems are often portrayed as requiring different technical skills and different computers to conventional computer systems. Although this is frequently exaggerated, it adds to the apparent cost of the undertaking.

Before considering the evaluation of a potential expert system, it is worth reflecting on the possible roles that an expert system might play. Expert systems have a powerful contribution to make in establishing a competitive edge. They do this by assisting the organisation to improve the performance of its most important asset — people.

4.2   THE MOTIVATION FOR AN EXPERT SYSTEM DEVELOPMENT

The motivation for an expert system development must lie in the benefits that will be gained. The early stages in the commercialisation of expert systems have been accompanied by interest in them as a new technology, but this cannot last into maturity without demonstrating a return. The benefits are those which will be gained by having practical, expert knowledge encapsulated in a form which is transferable to those who are not experts. The number of possible applications is enormous.

The specific incentive for investing in an expert system might be:

— To free experts from their more routine activities, so that they have more time to devote to the specialised, more demanding tasks which only they can handle.
— To allow experts to pool and refine their own expertise, especially where the tasks require a contribution from several individuals. The organisation acquires a 'knowledge bank' of good practice.
— To improve the performance of non-experts by providing expert systems which are readily available to those who need quick and ready reference to expertise.
— To provide training of a consistently high quality with the capability of being disseminated throughout the organisation.
— To provide a standardised approach to solving important, unstructured tasks which require expertise.
— To automate the application of expert judgement to a large mass of data, e.g. identifying exceptions within management reports.
— The opportunity for the expert who built the system to improve his own understanding, and hence improve his own performance.
— The opportunity of integrating the latest and most powerful information technology with the conventional systems currently in use. This goes beyond the idea of distributed information, to achieve distributed knowledge.

Increasingly, the benefits being sought are those of competitive advantage rather than cost savings.

4.3   EXPERT SYSTEMS AND DECISION MAKING

The success of a business depends on the ability of the staff to make good decisions, and to make them at the appropriate time. In fact the organisation is continuously engaged in a host of decision making processes at all levels. The better the quality of the decisions taken and the greater the harmony between the different decision making activities, then the more chance that organisation has of out-performing its rivals.

Expert systems lend themselves to supporting decisions which are not well structured, and rely largely on experience and acquired knowledge. By harnessing the practical know-how of experts in the field, expert systems provide a new form of support to decision makers that conventional computer systems have been unable to provide. The difference is that instead of assisting the decision maker by providing ever more data, the expert system tackles the decision making process itself. The expert system will not only recommend solutions to complex problems but also has the power to explain the reasoning behind that recommendation. These explanations should mirror the explanations that an expert would give if he were available at the time.

Decision making activities within an organisation are normally assigned on a hierarchical basis. At the most junior level, tasks are highly structured. That is, there exists a procedure which the employee is expected to follow to achieve a predetermined result. There is little or no opportunity for deviation from the set procedure. As one moves to more senior levels, the decision making demands greater experience, initiative and discretion. The problems that arise are less clearly definable, and the optimal solution may be less evident. At the most senior level of an organisation, management is faced with highly unstructured problems surrounded by a great deal of uncertainty. The decisions to be taken have a strategic impact, and therefore the implications of making good or bad choices can be very severe indeed.

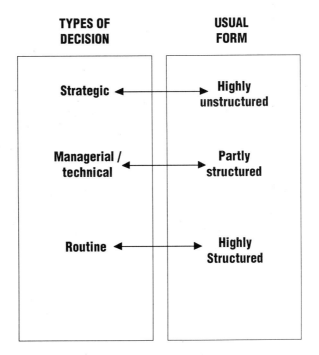

Fig. 4.1 — Levels of decision making.

For example, in a venture capital organisation we might have:

— The highly structured task of administering existing contracts. This would be carried out by a clerk, perhaps supported by a conventional database.

— The partially structured task of evaluating a particular business as a prospect for funding. This would be carried out by an investment manager, and draws heavily on experience.

— The unstructured task of deciding where to seek new business. This would be carried out by the Chief Executive, and requires a breadth of experience plus good current information.

The most evident use for expert systems is ·in the middle ground, i.e. addressing those problems which are neither highly structured nor totally unstructured. These are beyond the reach of conventional computer systems, and will include many technical, professional, and managerial tasks. By addressing the middle ground, it is also hoped that expert systems will promote the flow of expertise *across* an organisation. For example, a design team might share their know-how with production, and vice versa. At present, information normally flows only up and down an organisation, and expertise rarely flows anywhere at all! Expert systems can create horizontal exchanges where none existed before. If this serves to reduce inter-departmental barriers then it will contribute to innovation and competitiveness.

There are also many potential applications among the junior members of an organisation. Some of their information processing tasks will follow well specified procedures, and are therefore highly structured. These are often well supported by conventional data processing, and expert systems are not about to replace these methods. However, others call for significant amounts of know-how, for example fault finding and repair or securing a prompt delivery. These expert systems represent a 'sideways' extension of computer usage within the organisation.

At the other end of the scale, highly unstructured tasks call for too much knowledge, and accessed in ways which are too subtle, for it all to be encapsulated in a computer system. This means that expert systems are likely to support only particular aspects of the work. However, expert systems can be outstandingly useful as an aide-mémoire, particularly when a multi-faceted approach is called for. The expert systems provide specialised help, second opinion, or simply confirmation.

In summary, expert systems are most effective at handling specialised tasks which would otherwise require an experienced human. These occur at all levels of an organisation. Within this scope, expert systems are most successful when a well-defined area is selected (one which has clearly recognisable boundaries), and objectives which can be determined in advance.

4.4   A BUSINESS STRATEGY

A strategy for business success using expert systems must focus on those applications which will have the maximum effect. In principle, the selection process involves focussing on business priorities, selecting the most favourable developments, and using pilot systems to verify the potential benefits.

However, there are two important prerequisites:

(1) There is management support for expert systems.
(2) There is an experienced development team to do the work.

Both of these conditions must be satisfied before a corporate view of expert systems can be taken.

4.4.1   Management support

A reluctance to be involved with technology may prevent top management from viewing their business priorities as knowledge-based activities. Directors who are responsible for setting the business priorities may be unwilling to spend time evaluating the contribution of know-how (and hence of expert systems) to key tasks. In such cases it is necessary to develop demonstrator applications which illustrate the business benefits, and thereby secure management support.

Successful demonstrators are crucially important to the process of establishing an awareness of expert systems in an organisation. Their requirements are quite different from those for a pilot system intended to pave the way for a full development. If this point is not appreciated, an apparently sound system may be built which completely fails to win management approval. Such a project cannot expect further funding.

It follows that the development team must be aware of whether they are developing a demonstration system or a pilot application. If the project is presented as a technical exercise, the danger is that the developers may fail to appreciate the wider implications:

> if an inappropriate system is built
> then it will not survive the political battle for funding
> however accomplished a piece of work

It is a common experience that management will require a demonstration of a prototype system early in its development. Moreover, they may only allocate half an hour of their time and give very little advance warning. Such a demonstration must go well. If the management receives an impression that the system fails to contribute significantly to the business, then any amount of protest about the system being incomplete will not win their support.

The over-riding objective of a demonstration system is to illustrate benefits and to contribute to management understanding and support. What is successful as a demonstrator is likely to be inadequate as a pilot, and vice versa. For management, the key qualities in a demonstration are an attractive dialogue and obvious relevance to the business. Intelligibility and 'gloss' are essential; technical accomplishment generally counts for little. (See section 11.6 for guidance on the technical approach.) The manner of the demonstration also contributes greatly to the impression given. This implies acceptable surroundings, a good view of the computer screen(s) for the whole audience, clear explanations by the presenter, no unexpected 'crashes', and of course interesting cases run on the expert system. It is more important that the presenter should be a good speaker than a good technician — others can be on hand to answer technical questions. Whoever speaks, they should of course rehearse their demonstration beforehand.

4.4.2   Gaining experience

Gaining experience of developing expert systems is obviously a matter of completing projects. This is fully described in Part V of this book. However, management has a role to play by allowing for the inevitable learning period. In section 13.2.2 we recommend that the developers should gain experience with a 'toy' system initially and then rapidly move up to modest, but real, applications.

A key point is that an organisation's first substantial project should not tackle a major strategic issue. This may be a prime business objective, but it is certain to be difficult and may not be tractable at all. The project will also be exposed to the glare of corporate scrutiny, and any problems will be highly visible. This can make it very difficult to take sensible measures such as scrapping a design and adopting a better one, or halting a line of investigation which has outlived its usefulness. These are not good omens for an inexperienced development team.

This is not to say that the business concerns are secondary — quite the opposite. If the investment in expert systems is squandered on minor objectives then the payoff will also be minor. Therefore the correct strategy is to gain experience on useful but non-critical applications and then to be guided by what is relevant to the business, as described below.

4.4.3   A mature strategy

Once there is a culture which is receptive to expert systems and a body of experience gained on successful projects, then a corporate view of expert systems can be taken. The logical steps are as follows:

— know the business objectives of the organisation and how these are best achieved,
— identify those areas where expert systems can further these objectives, i.e. identify the potential applications, and
— target specific expert system developments by selecting from the potential applications according to their technical feasibility.

The process of identifying target applications will provide objectives for specific expert system developments. These will be business-oriented, since they derive from business priorities. They are the 'desired objectives'. It is necessary to refine these into 'achievable objectives', i.e. those which can be achieved within acceptable limits of time, effort, and technical difficulty. This is usually done by means of a pilot system. A pilot system is necessary because any expert system development is an exploration. The feasibility, eventual cost, and final facilities cannot be known with certainty at the outset.

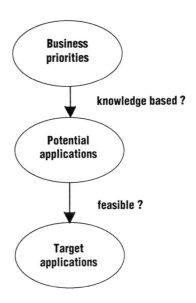

Fig. 4.2 — Targeting expert system applications.

Even when the objectives for the full system appear to be clear cut, we would still recommend distinct stages of piloting, review and full implementation. This is to ensure that the pilot does not itself evolve into the full expert system without a detailed review of its objectives, and how it is to deliver benefits to its eventual owners and users.

The pilot system is a small expert system which implements some part of the full scope envisaged for the complete expert system. Its purpose is to explore the problems involved in building the full system, and to sample the benefits, without committing to the full costs. The key issues are problem-solving power and user-acceptability. Presentation is less critical than in a demonstration, but it will still be important for review purposes.

Therefore the overall development of an expert system's objectives is as follows (Fig. 4.3):

- The desired objectives are set by the business requirements.
- Scaled down objectives are set for a pilot system. These are carefully constructed so that when the pilot system is evaluated, it will be possible to:
  - identify achievable objectives for the full system,
  - be confident of the technical feasibility,
  - estimate the total costs, and
  - assess the business benefits.
- The pilot system is implemented, and then evaluated against the business

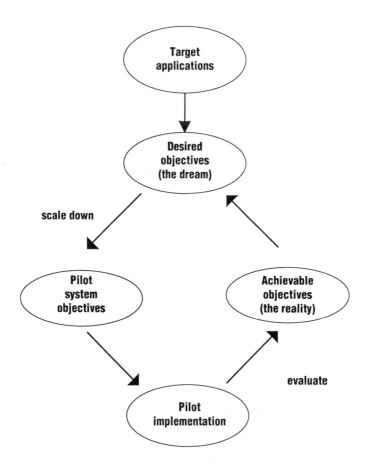

Fig. 4.3 — Developing the objectives.

requirements. This feedback is combined with the desired objectives to produce achievable objectives for the full system.

In an expert system for sharing expertise (as described in this book), the technical risk is expected to be low. Therefore the pilot system usually covers only one or two topics in depth, and neglects the others. The presumption is that the other topics will be of comparable difficulty. The resulting system should work effectively, but only on a narrow sub-set of problems. Its main purpose is to sample the user reactions and to estimate total costs. By contrast, in a system which is to replace some human judgement then the technical risk will be large. This means that the pilot may have to sample many topics to verify that the task can be accomplished at all. It will have to demonstrate that reaching the desired level of problem-solving really is feasible. The key problem-solving activities should obviously be tackled first.

When preparing scaled down objectives for the pilot, it is important that the real difficulties are not scaled down to the point where they cease to be difficulties. The main culprits are generality and size. For example, a pilot system which is restricted to small manufacturing businesses is a very different proposition from a full system which is intended to deal with all industrial companies. Not only are there in the latter case many more types of business, but the issues involved become more complex and there are fewer widely applicable guidelines. The aim should be to accommodate all expected users and uses, and to pilot the functions involved. Concerning size, it is often possible to process a small number of possibilities using straightforward methods. But if the real system has to cater for a hundred times more possibilities, will these methods still be adequate? It is the responsibility of the development team not to 'design out' their difficulties by setting carefully designed objectives. An experienced and professional team will tackle the key problems during the pilot project.

A pilot system should be implemented as an expert system in its own right, and carried through to evaluation with users. It should be a model for the full system, but on a smaller scale. The principal reviewers should be the future users and their management, preferably by a period of trial use. This will ensure that the evaluation is done on business impact and not on technical merit. This is the only basis on which a subsequent proposal to implement the full system is likely to succeed. By failing to recognise this, some organisations become involved in a series of prototyping exercises. This is a sign of the developers looking inwards to the technology rather than outwards to the desired benefits.

The results of the evaluation, together with the implementors' own input about what is feasible, should be used to set objectives for the full expert system. The whole system's purpose and objectives should be open to reconsideration. Indeed, since the building process itself involves continuous feedback, the objectives will already have been modified and/or clarified during work on the pilot system. The objectives set for the full system will then form the basis of a proposal to proceed.

Assuming management approval, the full system can be implemented using the same techniques of analysis, incremental building, and refinement that will have been used for the pilot (see Part V for details). Implementing the full system also involves feedback form experts, users, and management. Therefore the final form of the system and definition of what it achieves will be but the latest stage in an evolutionary process.

To summarise the strategy:

- Applications should be selected against the organisation's overall business objectives. Potential applications start with the business priorities and are then filtered according to the contribution that an expert system might make, and lastly against the technical feasibility.
- A pilot phase is used to establish feasibility, costs, and business benefits.
- Experience gained in the pilot phase is used to revise the desired objectives in the light of what is achievable. The full implementation can then proceed with confidence.

4.4.4   Natural selection

Du Pont in the USA have adopted a totally different strategy from the one outlined in section 4.4.3. Their expert systems group observed that it would be difficult for them to pinpoint the most suitable applications within such a large company, and a great deal of user education would be required. Therefore they opted to encourage a large, mixed population of applications, and subject them to natural selection.

Owing to the perseverance of an independently minded manager, Du Pont accepted a policy of allowing almost any interested employee to try building an expert system for himself. They equipped each expert with an expert system shell (section 9.2) running on a personal computer, and allowed him to get on with it. Out of perhaps seven hundred applications started, Du Pont now have some seventy expert system applications in routine use. The attrition rate has been high, but the argument is that genuinely useful systems will survive because of their value to the users. The corporate investment per successful application has undoubtedly been much smaller than in many other organisations.

Most of these systems have been built by the experts themselves, either for their own use or for their immediate colleagues. They are all 'rabbits', i.e. small systems with less than about 200 rules†. The breeding philosophy is the same: produce in large numbers, and the species will prosper even though many die in infancy.

Whilst Du Pont have made remarkable progress, we believe that their future strategy should provide more knowledge engineering support for the experts. Their experience appears to mirror our own, i.e. that experts working alone tend to produce systems which are only really suitable for the experts themselves (see section 7.3). At Du Pont, the great majority of the live systems are only used by one person. They have yet to capitalise on their success by making the know-how available throughout the organisation, as opposed to only at its source. Sharing the know-how would greatly increase the leverage of what has already been achieved. However, this will not happen if all the work remains at an individual level. Corporate support should be provided for those applications which have corporate benefits.

If other organisations choose to follow this 'natural selection' approach, we strongly recommend that the amateur system developers should have access to experienced help. This should multiply the effect of the knowledge engineering skills which already exist within the organisation, minimise time lost due to small difficulties, and promote the development of systems with shareable know-how.

4.5   IDENTIFYING MEANINGFUL APPLICATIONS

We have suggested that expert systems can contribute to the overall performance of the business, potentially provide a competitive advantage,

† There are rabbits, buffaloes, and elephants. See section 6.2.

and enable users of the system to be not only clever but also wise. A major contributing factor to the effective delivery of these promises lies in the selection of the applications.

The criteria for selecting an application can be summarised as follows:

- The application must contribute to the overall objectives of the organisation. It should not focus on a task which is relatively inconsequential, however much it may lend itself to an expert system development.
- The task should preferably be one for which success has material value (although not always demonstrable in cash terms). Some examples include:
  — selling aids
  — coping with a sudden loss of services
  — handling employee relations correctly
  — configuring complex products
  — maintaining safety standards
- The experience and know-how being applied by the human expert must make a real contribution to the success of the task.
- The know-how to be included must be reasonably well understood.
- Solving the problem must rely on reasoning rather than calculating or physical skills.
- The expert who will be the source of the know-how must believe in its potential value to non-experts.

Specific benefits which can accrue from a well-chosen application are:

External (i.e. to enhance competitiveness and the ability to perform in the market place)

— improved competitor analysis
— increased sales effectiveness
— better information dissemination to and from customers
— raised quality of service
— reduction in errors and omissions
— cross-fertilisation within the organisation
— enhanced image
— higher quality staff
— on-the-spot response to specialised requests
— improved knowledge of products and services
— enhancements to existing services

Internal (to enhance efficiency and effectiveness)
— improved delegation of tasks
— less experienced staff handling a higher proportion of the work
— experts freed to handle novel problems
— specialist expertise available 24 hours, seven days a week, and in all locations

— vigilance on repetitive tasks
— consistent thoroughness in the performance of tasks
— standardisation in the execution of important tasks
— reduced dependence on key individuals
— the establishment of a corporate reservoir of pooled experience
— increased staff morale
— improved training facilities

Some business functions are more strategic to the organisation than others. For example, the new product development department and the marketing function are both crucial for long-term survival. These areas promise higher and more visible returns than improvements in, say, administration or record keeping. However, this does not mean that only high profile applications can generate an acceptable return. There are many instances of expert systems which only generate modest feedback, but do not suffer from excessive user expectations and can deliver useful results.

Selecting potential applications is the process of identifying priority tasks where an expert system would be:

— useful,
— feasible,
— sensible, and
— worthwhile.

The following checklists set out guidelines for making the assessment.

Checklist 1 — Is it useful?
That is, will the expert system provide a real benefit for the organisation?

- Is this a valuable skill, with few experts?
- Is this a skill which is important, but rarely used?
- Is there a risk that the expertise may be lost from the organisation?
- Might key staff leave or be head-hunted?
- Is it necessary to rush key personnel to trouble spots?
- Do the existing experts get called out at unsocial hours?
- Do the experts spend much of their time handling relatively routine requests?
- Is it often necessary to refer back to the expert?
- Is there a problem of consistency across the organisation, or between head office and the branches?
- Are new projects interrupted by the need to support established ones?
- Are staff obliged to make decisions for which they do not really have the know-how?
- Are staff expected to respond to customers, or otherwise handle the situation, with little support?
- Are staff expected to be familiar with extensive manuals, laws regulations, or codes of practice?

- Could the staff who deal with customers sell a wider range of the company's products or services?
- Do staff have to be frequently updated with new products or new policies?
- Is it necessary to provide extensive customer support, or a 'hot line'?
- Is there a rapid turnover or rotation of key staff?
- Is there a large spend on training or re-training?
- Is there some particular reason why the project should be implemented as an expert system (e.g. to gain experience)?

Scoring: 'yes' to any of these indicates a possible benefit from an expert system. If the answer to every question is 'no' then it is not clear what benefit the expert system will provide.

Checklist 2 — Is it feasible?
That is, can the problem be solved using an expert system?

(Existence of know-how)
- Are there generally recognised experts?
- Do the experts perform substantially better than novices?
- Do the experts usually agree on major points?
- Can the problem be solved by applying past experience, rather than requiring new insights?
- Can the problem be solved without creativity or imagination?
  If 'no' then does all the creativity come from the system's users?
- Is the know-how structured in some way rather than just being a mass of experiences?

(Availability)
- Is an authoritative expert available to help on the project?
- Is the expert willing, even enthusiastic?
  If 'no', can they be intrigued into helping willingly?
- Is the expert reasonably articulate?

(Use of reasoning)
- Can the problem-solving be meaningfully described, rather than just demonstrated?
- Can the problem be solved without physical skills such as manipulation or balance?
- Can the problem be solved without human senses such as sight, touch, or smell?
- Could the expert solve the problem by talking to the user over a telephone line?
  If 'no', would it be sufficient if the user could also be shown pictures or drawings?

(Size)
- Can the problem be solved without referring to common sense?
- Is the extent of the problem clear?
  If 'no' can it be defined so that it is possible to say which tasks are a part of it, and which are not?

- Can a single expert solve the problem within a few minutes or hours, rather than days?
  If 'no', then can the problem be segmented and tackled one piece at a time?

(Other points)
- Will there always be a human to interpret the system's output and filter out 'obvious' errors before action is taken?
- Can the expert ignore what the user is thinking?
- Is the expert's knowledge of six months ago still useful?
  If 'no', is the purpose of the exercise to capture know-how as it accumulates?

Scoring: a reply of 'no' to any of these means that an expert system may not be feasible. (In the case of physical skills or senses then it will definitely not be feasible.) At the very least, the difficulty, and therefore the expense, will be increased. 'if no ...' shows how the issue can be avoided in some cases.

Checklist 3 — Is it sensible?
That is, is an expert system a good choice for the application?

- Is practical skill a crucial factor in solving the problem?
- Does the skill lend itself to rules of thumb (heuristics) for short cuts, recognising familiar situations and deciding how to proceed?
- Is it acceptable that the system may sometimes take much longer than usual to reach a solution, or may not reach a solution at all?
- Does the solution entail reasoning about ideas and concepts ('symbolic reasoning') rather than performing calculations?
- Do the data remain fixed during a run (or only change slowly)?
- Is it possible to reach the solution without having to work with several, partly formed solutions simultaneously ('hypothesise and test')?
- Is the system aimed at serving a clearly identified group of users?
- If the system were made available to users, would it be sufficiently interesting and/or useful that they would examine it more than once or twice?
- Can the users be involved in the development?
- Will the system be made freely available to the users at the location where they take their decisions?
- Will the users be rewarded for using the system (not necessarily in cash)?
- Is there a plan for long-term development of the system, and does this have management support?

Scoring: the more 'yes' the better. The early items in the list above are important in establishing whether an expert system is the best approach and how difficult it will be to implement; the later items are relevant to its success in service.

Checklist 4 — Is it worthwhile?
That is, is the expert system likely to be a good investment?

- Is it possible that the benefits might justify the proposed expenditure and commitment of skilled staff time?
- Is there sufficient evidence and/or incentive to build a prototype to test the feasibility?
- Would an alternative solution be better (not necessarily computer-based)?
- What are the consequences of *not* having the expert system?

Scoring: these are the issues. Managers must ascertain the scale of the benefits for their own organisation, balance these against the likely costs, and form their own judgement.

4.6   BENEFITS AND COSTS

The benefits to be derived from an expert system are harder to quantify than for a conventional computer system. The advantages of the expert system often appear to be qualitative rather than quantitative as they are largely to do with improved human performance. For example, what price should one put upon better product design? The advantages are all too obvious in one's competitors, but the internal benefits may only be measurable with hind-sight, once the system has been in service for some time.

The best-known business success is X/CON, used by the US computer manufacturer DEC. This system is unique in the length of time it has been in use, and the detail in which its benefits have been monitored. X/CON is used to configure orders for DEC's VAX range of computers, i.e. to prepare a detailed parts list to fulfil a customer order. Configuring these machines is a lengthy and complex process which requires a high level of specialist skill. Since the task is also highly repetitive, mistakes were inevitable when done by humans. In fact only 37% of configurations were correct in every detail at the first attempt when prepared by hand.

X/CON is huge. It is believed to be the most complex expert system in commercial use. It now contains over 8,000 rules expressed in a computer language called OPS-5, and is still growing†. DEC has invested perhaps 50 man-years development effort, at a cost of several million dollars. The obvious benefit is that the team of specialist configurers has remained at a constant size of about 12 people, whereas it has been estimated that well over 100 configurers would now be required to cope with the current workload. Since 30 staff are now employed in X/CON's continuing develop-ment, the direct saving is the cost of at least 60 staff.

However, greater savings lie elsewhere. Mistakes in configuring are always an embarrassment to the supplier and an irritation to the customer. Considerable sales, support, engineering and administrative effort is

---

† We are grateful to Peter Sell of DEC for this and other details.

required to resolve them, not to mention the loss of credibility. For X/CON, this saving has been put at over $100 million in total, as a direct result of the reduction in configuring errors.

There is more. The greatest benefit of all relates to DEC's long-term survival in what is one of the world's most competitive industries. It is DEC's policy to offer customers a completely tailored product: the company will provide any technically compatible mix of components to match the customer's exact requirements. This gives DEC a clear marketing edge over competitors who can only offer a limited choice of equipment packages. This marketing policy is only sustainable because X/CON provides the ability to configure the large flow of orders in precise detail.

A much more modest system was cost-justified on the basis of revenue and break-even, and not on savings. Expertech Ltd and Robson Rhodes have developed an expert system application which helps its users to apply the UK law relating to dismissing employees in a fair manner. (Expertech is a leading UK supplier of expert systems software. Robson Rhodes is a London firm of chartered accountants.) The system is sold as a commercial product. It was built by three specialists (one knowledge engineer and two experts on employment law) in a total of about 5 man-months. The most conservative basis would be to take the opportunity cost of using these staff, say £500 per day, giving a direct cost of approximately £50,000. If we assume a selling price of £250 per unit, 50% of which was absorbed by marketing and distribution, the development cost would be recovered after 400 sales. Since the head of every medium or large business unit in the UK was a possible customer, this was deemed to be an acceptable risk. However, even in this case, the major benefits were intangible. The system contributed to competitive edge by raising market awareness of the contributing companies, and possibly creating opportunities to sell associated services and products. These latter were likely to be much more valuable than the package itself.

Notice that for the purchasers, a different cost justification applied. Most of the law on employment provides for fair treatment of employees. Employers who wrongfully dismiss an employee can be penalised by an industrial tribunal, and perhaps fined many thousands of pounds. They also risk damaging their industrial relations. Handling just one such case correctly would justify the purchase price of the expert system many times over. However, the system's real use is not for dismissal litigation at all, but for avoiding it. The key benefit for business managers lies in the system's guidance on how to conduct serious disciplinary proceedings in an ethical and fair manner. In all likelihood, dismissal will not then be necessary. Interestingly, this system has also been purchased by at least one trade union: the know-how can equally be applied to supporting an employee's position.

These cases illustrate the general statement made above, that the benefits of an expert system are often in quality and effectiveness, and may only be measurable with hindsight. The direct financial savings may be no more than a bonus.

We are hesitant to suggest typical costs for projects since there are so many influences. Any figures quoted might be taken too literally. However, by way of illustration, Appendix D gives examples of projects with total budgets ranging from £30,000 to £500,000.

4.7   JUSTIFYING THE INVESTMENT

Investment decisions usually gain approval on the basis of a positive cost/benefit analysis. However, it has already been shown that the benefits can rarely be estimated accurately. This leads to a paradox:

(1) formal cost justification is meaningless because it cannot be done properly (this from the expert systems specialist), and
(2) cost justification is the only valid basis for approving funds (from the conservative manager).

Both of these viewpoints have merit. Certainly, there are real difficulties of estimating costs and benefits. However, in real life it is always necessary to compete for funds with other projects. To compete within the organisation it will be necessary to have a cost justification document, however great the uncertainties involved. The decision by the Board of Directors may still be made on emotional criteria, probably influenced by internal politics, but the cost justification remains a necessity.

The other motivation for performing a cost/benefit analysis is the value of the investigation itself. The enforced discipline of estimating costs and benefits is an excellent means of clarifying the developers' own thinking. It may well lead to better objectives being set for the development.

'The plan is nothing.
To plan is everything.'

A standard cost/benefit analysis is calculated by projecting the incremental cash flows attributable to an investment. In other words, this is the detailed projection of cash inflows and cash outflows that occur as a result of the investment. These are estimates of the potential revenues that will be generated and the expected costs in order to generate those revenues. The 'revenues' may also be in the form of cost reduction.

Long-term investment decisions are seen as high risk. The financial risk lies not only in the absolute size of the investment, but in the timing of the cash flows. Therefore the longer it takes a project to deliver a working system, the greater the perceived risk. Furthermore, the eventual costs of an expert system are not always clear at the outset, and the estimates will evolve as the project progresses. This is one very good reason for managing the development in small steps, so that costs can be closely monitored and the risk contained.

Costs are usually assessed by comparison with similar projects; there is no better method at present. The obvious difficulty is that similar systems are not readily found, and/or many firms keep their expert system developments confidential. Additionally, it is usually the case that only the next step in a development can be estimated with any confidence. An initial estimate of the resources for the entire project is only sensible as a budgetary provision. The correct strategy is to estimate the first stage of development in detail, and to have provisional estimates for the remaining stages. After each stage, the estimates are revised to reflect the experience gained, and possibly to accommodate changing objectives.

A cost/benefit analysis is then arrived at by, inter alia:

- estimating the investment in cash flow terms, taking careful account of the amount and the timing of the outflows.
- forecasting the potential cash in-flows (revenues and savings), again by amount and by timing.
- discounting the cash flows at the company's weighted average cost of capital.

If the net effect of the above is a positive net inflow, then the project should, in theory, be undertaken.

The reality is usually different. The benefits being sought from the expert system are often in the form of better human performance, or competitive edge. It is hard to count the effectiveness of people directly — only their ineffectiveness is obvious! Similarly, competitive advantage can only be valued with hindsight. Therefore the value placed on the benefits is a subjective one, and requires a consensus on what the impact of the expert system will be. Factors such as expressing the costs in real terms become secondary. If discounting the costs to today's prices has a significant effect, then either the project is exceptionally long or the benefits take a long time to accrue.

Most systems are built on the basis that the result is obviously valuable, e.g. preserving life, securing a vital skill, or enabling the company to survive. Typically the consequences of failing in the task are disastrous and/or unreasonably expensive. For example, what is the value of improving the performance of an oil trader buying and selling lots on the international market? Avoiding just one poor decision could justify the costs of the system in full. However, no one will ever measure its success because there is no control to measure against. The vagaries of the oil market are so great that an improvement would have to be spectacular to be evident in the short term. Similarly, an expert system which helped its users to develop success-ful new products could make a crucial contribution to its owner's prosperity. It is unlikely that the system would be given credit directly, since its role would be to further the skills of its users.

Therefore the real discussion of costs and benefits centres around the extent to which an expert system can promote success in the chosen task, and the value to the organisation of that success. Management is then asked to take a limited risk by investing in a pilot project. This pilot is used to test the effectiveness of the system by trial use with users. When complete, the pilot can also be used to obtain a better estimate of the total costs. Management can now make a judgement about the next phase, since the uncertainties are much reduced.

For expert systems, both the costs and the potential benefits are likely to include a high element of 'the price of time'. The productive use of time is always a highly subjective issue. Nevertheless, many organisations are now going ahead with expert systems projects even where the formal cost justification exercise does not guarantee clear returns in advance. A forward-looking organisation is always required to take some calculated risks — especially if it believes that it can secure the benefits.

4.8   SECURING THE BENEFITS

The greatest contribution of an expert system is to improve the performance of its users. If this is not evident after the system has been accepted into use then it has failed in a major objective. To ensure that an organisation receives the expected benefits, it should set very clear objectives and expectations for the expert system. All the justifications in the world will not ensure that the benefits manifest themselves in an acceptable manner without being supported by a well-thought-out development plan which includes the deployment of the necessary ingredients of know-how, people, technology and methods.

4.9   THE FIRST APPLICATION

Selecting the first application is both important and difficult. Its importance lies not only in the fact that the choice of application will affect the outcome of the project, but also that success or failure will be a precursor of how expert systems are generally viewed within the organisation. Our experience is that the first project has a disproportionate effect on views as to what expert systems are, where they can be applied, and how effective they will be. This appears to hold true however atypical the application, and regardless of the view of the implementation team.

Added to this, by definition the first project will have no history to call on when problems or complications arise. There are always cynical types in an organisation whose theme tune of 'I told you so' will resound at the slightest hint of a setback. The message is:

> if you intend taking expert systems seriously
> then start with a relatively simple application
>> and aim for modest results
>> and split the project into small steps
>> and monitor and support the project team
>> and avoid announcing any triumphs until the benefits can be
>>> adequately demonstrated

As with all system developments, tenacity and prudence are the keys to success. For expert system developments, a strong dose will be useful!

The first application should call on the skills of an experienced and confident expert who is prepared to venture into uncharted territory. The expert should be prepared to give of his time to understand what an expert system really is, rather than what others might say it is. A motivated and involved expert will pave the way for other experts.

Similarly, the organisation should select an experienced knowledge engineer if at all possible. In our experience it has been worthwhile for an organisation to call on the services of experienced outside consultants to act as knowledge engineers if there is no experience internally. Not only will this increase the chances of success, but it will provide great assistance to the expert. The relationship between expert and knowledge engineer is discussed in detail in chapters 13 and 14.

5

Make or buy

5.1 DECISION CRITERIA

The decision as to whether the resources to build an expert system should come from within the organisation, an external supplier, or a mixture of both depends on:

- any existing corporate culture,
- the views of the sponsoring manager,
- the strategic importance of the application,
- possible confidentiality,
- any existing in-house capability,
- the required timescales,
- the budget available,
- support for ongoing maintenance and development.

The last point is probably the most important to a satisfactory long-term strategy. The owner of an expert system must always plan for its continuing development, for if the system is not developed it will fail to reflect current thinking. This means that it will no longer be a useful assistant for its users, and it will fall into disuse. (Since conventional computer systems can hardly respond to changes in requirements at all, fossilisation is a main cause of their being abandoned.)

Sources of help are identified in section 5.3. The decision for management is whether to rely on external resources, or to develop an in-house capability.

5.2 BUYING IN APPLICATIONS

The great majority of expert systems are developed for use by a specific organisation. This is to be expected, since the prime aim is to capture the specialised know-how within that organisation. However, there are applications where the know-how is not held by the user, and the purpose is to buy it in. These applications may or may not allow the purchaser to modify the know-how for his own purposes.

There are a small number of large, off-the-shelf applications. The best known is called Intellect, which is a front end for databases. It can accept enquiries in American English, and translate these into calls on the data-base. The sentence analysis is quite sophisticated, so that it appears to the user that the software can understand colloquial American. It also retains the context, so that for example 'print it' is understood to mean 'print the last table of items retrieved'. This system is sold for its clever performance: it is a rare example of commercially applied artificial intelligence techniques.

A recent development is the availability of a small number of low-cost business applications built using expert system shells, and running on personal computers. Here, the product being offered is the know-how itself rather than the program. Topics covered include company financial health, employment law, licensing of databases holding personal information, and payments to staff on sick leave or maternity leave. For obvious reasons these are biased towards applications which might be of use in any company. Whilst the potential is large, this market has yet to take off.

Business applications will multiply with the arrival of 'skeleton' systems. These overcome the problem of know-how being specific to an organisation by providing only the structure and the general principles of the domain. The purchasers then develop the system for their own use by providing expertise which is specific to their own organisations. The system which is sold provides a 'skeleton' on which the customer provides the 'flesh'. This requires considerably less knowledge engineering effort and skill than starting the system from scratch. Additionally, the difficult process of establishing an overall structure and identifying generic principles will already have been done. Therefore the purchasers can achieve customised applications at much lower cost than doing all the work themselves. There can easily be a saving of six to nine months involved. Once this trend becomes established, it will be possible to involve leading experts to develop the skeleton, and to defray the costs of development and refinement over many purchasers. We expect this to be a growth market over the next few years.

5.3   USING OUTSIDE SERVICES

An organisation's own staff should always be involved to some extent in an expert system project. However, it may be wise to subcontract all or part of the work to an outside organisation in the following cases:

- To provide a demonstration for management
  Where there is no previous experience of expert systems in the organisa-tion, user management may be unwilling to proceed without a realistic demonstration. Indeed, lack of awareness of expert systems among user management is often cited as a major barrier to their introduction. As described in section 4.4, the recommended approach is to implement a 'slice' of a favoured application and to use this as a demonstration. Provided that an able contractor is chosen, then contracting out the building of the system will be the fastest and most certain way of achieving a demonstrable system. This also has the benefit of fixing the financial

commitment. However, we would strongly recommend a degree of involvement by internal staff, otherwise there will be no contribution to in-house skills.

Naturally, the system builders will need access to experts and to trial users. The purchaser should also assign a project manager to monitor the system's objectives, since if the system fails to address a genuine organisational need then it will fail to impress as a demonstration.

- To test the feasibility of a hard problem
  It may be that the problem chosen goes beyond expert know-how, and will require research into previously unsolved problems. This suggests a need for artificial intelligence skills and the associated paraphernalia of workstations and knowledge engineering environments. Since the skills and the equipment are so expensive to acquire, it may be decided that the whole system should be built by a specialist supplier. Note that if this is done, the purchaser will be buying a 'black box' program: it is unlikely that anyone other than the developers will be able to refine it in the future.

- To overcome staff shortages
  A shortage of knowledge engineering skills is sometimes perceived as the main barrier to expert systems development. For systems requiring research, this may well be true. However, systems based on know-how (as described in this book) require considerably less technical expertise. The majority of systems based on know-how have been built by amateur teams, often self-taught. Skills shortages can be overcome by allowing for a learning period at the beginning of a project and selective use of outside consultancy and knowledge engineering help.

  Outright shortage of resources is a different situation. There may be no suitable staff available, or none available within the desired timescale. In that case there is no alternative but to use outside resources. The comments made above (concerning demonstration for management) apply here also. At least one member of staff should be closely involved in the project and undertake some of the building work to ensure continuity.

Knowledge engineering services can be purchased either to carry out the bulk of the building work, or to assist an in-house team. The usual sources are:

— The software supplier, which is the preferred source for assistance in using their particular products. At least one member of the in-house team should acquire a thorough understanding of the software.

— Consultancies, including systems houses. All of the major firms have an interest in expert systems because it is an attractive growth area for them. Consultancies are not always as objective as might be supposed, since some have an established preference for particular methods or products.

— Some universities have artificial intelligence activities, and their staff are often available for contract work. Both their skills and their motivation are relevant to projects which require an element of research into unsolved problems.

5.4   DEVELOPING IN-HOUSE SKILLS

The alternative to purchasing outside services is to develop an in-house capability. In the long term this will be more economical since the permanent staff will have a better knowledge of the organisation's aims and operations. Two factors should be anticipated when setting up an expert systems activity: time to gain confidence, and critical mass.

There will be an initial delay while the team gain experience with the hardware and software to be used, and tackle their first projects (see section 13.2.2). The first projects should be small and not strategically vital — so that the budding knowledge engineers are not pilloried for their early mistakes.

The emphasis should be on user applications from the beginning, not on 'learning exercises' carried out in a vacuum. Having to deliver a working system has a salutary effect. Also, the systems should be exposed to users early on. There is a tendency in newly formed groups to hide their first application until they feel it is as perfect as they can make it — in some cases this has meant no applications being reviewed with users for over a year! Such a defensive view is quite wrong. Knowledge engineers must learn to thrive on comments from users, critical or otherwise, and the sooner they gain experience with users' likes and dislikes the better.

When an initial project is undertaken using Research and Development funds, then there is a danger that the potential user department will have little commitment to it when the time comes for implementation. Barriers may then be erected to justify inaction. Difficult though it may be to get agreement, the chances of success will be much improved if the user department has a financial stake in the system's success. 'You don't value what you don't have to pay for.'

Critical mass also has a major effect on the productivity of the knowledge engineers. Where expert systems are not part of the organisational culture, the environment will be hostile, or indifferent at best. In a large company, a sensible minimum is to plan for four to six staff once there is a commitment to expert systems development. Where there are existing expert systems which are seen as successful, or there is solid support from management, the central team can be reduced to three or four. The group should always be accommodated together and have opportunity to share experiences and problems. Isolating the group members, for example one in each business unit, will have a strongly negative effect.

An expert systems group will effectively be introducing a new technology into the organisation. Barring a spectacular success bringing them to the attention of top management, the process is likely to call for skill and persistence. The group manager should be a strong-minded individual. Also, the experience is that some data processing departments have been unsupportive, even downright antagonistic. This is damaging, since their skills will certainly be needed at some stage. A stance of 'support when needed' is the most helpful. An expert systems group should not be made part of the data processing department to avoid the risk that expert systems might be used as just another software technique. This would be to waste the main benefits.

Some expert systems groups have been set up as research activities. Rather than being focused on producing applications, their brief has been to 'evaluate the technology' or somesuch. However, technology does not earn profits, only its successful application does. The technology of expert systems is already ahead of commerce and industry's ability to apply it. Therefore it is strongly recommended that any expert systems activity should be firmly directed towards useful applications from the outset.

5.5   RECOMMENDATIONS

The optimum course of action is to pick up speed by using expertise which already exists in service organisations, while developing in-house skills. The in-house skills can be applied to developing the early applications after they go into field use, and can be expanded towards self-sufficiency at any desired rate. The use of experienced help provides speed and safety: speed in getting the organisation's own staff up the learning curve, and safety by avoiding wasted effort pursuing 'blind alleys'. A novice team working with an experienced consultant can easily halve the time to produce their first live application compared to the time it would have taken unsupported, with a better finished result.

Obviously it will be necessary to identify an experienced source of help. Track record (i.e. systems successfully produced) is the only real guide. Be cautious of public profile alone.

The most useful points to seek help during a project are:

— During the initial investigation, to identify a suitable application from among the possibles. This will avoid the risk of a discouraging 'false start'.
— During the early, structuring phase of a project. Skilful work here will lay a sound foundation for the whole project and will repay itself many times over.
— As and when the application reaches a complexity where detailed knowledge of using the software is required.
— When an application is being readied for trials with users, to advise on style, presentation, intelligibility, and user facilities.

In a project carried out by an inexperienced knowledge engineer over a period of two months, it would not be unusual to use a consultant for one day a week, say eight to ten days in total.

Part III
Technology

6

How expert systems work

This chapter gives a technical description of how expert systems work, and the functions of the key components.

6.1 AN OUTLINE

Put simply, an expert system works by taking data in from the user, applying know-how to it, and thereby generating useful conclusions (fig. 6.1).

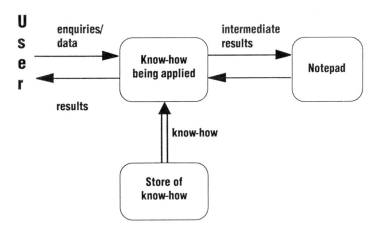

Fig. 6.1 — An expert system in use.

For example, during a session with an expert system about taxation, we might have the following:

— data from the user, perhaps an enquiry about tax liability followed by a series of answers to questions;
— know how about taxation which is applied to assess the liability;
— conclusions being reported to the user about whether there was a liability, why, and how much.

These functions are carried out by four key components within the expert system (fig. 6.2):

(1) the knowledge base, which is where the know-how is stored;
(2) the inference engine, which carries out the reasoning;
(3) the database, which is used by the inference engine as its 'notepad', or short-term memory;
(4) the user interface, which handles the conversation with the user.

In addition, many systems have two further components:

(5) a developer's interface, which provides facilities for building and modifying the knowledge base;
(6) an external interface, which allows for data to be passed to and from other programs and files (i.e. not just to and from the user).

This structure is common to nearly all expert systems, whatever their application area.

This characteristic structure is quite different from the structure of a conventional computer program. In an expert system, the know-how (in the knowledge base) is separated from the routines which make use of it (the inference engine). This is a crucial feature because it means that the two parts can be developed independently. In a conventional program the know-how is buried in the coding of the program, and is effectively lost.

6.2 THE KNOWLEDGE BASE

The knowledge base is the heart of an expert system since it contains the detailed knowledge supplied by an expert. It is usually in the form of rules (section 3.3), expressed in whatever language is provided by the software tool being used. The languages vary enormously, from the very simple to the hugely complex, and from easily readable to some kind of cipher.

In practice, knowledge bases also contain facts, questions and other items needed to make the system work as required — but the rules express the expertise. A knowledge base can contain just a few rules, or thousands, depending on its scope. Additionally, what requires a single rule in one software system may require ten or twenty rules in another.

Therefore, quoting the number of rules in a knowledge base is an even less accurate measure of content than quoting the number of pages in a book. Like the pages in a book, individual rules can be of great merit or trivial and repetitive. However, Professor Ed Feigenbaum has coined some amusing (and very approximate) categories:

Rabbits	up to 200 rules	small systems and demonstrations
Buffaloes	200-3000 rules	typical business systems
Elephants	over 3000 rules	major developments

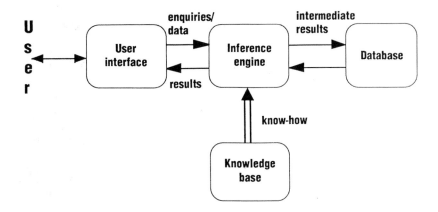

Fig. 6.2 — Key components of an expert system.

There is a strong trend towards larger knowledge bases. This is a result of accumulating knowledge engineering experience and the tackling of more serious business applications. We expect that expert systems of several thousand rules will be commonplace by 1990, and that these categories will have to be revised upwards.

6.3   THE INFERENCE ENGINE

Know-how is only useful if it can be applied, and that is the function of the inference engine. In a rule-based system the inference engine is essentially a rule interpreter. Its function is to use the rules, facts and other items in the knowledge base to solve the problem set by the user.

The inference engine is the 'reasoning' component of the expert system. The word 'inferencing' is actually more accurate, since it reflects the strictly logical processes carried out by the computer, as opposed to the richness of human reasoning. The inference engine is a set of routines which carry out deductive reasoning by applying the know-how in the knowledge base. Note that the inference engine has no understanding of what it is doing, or what it achieves, any more than a wristwatch understands the meaning of the time it shows. The process is simply a mechanical one.

In human terms, the inference engine has two possible decision making strategies (fig. 6.3):

either   eliminate alternatives
or: search for a match with a known solution.

When following the strategy of eliminating alternatives, a human would begin by identifying the possible solutions to the problem, and then work through them until a satisfactory solution was found. Typically, each

Eliminate alternatives

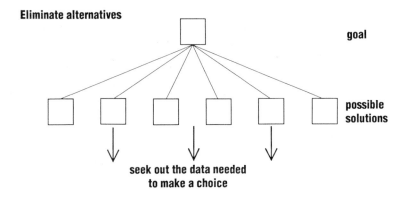

goal

possible
solutions

seek out the data needed
to make a choice

Seek a match

gather data

respond according to
previous experience

Fig. 6.3 — Basic inferencing methods.

solution would have to be explored to some extent before it could be
rejected or accepted. In expert systems jargon, this is known as 'goal
directed reasoning' or 'backward chaining'. The 'goals' are possible solutions, usually identified by the user. For example, in an expert system about
personal financial planning, the user might set the following goal:

'Which pension plan should I choose?'

Using backward chaining, an expert system would use know-how from a
pensions adviser about how to choose between the various options. It might
then respond to this enquiry by recommending one or more plans.

The second style of searching for a match is different. Instead of referring
to a list of pre-specified alternatives, the strategy is to gather data until a
known pattern is recognised. The data 'sparks off' a response based on
previous experience. To continue the pensions example, the user of the
expert system might volunteer:

'I am 58 years old. So what?'

The user is searching for a reaction, testing to see what conclusions might emerge from this new information. This process, where the user provides data and lets the system run from that, is known as 'data driven reasoning' or 'forward chaining'. It will be apparent that, unlike backward chaining, the conclusions can be more wide ranging and less predictable. Such differences are explored further in section 6.3.3.

The word 'chaining' is used because both of these inferencing methods involve threading through a chain of rules. This can be seen if we examine the mechanisms involved in more detail.

6.3.1   Backward chaining

Consider how a sales manager might examine a business problem of poor profitability. What should he do about it? We can use his imaginary train of thought to illustrate how an inference engine could tackle this question. This section on backward chaining illustrates the process used to eliminate alternatives.

One of the sales manager's options is to step up the sales effort. This will be expensive, so it should not be undertaken lightly. However, he reasons that if competitors are winning orders from his customers then it might be a necessary expense. (Obviously there are many other options in real life, but exploring just this one alternative will serve to illustrate the process.) The sales manager has identified a rule of thumb, or heuristic:

rule 1

> if competition may be a problem
> then try increasing the sales effort

So far, so good. But how is the sales manager to know if competitors are becoming a problem? The obvious effect will be that his volume of sales will fall. But that is not sufficient in itself: there might be other reasons for a fall in sales. For example, the customers may not be doing as much business themselves, or may have improved their methods so that they do not have to buy in so much material. The sales manager knows that competitive activity is signalled by a combination of falling sales and the customers still using the same amount of his type of product. This is his second rule:

rule 2

> if your volume of sales is falling
>   and your customers are still using the same amount
> then competition may be a problem

The sales manager has now arrived at questions which he can ask. The volume of sales can be found from his own statistics, and the quantity being used might be checked by telephoning a selection of customers.

What the sales manager has done is to start from his goal (what action to take), list the possible solutions (we have only considered one, increasing the sales effort), and work back to the questions which he needs to ask. An expert system using these same rules might ask the questions like this:

What is the trend in sales?

Choose: rising
           flat
           falling

How much of your type of product are your regular customers using?

Choose: more than they were
           the same amount
           less than they were

Finding these questions involved going through a chain which started from the goal 'try increasing the sales effort', went via 'competition may be a problem', and then on to the two items 'your volume of sales is falling' and 'your customers are still using the same amount' (fig. 6.4).

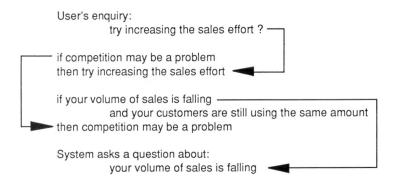

Fig. 6.4 — Backward chaining.

Backward chaining always goes from the conditions (the if part) of one rule to the conclusions (then part) of another, to the conditions of that same rule, on to another conclusion, and so on. Whilst only two rules were involved in the sales example just given, backward reasoning chains can involve any number of rules.

Although backward chaining has been described for a particular example, the process can obviously be generalised. The user starts the system running by specifying a goal, perhaps by selecting it from a menu, by typing in a command, or by having the goal built into the system. The inference engine then searches its knowledge base to find a rule which contains a relevant conclusion (i.e. one which might satisfy the goal). If the inference engine could show that the conditions of this rule were true, then the rule could be applied and the desired conclusion would have been found. (A rule whose conditions are shown to be true is said to 'fire'.) Therefore the inference engine proceeds to check each of the rule conditions in turn by applying the backward chaining process to each condition as if it were a goal itself, i.e. if a condition is itself the conclusion of another rule, then the conditions of that other rule are examined, and so on. The cascade comes to an end when there is a question to ask, or a fact is found, or there are no rules in the knowledge base which can satisfy the condition.

If the conditions of a rule are not true for a particular case then the rule is said to 'fail'. This means that for the case being considered, one or more of the conditions is not true and the rule does not apply. When a rule fails the inference engine searches for other rules which might yield relevant conclusions — these are the other alternatives in the 'eliminate alternatives' strategy. If all of the rules fail then no result will have been found, and the result is unknown.

Note that when a rule fails, this does not mean that the conclusion is false. This is a major distinction between formal logic and reasoning about know-how. For example:

> if the animal is a horse
> then it has four legs

If we knew that the animal was not a horse, it would obviously be wrong to conclude that it did not have four legs. When the conditions fail, it simply means that the rule cannot be used for this particular case.

Returning to the example about sales, we can also see how the expert system can explain its line of reasoning. Given that the inference engine is attempting to apply a chain of rules, then the user can be told what those rules are. Provided that the rules are understandable, they help to explain what the expert system is attempting to do. For example:

Expert system:
   Is your volume of sales falling?

User:
   why?
   (i.e. why ask this question)

Expert system:
   Because I am trying to show that 'competition may be a problem' using rule 2:
      if your volume of sales is falling
       and your customers are still using the same amount
      then competition may be a problem

   which is needed to establish 'try increasing the sales effort' using rule 1:

if competition may be a problem
then try increasing the sales effort

because you asked about 'try increasing the sales effort'.

The explanation shows the backward chain of reasoning which is currently being tried.

An important feature of this reasoning is that the inference engine picks out the rules which are needed. The system builder (knowledge engineer) does not have to specify how the rules are to be used, or in what order. If rule 2 above had actually been rule 102 then it would still have been found because the inference engine was searching for 'competition may be a problem'. This is the 'declarative' aspect of expert systems mentioned in chapter 3. The inference engine makes its selection using pattern matching, matching the data it is seeking against the conclusions of the rules in the knowledge base.

To complete the sales example, consider what would happen if the user were to answer 'falling' to the question about sales volume. The condition 'the volume of sales is falling' would then be true. The inference engine would apply rule 2 again, leading to the second question about 'your customers'. If the user replied 'your customers are still using the same amount', then rule 2 would fire, followed by rule 1, and the expert system would reply to the user's enquiry with a message such as:

Answer to your enquiry:
try increasing the sales effort

This illustrates the simplest way of using an expert system. The user makes an enquiry, responds to the questions as they are asked, and eventually receives a reply.

In practice there are some added complexities in backward chaining:

- If there are several rules which could all provide a result being sought, then the inference engine needs a policy for choosing the order in which to try them (known as 'conflict resolution').
- If a particular reasoning chain fails to produce the result being sought, then the inference engine must automatically try any alternative paths (known as 'backtracking').
- There are usually other sources of data apart from the rules, for example via the external interface (see section 6.7).

All of these are usually handled by the inference engine designer, and are invisible to the user.

6.3.2 Forward chaining
Forward chaining works in the opposite direction to backward chaining. Instead of being given a goal and working back to the necessary data,

forward chaining begins with data and works forward to see if any conclusions can be reached. It corresponds to the strategy of 'search for a match with a known solution'.

This can be illustrated using the same example about sales problems as was used in section 6.3.1:

rule 1

       if competition may be a problem
       then try increasing the sales effort

rule 2

       if your volume of sales is falling
         and your customers are still using the same amount
       then competition may be a problem

On another occasion, suppose the sales manager had just received a management report and noticed that 'your volume of sales is falling'. This is a piece of data, and can be applied to his rules of thumb. What would happen? Nothing. As already pointed out, knowing that the volume of sales is falling is not sufficient in itself. The first condition of rule 2 is satisfied, but we do not yet know if 'your customers are still using the same amount', therefore rule 2 cannot fire.

Suppose now that the sales manager also discovered that 'your customers are still using the same amount', by whatever means. Both conditions of rule 2 are now satisfied, and he now concludes that 'competition may be a problem'. This is a new piece of data, and can take part in further forward chaining. Using rule 1 the sales manager can immediately conclude 'try increasing the sales effort', which he may decide to act on. The forward chain started with the new information 'your customers are still using the same amount', which fired rule 2, which concluded 'competition may be a problem', which fired rule 1, which then concluded 'try increasing the sales effort' (fig. 6.5). Since there were no rules which included the condition 'try increasing the sales effort', forward chaining stops at that point.

Like backward chaining, forward chaining can also provide an explanation for any conclusion in terms of the rule which was used to deduce it. For example:

User:
    How did you conclude 'try increasing the sales effort'?

Expert system:
    By using rule 1:
        if competition may be a problem
        then try increasing the sales effort

Note that as described here, forward chaining does not lead to any

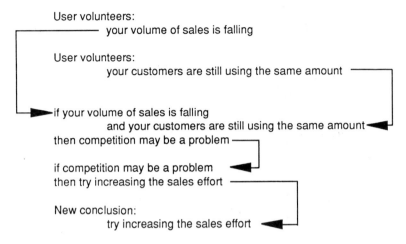

Fig. 6.5 — Forward chaining.

questions being asked. If the user is expected to supply data by answering questions, then the questions must be asked explicitly. This is usually done by a command in the conclusions of a rule, for example:

rule 3
    if your volume of sales is falling
    then *ask question*
        your customers are still using the same amount

This is one illustration of the way in which forward chaining lends itself to expressing procedures: if this-has-happened then do-this-next.

6.3.3   Comparison of backward and forward chaining

Forward and backward chaining are complementary, in that they have different uses and different effects (fig. 6.6).

	Backward chaining	Forward chaining
Also called	goal directed	data driven
Starts from	possible solutions	new data
Works towards	necessary data	any conclusions
Progression through rules	conclusions to conditions	conditions to conclusions
Style	conservative	opportunistic
Processing	efficient	possibly wasteful
User's impression	plodding but predictable	responsive but quirky
Obvious usage	selection between alternative solutions	building up solutions and 'leaps' in reasoning

Fig. 6.6 — Comparison of backward and forward chaining.

Perhaps the greatest virtue of backward chaining is that it is efficient. Because the backward chain only follows paths which may yield a useful solution, the only questions asked will be necessary ones. However, for the user the reasoning style can seem to be pedestrian. Backward chaining will dutifully explore a chain even when the user knows in advance that it will fail. It is like talking to a clerk who insists on going through every question on a form, even when you know he has the wrong form. The positive side is that it is predictable, and therefore easy for the knowledge engineer to control and for the user to follow.

To use backward chaining, it must be possible to identify the possible solutions in advance. This sets a practical limit on how many can sensibly be specified. Therefore backward chaining is basically suitable for choosing among a set of known alternatives, or for exploring a predetermined set of topics. This is sometimes called 'complex selection'. The results achieved can be far more sophisticated than this phrase suggests, even though the logical process is indeed one of selection between alternatives.

If backward chaining is cautious, then forward chaining is impetuous. Rules may fire at a complete tangent to the current line of reasoning, triggered off solely by their conditions becoming satisfied. This means that the expert system will respond to known situations (combinations of conditions), whether or not they have been specified as goals. By contrast, backward chaining will ignore any combination of circumstances which is not relevant to the goal it is currently seeking. Forward chaining has an important role here to implement the expert's short cuts: recognising a familiar situation may allow the inferencing to leap forward, bypassing much tedious analysis.

Forward chaining may generate all manner of conclusions without them having to be specifically requested. However, there is no guarantee that the user will be interested in any of these! Therefore forward chaining can absorb considerable processing time without any apparently useful effects. Forward chaining can be controlled by arranging specific paths through the rules, perhaps by ensuring that there is only ever one rule which can fire next. This is the responsibility of the knowledge engineer.

Forward chaining is the obvious choice when the system has to respond to new data (e.g. in industrial alarm processing) or where a solution has to be built up from many components (where there are too many outcomes to list individually as goals). For example, selecting a particular type of investment may be amenable to backward chaining, since the task is to choose from the available list. However, to suggest changes to a client's portfolio it will be necessary to start from the present situation and forward chain to see what opportunities present themselves.

It is important to realise that forward and backward chaining are not problem solving methods in themselves, i.e. they are not strategies used by experts to solve problems. Humans are much more subtle. Rather, they are two forms of logical processing which can be used as a means of emulating the expert's approach.

In practice, many problems call for a combination of backward and forward chaining. For example:

— in financial advice, forward chain with the current portfolio to identify

possible future strategies, backward chain to select one of these strategies, forward chain to identify possible new investments under the selected strategy, and backward chain to investigate each one;
— in fault diagnosis, forward chain from the fault symptoms to find likely problem areas, followed by backward chain to work through them. Perhaps forward chain out of a likely problem area before it is fully explored if the circumstances show it to be irrelevant after all.

Few expert systems control their reasoning in such a complex way: most have just one, fixed style. This may well be due to the small number of software products which cleanly integrate backward and forward chaining. Also, experienced knowledge engineers can usually force a problem into either just backward chaining or just forward chaining as they choose, although this may call for some contortions.

6.4   THE DATABASE

The database is relatively simple to describe. It is a working store, a 'notepad' which the inference engine can use to hold data while it is working on a problem. It holds all the data about the current task, including:

— the user's answers to questions,
— any data from outside sources (see below),
— any intermediate results of the reasoning, and
— any conclusions reached so far.

For example, at the end of the enquiry about increasing the sales effort described in section 6.3.1, the database would contain the following items:

the volume of sales is falling
        (provided by the user)
your customers are still using the same amount
        (provided by the user)
competition may be a problem
        (from rule 2)
try increasing the sales effort
        (from rule 1)

There is a clear distinction between the knowledge base and the database. The knowledge base contains know-how, and it can be applied to many different cases. Once built, a knowledge base will be saved and used many times over. The database contains data about the particular case which is being run at the time. For example, the knowledge base about sales problems might be applicable to any small manufacturing business. During a run, the database would contain data about a specific company and its trading performance.

Confusingly, there is little connection between the database within an expert system and databases as known to data processing. An expert system database is just a table in the computer's memory. For lovers of jargon, the database can also be called 'the world model'.

6.5   THE USER INTERFACE

Obviously an expert system needs to communicate with the outside world, and it does this via its interfaces. The user interface is provided to manage the dialogue with the user, typically via a standard computer terminal. A good user interface to an expert system will allow:

— the user to make enquiries of the expert system,
— the user to volunteer data before being asked,
— the system to ask questions of the user and to accept replies,
— the user to correct any wrong answers,
— the system to inform the user of any conclusions,
— the user to request help and explanation (both about the application being used and the system's own facilities),
— the user to examine the state of the reasoning at any time and to explore any conclusions reached,
— the user to examine the effect of changing some answers, i.e. to do 'what if', and
— the user to break off from a session and resume it later.

The key point is that the user can 'see into' the system to determine what conclusions have been reached so far, why those conclusions were reached, what the system is doing now, and why it is doing it. The user interface should be like an open window into the system. This is referred to as 'transparency'. It is in great contrast to conventional systems which are always 'black boxes'.

Some research work has attempted to produce 'natural language' interfaces for expert systems, i.e. to allow the user to enter requests and to volunteer information in a highly informal style. The aim is to remove the need to be familiar with using the software. These interfaces are not even remotely near the standards of everyday conversation. However, it is possible to produce 'chatty' interfaces with an apparently informal style, analogous to the way in which rules have been expressed in an informal style in this book. These rely on simple, but rigid, grammars.

There have also been projects to investigate the use of windows, icons, mice and other devices for the user interface†. Mouse-driven systems are strongly preferred by those who have learnt to use them, but can seem awkward for newcomers. Additionally, since virtually all business users only have a character-based screen and a keyboard (i.e. no high quality graphics or mouse), product suppliers have tended to tailor their software for such

† An 'icon' is a small picture on the computer screen. A 'mouse' is a small, hand-held device which controls a pointer on the screen.

equipment. The usual solution is to have a menu-based user interface. This
will change as mice and quality graphics become standard equipment. When
expert systems are made available to the public, touch screens and highly
simplified keyboards will become important.

6.6   THE DEVELOPER'S INTERFACE

The developer's interface is an extension of the user's interface because the
developer needs to be able to build knowledge bases as well as to run them.
In well integrated expert system software, the developer's tools will appear
as an extension of the user facilities. Other systems provide an interface
which is completely separate, for example the knowledge base being built
using a separate text editor and subsequently loaded into the expert system.
Integration is a considerable advantage because development consists of
rapid cycles of making changes and testing them, perhaps as often as every
few minutes.

The developer's, or knowledge engineer's, interface will be used for
building the knowledge base, running it with example data, finding errors,
making modifications, and running again. It should offer:

— A means of building and editing the knowledge base, and checking that
  the know-how is expressed in a way which the system can accept (i.e.
  checking the syntax). The more support there is for entering knowledge
  base items, the better.
— A means of examining the work so far, preferably allowing items to be
  selected according to their contents. This is like automatically indexing a
  document as it is being written. A graphical display of the knowledge
  base showing the relationships which have been established is very
  useful.
— A means of setting up links to other programs, if the expert system
  software allows this (see section 6.7).
— all the facilities of the user interface for running the expert system.
— diagnostic facilities such as logging the dialogue, tracing the reasoning
  and the state of the database, and displays of the chains of rules being
  used. The diagnostics should make it easy to find how any conclusion was
  reached (for investigating wrong conclusions) and exactly what the
  inference engine attempted to do (for investigating conclusions which
  should have been reached, but were not).

Developers are keenly interested in automatic tools for checking the
validity of a knowledge base. There are substantial gains to be had, since
testing a large knowledge base is very time consuming. A few expert systems
products do provide tools for checking logical completeness, redundancy,
consistency and so forth. Note that all these can do is to test for strictly
logical errors — they have no bearing on whether the know-how is valid or
not. An alternative ploy is to restrict the developer to a 'top down' approach
which reduces problems of completeness. This is attractive to novice system

builders but makes it difficult to keep up with an expert. Experts provide know-how when it occurs to them, not in top down form.

Research is also in progress into formal specifications of expert systems which might be provably correct. This seems to neglect a basic issue. Even if it were possible to produce a complete specification of the know-how (not true at present), and to convert this completely reliably into a working system (also beyond the bounds of today's software technology), then because the system was based on heuristics it could still make mistakes if these heuristics failed.

6.7   THE EXTERNAL INTERFACE

The user interface is responsible for handling all data going to and from the user. However, it is useful to be able to exchange data with other sources, e.g.:

— data files,
— other packages (such as spreadsheets or databases),
— other programs (for any specialised processing such as detailed calculations or looking up tables),
— other computers and communications networks (perhaps to fetch marketing data held on a corporate mainframe, or stock market information from an external information provider),
— measuring instruments and sensors (especially in industrial plant),
— specialised devices such as video disk or CD-ROM.

Note that the expert system need not be concerned with where the data comes from, or goes to. The inference engine simply calls upon the external interface to get the input it needs, and to transmit output to its proper destination.

In the past, expert systems have had very weak or nonexistent external interfaces. Basic data handling facilities like accessing files were sometimes completely missing. Even user interfaces were primitive, perhaps just a line-by-line display with the user having to type replies in full (i.e. no menus, prompting, or screen layout). This reflected the builders' motives in creating interesting programs rather than productive business tools. However, the demands of commercial use have created a strong trend towards better interfaces which allow relatively easy integration with other packages. Even so, the data handling capabilities of expert systems are still well behind those of the established data processing languages.

7

Published methods of building systems

This chapter is concerned with published methods of building expert systems. It is not an exhaustive review, but is a summary of methods which have been discussed in the literature.

These topics are important because there is a legacy from research work which needs to be kept in perspective. Most of the work described in scholarly papers is based on a theoretical approach, the implicit goal being a better intellectual understanding rather than a more useful computer system. This manifests itself in the pursuit of 'intelligence'. By contrast, most of the work on industrial and commercial applications goes unpublished. It follows that in the absence of personal experience, those who study the literature may gain a very theoretical view of what is important when building expert systems. Indeed there is an established school of thought within the expert systems industry itself which views both the use and the development of expert systems as a research-oriented activity. These organisations often have a high profile, since their professed aim is to push back the frontiers of computer technology.

Our own methods are somewhat different, and endeavour to be both pragmatic and profitable. One might then query why this chapter is included at all. The answer is that we are all still learning, and are certainly not above learning from others. That would be too ironic in a book devoted to shared expertise!

7.1 THE CURRENT POSITION

There is an obvious desire to have well understood methods which can be taught to others. This is the training alternative to apprenticeship. However, at present there is nothing approaching a consensus as to which methods of knowledge engineering are effective, or when they should be used.

Learned papers about expert systems often refer to 'inarticulate experts'. There is talk of 'the usual difficulty of extracting knowledge from the experts'. This is so prevalent that it is often treated as self evident. It has become a part of the folklore. Accordingly, several years of research into methods has been concentrated on techniques of acquiring knowledge, and these techniques are described in the following sections. However, in business, problems of experts not being able to say what they do are rare (section 12.3). On the contrary, experts usually delight in talking about their speciality. Despite this, it would be foolish to dismiss these methods since some developers obviously find them useful. Our view is that they should be freely used if and when they are found to be helpful.

Recently there has been considerable interest in the idea of an expert systems 'methodology'. We are averse to this for two reasons:

— having a 'methodology' implies having a single recipe for success, and
— the accompanying jargon is often a major obstacle.

In addition, the development work must accommodate the highly subjective criteria of experts and users so there will always be a requirement for flexibility. Our view is that there are many useful guidelines, but it is premature to speak of a methodology. The negative contribution made by jargon does not always seem to be appreciated.

There is no single method which knowledge engineers and experts can follow which will guarantee success, any more than there is a method which will guarantee learning a particular skill. Even if a particular approach works for one expert, it may not work for another. We believe that knowledge engineers should have a 'tool bag' containing a variety of techniques. Many of these are concerned with attitude and strategy, and may not be in the form of checklists or software tools. That would require that the method had been reduced to a procedure. It is up to knowledge engineers to gather their own resources and to deploy a piece of one with a fragment of another as the moment demands. One can liken this to a physician adapting his bedside manner according to the difficulty of the diagnosis, the urgency of the case, and even the mood of the patient.

7.2   THE APPROACH TO KNOWLEDGE ACQUISITION

Knowledge acquisition is the process of encouraging an expert to provide expertise, and capturing the significant elements in a permanent form. The immediate output is usually in the form of written notes and diagrams.

The techniques described here were mainly developed by those in pursuit of formal knowledge (see section 3.4). Therefore the knowledge engineers were seeking an underlying model, rather than valuing the expert's spoken knowledge for its own sake. Nevertheless, we have commented on the methods according to their value in obtaining know-how rather than formal knowledge.

The supposition is that much of the stated difficulty of obtaining knowledge arises from two sources. Firstly, experts do not describe their knowledge in a well-structured form which suits the idea of an underlying model. It seems harsh to blame this on the expert. Secondly, methods described in the literature make the assumption that knowledge acquisition is done by an analyst observing a subject. A knowledge engineer identifies the knowledge by examining what an expert says or does. It is our firm belief that knowledge acquisition must be interactive. The expert should be helped to form his own statement of the know-how rather than this being done by a second party. To treat the expert as one would a laboratory animal is to ignore the key resource — the expert's own appreciation of the problem.

All of the methods described here require a human expert. The heuristic is:

> if you do not have a human expert
> then you will not get an expert system

Or, more succinctly: 'No expert, no system'. This adage is frequently quoted, but less frequently understood. The key to a successful expert system is to capture a good quantity of practical expertise. This is different from a theoretical knowledge of the task, or a knowledge engineer's view of what the expert does. It can only be obtained from a practicing expert.

7.3 INTROSPECTION

Introspection means that the expert examines his own decision processes and also builds the expert system. This may seem ideal since it is the expert who has the know-how, but there are real difficulties:

— Some skills may be so deeply ingrained that they are hard for the expert to describe. Writing this book was just one example. The authors sometimes had difficulty describing what they intuitively knew. This has been called 'the paradox of expertise': the more proficient an expert becomes, the less they have to think about what they do (Johnson, 1983). In such cases the discipline of having to explain to someone else is very helpful. As an added benefit it also causes experts to review their own methods.
— Experts frequently assume that the users have a greater understanding than is really the case. They assume a level of 'common knowledge' which is not common at all. As a user once put it to an expert: 'I am still struggling to understand things which you have forgotten were ever a problem'. As a result, an expert system built by an expert alone may only be suitable for other experts.
— At a more basic level, an understanding of the concepts involved may be necessary even to discuss the problem. This 'implicit knowledge' is a result of familiarity rather than teaching or explanation, and can be very difficult to identify even for a knowledge engineer.
— An expert's time is usually at a premium. Working with an experienced system builder can reduce the time commitment considerably.
— The end result may be clumsy or poorly expressed because of the expert's inexperience in building expert systems. In extreme cases the disappointment may even turn the expert against the idea of expert systems.

Despite these barriers, many systems have been built by experts working unaided. However, introspection cannot be advised where there is a prospect of distributing the system to non-expert users. There is a real danger that the expert will invest a considerable personal effort, only to find that the end result does not appeal to others. This can only be discouraging. At the very least, it is wise to ensure that an experienced 'uncle' is on call to prepare the ground and to help with specific problems.

7.4 INTERVIEWING

Interviewing is the most familiar technique, and every project uses interviewing at some stage. A technique which has been widely reported in the literature is for a group of professional knowledge engineers to interview an expert for between one hour and half a day at a time. The knowledge engineers make copious notes, and may record the conversation on tape for later transcription. It is then up to the knowledge engineers to identify the expertise in what has been said, and to convert it into an organised form which can be used in an expert system. This may even involve designing a computer language specifically for the purpose of representing the knowledge. Subsequently, a team of programmers will implement this as an expert system, providing purpose built software to support the 'knowledge representation language'. The behaviour of the resulting system can then be examined by the expert. The whole process is regarded as one of 'extracting' knowledge from the expert, and herein (in our view) lies the danger.

It seems ambitious to assume that a knowledge engineer will be able to deduce how the expert actually thinks. However, many projects using formal methodologies appear to have followed this path. What they produce is a representation of the expertise which may have very little to do with the expert's own understanding. The expert system is built to behave like the expert does, rather than to use the know-how which the expert has. Frequently the system builders have chosen to record the knowledge in one of the more complex representations (e.g. semantic nets or frames, see chapter 8). These are chosen because they can be processed by the computer in ways which suit an elegant model of the reasoning. A sure sign is when the team have to invent a means of explaining the machine version of the knowledge to the expert, for example as a paper model.

If the knowledge engineering team hit upon a scheme which the expert understands, and recognises as being how he really does think, then bravo! They will have scored a considerable coup. We have yet to see this happen in practice. Persuading the expert that he or she actually does reason like the expert system is quite different. This can be a powerful influence, especially if the expert's vision of how an expert system should work has been provided by the knowledge engineers. Typically the expert does *not* reason like the mechanism which has been built, and the expert's role is to review the behaviour of the system rather than its content. The knowledge engineers are responsible for amending the knowledge to produce the desired changes in behaviour. The direct connection between the expert and the knowledge being applied in the expert system will have been lost.

It has to be said that this approach was the only one possible when the software tools could only be understood by computer professionals. This is no longer a restriction.

7.5 OBSERVATION

Rather than interviewing an expert, it is obviously possible to watch them at work. The process is recorded, perhaps on video tape, and the expert will probably be asked to give a verbal commentary. Subsequently the recordings are reviewed with the expert to determine what they were doing, and why. Memory fades fast, so it is essential that the analysis is done very soon afterwards, certainly on the same day.

The experience is that 90% of the information lies in the sound recording. Actions are usually too ambiguous to be of much direct help. Some research work has concentrated on methods of automatically analysing the spoken commentaries ('verbal protocol analysis'), which can also be applied to transcripts of interviews, but these have yet to bear fruit. The video images are mainly useful for prompting the expert during the analysis.

Great care has to be taken that real know-how is obtained during the analysis. Trying to be helpful, subjects frequently rationalise what they did. Alternatively, they simply acted intuitively and will afterwards invent a justification. The resulting explanation is likely to be plausible, logical, and consistent with what their management approves of. Seldom does it include the know-how which was actually applied. In such a formal analysis, the subjects tend to behave in the way they feel is expected of them.

There are obvious difficulties with placing experts under a video camera. Few will relish the experience. Additionally, the fact of recording has a tendency to increase the formality. Experts will willingly say things in conversation which they would not write down or be recorded saying. However, knowledge engineers can write down spoken expertise, and should do so. The sense of the expert being under examination also means that audio tape recording should be used with discretion, and always with the expert's consent. Any knowledge engineer who records an expert without his permission risks destroying all the mutual trust which has been achieved. This sense of trust and mutual openness is crucial to the transfer of real expertise. If either side feels threatened, or wronged, then real cooperation will cease.

Knowledge engineers should be prepared for the thousands of words which will be recorded during (say) a three hour session. The resulting transcript will also contain repetitions, half-expressed thoughts, mumblings, and mis-identified speakers. Transcripts are a weak source of expertise. The main use of a recording is to overcome the knowledge engineer's limitations on memory and note taking. It is often acceptable when the project is under way, but not at the initial meetings.

As a method of knowledge acquisition, observation has all the challenges of interviewing plus several of its own. Additionally, the knowledge engineer is denied access to the expert while the expert is concentrating on the task in hand. It may be the only option when the task is time critical, but then it may be unrealistic to expect the expert to give a coherent commentary. For example, financial dealing and commanding a low flying helicopter have both been studied in this way. For most purposes, observation should be regarded as a course of last resort.

7.6   PROTOTYPING

Prototyping is a development of the interview technique. The difference is that a version of the expert system itself is used as the means of discussion.

A prototype is built at an early stage. There is no attempt to make this complete: the intention is to lay the foundation which will be built on piece by piece (known as 'incremental refinement'). The expert reviews the system by running test cases, and provides explanation when it makes mistakes or takes wrong actions. The knowledge engineers subsequently modify the system, and the reviewing process is repeated.

The key point is that the expert is being prompted to provide explanation in a highly specific situation. We all know that it is very much easier to comment on a given instance rather to give an abstract description. It is correspondingly easier for an expert to provide relevant know-how, and its justification, when prompted by a particular case.

Our own preference is for a version of prototyping taken to the extreme of involving the expert, the knowledge engineer and the developing expert system as equal partners (see section 11.4).

7.7   INDUCTION

The aim of induction is to detect a pattern in the past which can be used to predict the future. The past is represented by a set of example decisions, and the prediction is in the form of a set of rules which can be applied to future cases. The user provides the examples, and the induction algorithm automatically generates a decision tree, or an equivalent set of rules (fig. 7.1). The algorithm is usually derived from original work by Ross Quinlan (the ID3 algorithm). The resulting decision tree can be run as a 'decision maker', and will correctly classify all of the given examples using the minimum number of questions.

This process seems very attractive. We are all familiar with the idea of examples, and induction will generate the rules. Could this be the end of knowledge engineering? The answer is no.

Induction does not generate new knowledge. What it does is to identify the rules which *appear* to apply within the examples. There is not necessarily any connection between the rules and our understanding of what is going on. An anecdote about an alcoholic illustrates the point. He became concerned about constantly getting drunk after drinking several gin and tonics. So he changed to whisky and tonic — but he still got drunk. So he tried brandy and tonic, and still got drunk. The answer was clear. He had to give up tonic.

The examples below were provided by an amateur mechanic as instances of what to do to restart a car which had stopped at the roadside. The attributes chosen were:

starter   whether the starter motor spins the engine
engine fires   whether the engine fires at all
petrol gauge   whether the petrol gauge shows petrol in the tank
ignition   the type of ignition system fitted to the car

	starter	engine fires	petrol gauge	ignition	suggestion
1	dead	★	none	★	get help
2	spins	no	some	electronic	get help
3	spins	no	none	★	fetch petrol
4	spins	yes	none	★	fetch petrol
5	spins	yes	some	electronic	get help
6	dead	★	some	★	kick it!
7	spins	no	some	standard	try again later

The symbol '★' means 'any value', i.e. the example applies whatever the value in that column. Therefore the first example means 'if the starter motor is dead, whether the engine fires or not, and the petrol gauge shows no petrol in the tank, whatever type of ignition is fitted, then get help'.

Induction generated the following decision tree:

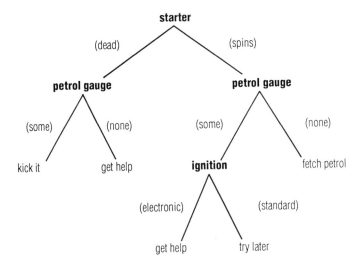

Note that the information about 'engine fires' has not been used. According to the examples this information is not needed to establish which suggestion is appropriate. Induction has simply picked out the pattern which seems to exist. The decision tree can also be represented as rules. For example, the far right suggestion in the tree is equivalent to:

> if the starter spins the engine
> and the petrol gauge shows no petrol
> then the suggestion is to fetch some petrol

Fig. 7.1 — An example of rule induction.

Induction must be treated with caution for these reasons:
- The rules produced may not be meaningful to the expert, or to users.
- The rules will only be as complete and correct as the examples supplied.
- The system has no method of recognising exceptions and special cases. Induction treats the examples as the sum total of expert knowledge.
- Induction cannot identify useful intermediate ideas, which are a key step to simplifying a problem.
- The expert may use particular strategies on different occasions. This is not shown by the examples, and will be missed (ID3 establishes its own sequence of questioning).

It follows that induced rules should never be used without the approval of an expert.

Despite these undoubted drawbacks, induction is still a powerful tool. It is the *only* automatic method available for acquiring rules, and has had some commercial success. It is said to have been used to analyse the operation of a nuclear fuel reprocessing plant in the USA using examples supplied by skilled operators. Some of the resulting rules were new to those same operators, and were used to improve the efficiency of the plant.

Induction is particularly useful for:

- Making a start on a project by obtaining an initial set of rules prior to discussion with the expert.
- Identifying an experimental set of rules where there is a shortage of human expertise.
- Sieving through large amounts of data to identify patterns (e.g. within historical data held in a database).
- Acquiring a set of rules for the expert to criticise (i.e. playing 'devil's advocate'), thereby provoking him to examine what he really does believe. This can be very effective for overcoming 'blind spots'.
- Reducing a set of symptoms and diagnoses (e.g. a fault matrix) to an efficient decision tree. The induction process will frequently indicate that some of the tests are not required at all, which has obvious commercial value.
- Scanning a set of examples to detect repeated cases, conflicting cases, or missing examples. This is difficult to do in any other way.

During 1986, a novel use of induction emerged within British Petroleum's Engineering Division. They found that even sceptical experts were excited by seeing their own know-how running on a computer. Since we can all quote examples of familiar decisions, BP staff were able to induce some rules and demonstrate them running in the space of only a few minutes. Although very small, this was often enough to spark an interest. Even if the toy system was discarded, it had served its purpose in recruiting the expert.

In summary, induction is not a substitute for knowledge engineering. It is a method of acquiring rules rather than knowledge. Its modern usage is in identifying what the rules appear to be for well defined problems, and discussing these with the expert to identify the real know-how. In this it can be a powerful prompt, and hence it has a worthy place in a knowledge engineer's tool kit. One can draw an analogy with a screwdriver which is adapted to grip a screw. Such a tool will not be needed often, but when it is needed then it is invaluable.

8

Representing knowledge

This chapter describes the best known methods of representing knowledge. It will be of interest to those readers who are particularly interested in expert systems technology, rather than their application. At the present stage of development, rules are the only means of representing knowledge which is effective for expressing know-how.

8.1 REPRESENTING KNOWLEDGE

Representing knowledge is concerned with how to record knowledge in the computer. This is a central technical issue because it dictates how understandable the knowledge will be, how easy it will be to modify, and how efficiently it can be accessed by the computer. The three best known representations are rules, semantic nets and frames. Most existing software systems are based on just one representation, although there has been some research interest in using combinations ('multiple knowledge representation paradigms').

These three formats are used for expressing operational or organisational knowledge, i.e. the reasoning involved or factual descriptions of how ideas are related. People use words to express this information, and words can be readily handled by a computer. However, some knowledge is best expressed as a drawing or diagram, and this is often a problem to represent in a computer. Physical descriptions such as the shape of a range of hills or the layout of services in a building are good examples. Handling such descriptions in a generalised way is an unsolved problem.

8.2 RULES

The basic if–then structure of rules was introduced in section 3.3, as was the importance of their being independent units of knowledge (i.e. being declarative). This section explains the capabilities of rules in more detail.

Rules may have several conditions and several consequences, and may include alternatives and negations ('or' and 'not').

For example:

> if the context is publishing a newspaper
> and an important item is planned for the front page
> and extra items are not expected
> or the deadline has arrived
> then go ahead with the planned item

Most people will have little difficulty understanding this rule, especially if it is read quickly. However, there is ambiguity between the 'and' and the 'or'. Bear in mind that a human reader will be familiar with the notion of publishing, and will be aware that a deadline implies that the page layout must be finalised. Therefore they will realise that the conditions 'an important item is planned for the front page' and 'extra items are not expected' stand together, and that 'the deadline has arrived' is sufficient in itself. Therefore a person will understand the rule to mean:

> if the context is publishing a newspaper
> and
> > either   (an important item is planned for the front page
> >   and extra items are not expected)
> > or
> >   the deadline has arrived
> then
> >   go ahead with the planned item

The computer has none of this general knowledge about human life, and the interpretation must be specified in full. Ambiguity can be overcome by the use of brackets and priorities (e.g. a convention that 'and' binds more tightly than 'or'), but only at a cost to readability. A rule containing many brackets, possibly nested, may be clear for a computer but will usually serve to confuse a human reader. The structures which are actually used vary greatly from one software system to another, often governed by whether the software is intended for use by computer professionals or by experts and users. Computer professionals will usually tolerate an awkward syntax as the price of precision, but others will reject the lack of readability as an unacceptable burden.

Not all rules have the same expressive power. This means that two different software systems may have very different capabilities, even though they both use rules. The simplest form of rules is where the conditions and consequences are statements which can only be true or false (yes/no). For example:

> if fishing-rods-in-stock
> then order-for-fishing-rods-can-be-taken

where the hyphens emphasise that 'fishing rods in stock' is all one idea, which will be labelled either true or false.

The power is considerably increased if the expert system is able to reason about ideas, rather than simply to label the ideas as true or false. This is known as 'symbolic reasoning'.

Symbolic reasoning is important because it allows ideas to be expressed in the way that people do. In the same way that conventional computing would allow the idea 'number in stock' to be given a value '10' or '134', symbolic reasoning would allow 'availability' to be given values such as 'from stock', 'obtainable within 24 hours', 'on 3 weeks delivery', or 'no longer available'. The difference is that these latter are symbolic values rather than data values, and can be used to mean whatever idea is wanted. Instead of being manipulated according to mathematical rules (like data), symbolic values are manipulated according to the rules in the expert system. For example, the following rule might be applied:

if	fishing rods	in stock
or	fishing rods	obtainable within 24 hours
then	an order for fishing rods	can be taken

where the layout shows the component parts. Some expert systems allow verbs to be used as the link between the name given to an idea and its value. This requires an element of 'natural language understanding' in the software, but allows a wide range of expression. The rule given above can then be expressed in a most acceptable English-like form:

> if fishing rods are in stock
> or fishing rods are obtainable within 24 hours
> then an order for fishing rods can be taken

This is the current 'state of the art' for ease of understanding in rules. For reasons of intelligibility, this is the usual form in which rules have been quoted in this book.

The third, and last, step in power of expression is to allow rules which can apply to *any* idea rather than just a specific idea. (All the rules quoted so far have applied to specific ideas.) The rule about fishing rods could be generalised as follows:

> if ⟨particular item⟩ is in stock
> or ⟨particular item⟩ is obtainable within 24 hours
> then an order for ⟨particular item⟩ can be taken

When the rule is being used, the phrase ⟨particular item⟩ can be replaced by the name of any item which the expert system knows about. '⟨particular item⟩' is referred to as a variable. It can stand for 'fishing rods', 'guns', 'boots', 'mint cake' or whatever, and the rule would apply to all of them. Therefore this one rule replaces the many rules which would be needed to specify each item separately. This level of facility is termed 'symbolic reasoning, with variables'.

More importantly, the rule quoted above is actually a piece of know-how expressed at a higher level than the equivalent specific rules, since it gives the principle by which an order can be taken for *any* item. This principle would only be implied by many specific rules, whereas it is made explicit using the rule with variables. When building an expert system, these 'generic' rules which apply over many cases are some of the most powerful and valuable pieces of know-how which can be captured. Writing them in this explicit form means that they can also be communicated to users, a considerable gain.

Thus far only the 'if–then' way of writing rules has been described, but there are other forms. Rules express a logical connection between their conditions and their consequences, and the same knowledge can be expressed using formal logic, as in the programming language Prolog (see section 9.1). The rule about fishing rods could be expressed in Prolog as:

        can_be (an_order_for_fishing_rods,taken) :–
        are (fishing_rods,obtainable_from_stock)
        ∨ are (fishing_rods,obtainable_within_24_hours).

where ':–' is read as 'if' and the symbol '∨' means 'or'.

This strict, mathematical notation allows for precise specification of complex relationships, more than can be easily expressed in the previous English-like form. However, the unfamiliar syntax is quite a barrier to programmers, experts, and users alike. Additionally, compromises which are necessary to make programs run efficiently (such as 'cut') mean that most logic programs are much less clear than this example suggests. This difficulty of understanding how a logic program works means that most experts will be unable to comment on the knowledge.

Rules are very useful for expressing operational knowledge — how to respond to new information and draw new conclusions. However, they are generally poor at expressing descriptive knowledge. The descriptive relationships may be implied by the rules, but are not always expressed directly. (It should be obvious that the more directly knowledge is expressed, the better.) Therefore rules often need to be supported by facts. For example:

        fact fishing rods are a stock item
        fact orders for guns need a special licence

Facts are statements which are always true, and are equivalent to rules without conditions.

Rules are particularly inefficient at expressing tables of information. For example, to express a single entry in a table of financial commissions we might have:

        if the deal is a purchase
            and the transaction is made in New York
            and the amount is less than $1000
        then dealing through in-house channels costs 8%

To take just one example, the table of standard commissions for the Swiss stock exchange contains approximately ten thousand entries, which implies ten thousand rules. These will be slow to access using expert systems methods since each rule is treated as being independent, and the system will run very slowly. It is far more efficient to make use of the structure which is inherent in a table, and to access it using a fixed procedure (an algorithm) rather than rules. In a rule-based expert system, this means that large tables are more efficiently handled by a conventional computer program which can be called via the system's external interface (see section 6.7).

8.3 SEMANTIC NETS

Semantic nets, or semantic networks, are a method of representing descriptive knowledge (e.g. Fig. 8.1). Each idea of interest is represented by a point

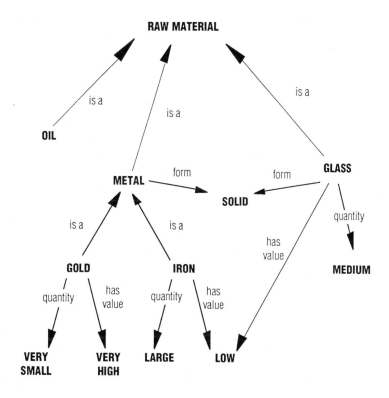

Fig. 8.1 — A semantic net.

in the network (a node), and the lines (arcs) between them show the relationships between the ideas. The term 'semantic network' is somewhat inflated, as it means no more than a network of concepts and relationships. The network can include many different types of relationship, for example 'is a' (which conventionally means 'is an example of a'), 'form' and 'has value'. A single idea may be connected to many others, and two ideas may be connected by many relationships. A semantic net may also contain ideas of totally different kinds, since the words used only have meaning to the reader. For example, 'very small' is a qualitatively different idea to 'raw material'.

The main value of a semantic net is its power to convey a complex set of relationships to the person viewing it. The techniques recommended in chapter 12 make use of an informal semantic network called a 'spider diagram'.

Within the computer, a different form must be used since a computer cannot handle diagrams directly. Therefore semantic nets are usually represented as tables of 'triples', such as:

(gold) (has value) (very high)

Each triple represents one link in the network. This form will be familiar to users of relational databases in conventional computing. A suitable computer terminal and graphics package are required to present semantic nets in their network form, and to allow for their updating.

8.4   FRAMES

Frames are used to represent a combination of descriptive and operational knowledge. Each frame represents an idea plus the items which are associated with it. A frame is a data structure and usually has a name, a type, and a set of attributes or 'slots'. Frames are linked together in a network to form a hierarchy, or possibly several interlinked hierarchies. Abstract thinkers can regard semantic nets as a simple case of frames, having only a single concept at each node instead of many.

The guiding principle when building frames is that any given idea is built up from more general ideas, only adding those features which distinguish the more specialised case. In the example shown in Fig. 8.2, a 'sales review' is specified as a type of 'meeting' with the nature 'formal'. The things which are special to a sales review are the chairman, coordinator, attendance and frequency. Naturally, in a live system there would be many other items too. This is implemented by the use of 'inheritance'. If a 'child' frame is a specialised type of a more general 'parent' frame, then the child is assumed to inherit all of the attributes of the parent, less any which are specifically excluded. In addition, the 'child' may have properties of its own which are not shared by the parent. Expert systems which support the use of frames provide automatic mechanisms for operating this inheritance.

8.5   COMPARISON OF THE REPRESENTATIONS

In business the use of different knowledge representations is clear: rules are used almost exclusively. This is because they are easy to understand, and are

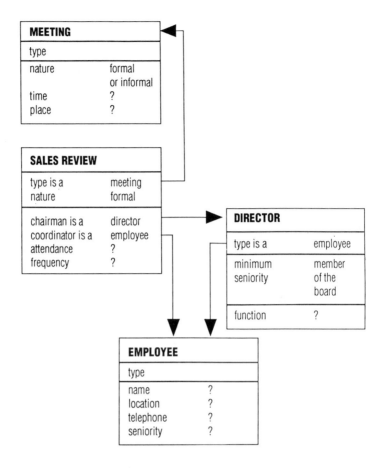

Fig. 8.2 — A family of frames.

an excellent medium for recording know-how. If well expressed, rules can be understood by the expert directly. This understandability has a considerable payoff when constructing and refining the system.

The main drawback of rules is that they are expressed at the finest level of detail. They are said to be 'fine grained'. This means that when a question is asked of the user, its significance is not always clear from examining the rules. This makes it difficult to understand the know-how involved. The saying 'you cannot see the wood for the trees' is very appropriate. The more powerful systems which provide for generic rules overcome this to some extent by allowing more general statements.

Explanation using rules suffers particularly if the builders try to express a formal model rather than know-how. In that case, the rules will simply show an incomprehensible mechanism, and it is most unlikely that the users will be able to acquire any expertise from them. If users cannot understand the rules, then they will rapidly give up examining them.

Semantic nets are only a partial knowledge representation, since something else is needed to express the operational knowledge. This extra component is often in rules, expressed so that the rules apply to all the different nodes (using variables). As mentioned above, the network can be held as a series of relations. These can obviously be expressed equally well as facts in a rule-based system, provided it has symbolic reasoning, and this is often used. The collection of facts effectively represents a network. For example, Fig. 8.1 shows a network concerning raw materials. The following facts represent three of the relations:

```
fact   iron    is-a        metal
fact   iron    has-value   low
fact   glass   form        solid
```

Some applications lend themselves to this style of expression. For example, a fault finding system for a communications network has been built by describing the connections, types of fault, symptoms, and fixes all as facts, and operating on these with a small number of generally expressed diagnostic rules.

The main virtue of a semantic net is that it can illustrate larger issues such as clusters of relationships, or many relationships to the same idea. These are difficult to discern among a large number of facts.

Frames are an attempt to gather up knowledge about a particular idea in one place. They also try to describe the world at an appropriate level of abstraction, the most general ideas being represented in the most general frames. The inheritance mechanism means that only the information which is specific to a frame need be specified, all the ideas which are common to frames of a similar type being inherited. This structure is elegant, and has obvious appeal for building systems with sophisticated reasoning.

Frames have two drawbacks which have prevented them from being widely used in business: intelligibility and computing requirements. It will be apparent from the example already given that real-world systems which use frames can be fearsomely complex. To obtain a particular value, the system may go through a whole series of frames before finding a frame which can provide the value it needs, and this may have little relationship with the context in which the value is needed. As a result, the operation of the system is usually quite incomprehensible to the users; they have to fall back on examining the results. The system has become a 'black box' for them. It is highly indicative that experts usually require a paper translation of such knowledge before they can grapple with it. This level of complexity also incurs a considerable computing overhead, with the result that existing frame systems tend to be much slower than their rule-based counterparts.

A frame is an elegant concept, but its advantages accrue mainly to the programmer and not to the businessman. Frames may yet become popular for business systems if they can be expressed as intelligibly as rules, and if their operation can be made equally clear.

8.6 UNCERTAINTY

Uncertainty may arise in an expert system due to any of the following:

— Missing data, which often occurs in business because the required information is not available at the time the decision has to be made.
— Data which is itself uncertain, for example based on opinion or on a forecast of future events.
— Incomplete and/or uncertain knowledge, which is nearly always the case.

In the first instance, missing data may be handled by allowing the question reply 'unknown'. A system which otherwise allowed only yes/no replies would be extended to allow yes/no/unknown. If the condition of a rule becomes unknown in this way, then the rule fails (see section 6.3.1). Nearly all commercial products allow 'unknown' or its equivalent.

Following the lead of early systems like Mycin and Prospector (see appendix B), some expert systems attempt to process the extent of the uncertainty. Various schemes are described below.

8.6.1 Dealing with uncertainty

Many expert system applications do not involve uncertainty at all. The only 'uncertainty' is the confusion of the non-expert because he lacks the necessary know-how. For the expert, once the necessary conditions have been established, then the course of action is clear. In fact this is a sign of well-honed expertise. For example, consider an expert system to identify the appropriate chassis, cab, body, engine, and drive train to be assembled into a truck. Such systems have been built by at least two truck manufacturers to assist their salesmen in tailoring their products to match the customer's requirements in the most economical way. It is hardly useful to give uncertain advice about which engine to fit, or whether to use a flat bed or a box body. The clear requirement is to make a definite selection. Where there are alternatives, then extra know-how is provided to discriminate between them.

The US minicomputer manufacturer DEC is undoubtedly the world's most experienced user of large expert systems. They have a rather clear view about uncertainty. 'There are over a hundred (expert) systems in use or under development within DEC. None of them use uncertainty' (Sell, 1987). All of these applications handle data which has no uncertainty, and use knowledge which yields definite results.

Other applications can ignore uncertainty because it would only serve to confuse. This can occur where the possible uncertainties are so numerous that it would be fruitless to consider even a fraction of them. The classic example is accounting. Corporate balance sheets and trading accounts are presented as precise information, neatly tabulated and balancing exactly. Yet such results depend on a host of estimates, assumptions, and educated guesses. For example, consider the valuation of 'work in progress'. Should this be valued at cost, at its potential sales value, or at its auction value if a forced sale were necessary? It is well known that companies adjust the stated value of work in progress to suit the level of profit or loss that they see fit to report. The same is true of asset valuations, bad debt provisions, and so forth. In addition, there are literally millions of permutations of assumptions about how the figures should be prepared. The only practicable way of proceeding is for the auditor to present all the information as precise, noting any unusual assumptions. It is then up to whoever uses the results to make allowance for the fact that there are uncertainties concealed within.

The next degree of uncertainty occurs where there is a genuine element of uncertainty in the data. For example, it may only be feasible to estimate the market image of a company. This is where a numerical scheme might be used (see below). If this course is chosen then the standard reasoning process is applied, but each step is labelled with a lower level of confidence (greater uncertainty) than would have been the case if the data were certain. We regard this as a mechanical response to a problem which people solve using know-how. There are better methods of handling uncertain data in terms of the expert's own descriptions rather than numbers.

A human expert will register the uncertainty but will use it to guide the reasoning process itself. i.e. Introducing uncertainty leads to different reasoning, rather than unchanged reasoning with a different level of confidence. For example, suppose we have an expert system which could help to decide whether to buy a used car — a topic where many of us could use more know-how! On examining a particular car, the expert notices that the carpets are well worn, even though the recorded mileage is low. Therefore he is suspicious that the claimed mileage may be incorrect. It is hardly useful to make a less confident assessment — the potential purchaser must decide between buy and don't buy. In practice the expert will look for other signs, e.g. wear on the pedals or the driver's seat, or may even contact the previous owner for verification. In this way the expert uses his know-how to respond to the uncertainty. The degree of uncertainty is usually of little interest in itself.

The last source of uncertainty is in the knowledge. As already discussed, it is in the nature of heuristics that they may not be definite. However, many heuristics are 'as good as you will get', and so still represent the best course of action. Therefore the reasoning itself usually ignores the uncertainty, whereas the results may be qualified by some degree of doubt. This means that the uncertainty is only introduced as a qualification to the results at the very end of the reasoning process as a means of giving the correct impression to the user.

There are very rare cases where the reasoning is clearly concerned with probability. The signal is that experts in the field discuss their expertise in terms of statistical quantities. The only commercial application of this kind which has been met by the authors concerned the mixing of populations of different types of grasses in a field. The expertise was truly statistical, and none of the schemes used for handling uncertainty in expert systems was appropriate. Indeed, being essentially numerical rather than knowledge based this application was not well suited to expert systems at all.

To summarise, many applications are best handled with definite reasoning, qualifying the results if necessary. Where there is real uncertainty, this is best dealt with by including the know-how which an expert would use to deal with it. This can be expected to include confirmation of doubtful actions and hedging against possible errors. Where the uncertainty itself is to be reasoned about, then it can be represented in the expert's own words or in numbers. Since humans do not think in terms of numerical certainties, our clear preference is for words.

The following sections illustrate how these different approaches would appear in practice.

8.6.2   Treating the reasoning as certain

Treating the reasoning as certain means that every statement within the system is treated as either true or false. For example, consider the rule:

> if sales volume falling
>   and customers still using the same amount
> then competition problem

which is a heuristic used when diagnosing profitability problems in small businesses. The statements 'sales volume dropping' and 'customers still using the same amount' are interpreted as either true or false (yes or no). To establish their values, the expert system might generate a question as follows:

> Is the sales volume falling?
>   yes
>   no

where the only permitted replies are yes and no. This is the simplest approach and can be handled by all expert systems software.

8.6.3   Describing uncertainty in words

Treating the uncertainty in words is the closest to our philosophy of 'do as an expert would'. The most obvious possibility is to expand the range yes/no into definite, probable, possible, don't know and so forth through to definitely not. In practice this is often a poor solution because the actual degree is not important.

A great improvement is to offer a scale which relates to the particular context. For example, salesmen have a scale for getting orders which runs something like:

> already signed
> next week
> next month

The cynical might translate this into everyday language as probable, possible, and not a chance. Another scale is used by doctors for describing the risks of unwanted effects of treatment:

> completely safe
> almost completely safe
> carries some risk

When used in context, these scales of uncertainty are far more relevant than abstract terms such as 'probable', and both more relevant and more meaningful then numbers. For example, the doctor's descriptions can be used in a rule about when to use a treatment:

> if the patient is not about to die
>   and using this drug carries some risk
> then try other treatments first

Statisticians will realise that both of these scales are highly non-linear in terms of probability. Probability ranges from 0 (impossible) to 1 (definite). It can be seen that the maximum of the doctor's scale 'carries some risk' may still only be 1 chance in 1000 (a probability of 0.001). Therefore the relevant part of the probability scale is only from 0 to 0.001.

Handling uncertainty using words requires a more powerful software system than systems based on yes/no. Instead of just labelling an idea with true or false (yes or no), the software must be able to give it a symbolic value such as 'probable', 'next week' or 'dropping', and must be able to reason with such values (see section 8.2).

8.6.4   Describing uncertainty with numbers

The basic principle of representing uncertainty with numbers is that the scale of 'definitely true' through 'neither true nor false' to 'definitely false' is mapped onto a range of numbers such as -100 to 100. For example, a statement such as:

> 'sales volume falling'

would be qualified with a confidence factor, giving:

> 'sales volume falling (confidence 70)'

which means that (on a scale of -100 to 100) it is fairly likely that the sales volume is dropping. The corresponding question to the user might then be expressed as:

> How certain are you that the sales volume is falling?
> (range -100 to 100)

where the user is being invited to enter a number in the specified range. Any convenient range of numbers can be used (table 8.1).

Table 8.1 — Measures of uncertainty

	Definitely false	Definitely true
Certainty factors	−1.0	1.0
Certainty factors again	−5.0	5.0
Percentage	0	100
Probability	0	1
Log odds	minus infinity	plus infinity

There are many ways of expressing these different degrees of certainty in rules. The rule about sales volume quoted in the previous section does not lend itself to being expressed in certainties. What should one conclude if the customers are probably not using the same amount? In itself, this says something about the limitations of working in probabilities rather than symbolic values (i.e. words). Consider instead a rule such as:

> going shopping (prior 0.0, max 4.0)
> > depends on
> > > having money to spend (true 3.5, false −5.0)
> > and
> > > today being a weekday (true 1.0, false 3.0)

which is an example of a rule using certainty factors in the range −5 to 5. Its translation is as follows. The certainty that we should go shopping is completely uncertain (0.0) if there is no evidence, and probable (4.0) if all the evidence is true. The evidence consists of whether we have money to spend, which increases the certainty quite a lot (in proportion to 3.5) if it is true, and decreases the certainty even more (in proportion to −5.0) if it is false. The certainty also depends on today being a weekday, which increases the certainty slightly (in proportion to 1.0) if it is true, and also *increases* (because the 3.0 is positive, not negative) the certainty rather more (in proportion to 3.0) if it is false (i.e. if it is not a weekday). Each of these factors has reduced effect if they are less than definite themselves.

There is obviously a need to combine these numerical scores by some means which preserves the correct range. For example, we cannot simply add a confidence factor of 3.0 (likely) to 4.0 (probable) to make 7.0, since the range only extends to 5.0. A more reasonable outcome is somewhere between 4.0 and 5.0 (between probable and definite).

The most common method for combining certainty factors makes use of Bayes' theorem. Bayes was a mathematician who devised a procedure for combining independent sources of uncertain evidence. His equation has the practical virtue that it behaves properly, i.e. with appropriate scaling any number of pieces of evidence with certainties in the range −5 to 5 will always yield a result in the same range. Bayes' theorem has only been proved for truly independent pieces of evidence, although this restriction is freely ignored in expert systems. A more sophisticated approach has been advocated by Shafer and Dempster, but this has had little impact. The reason is that the mathematical niceties are irrelevant.

When details of Mycin (see Appendix B) first became well known, mathematicians and logicians criticised its use of certainty factors as being non-rigorous and logically inconsistent. They were quite right. However, what those critics failed to address was that, within its narrow domain, Mycin performed as a top class medical consultant. It achieved results which no rigorous procedure was capable of. Mycin was effective because of its high class expertise, not because of any special reasoning prowess.

There is also a practical difficulty in using certainty factors, which is that experts do not know what values they should take — they have to guess. Humans reason qualitatively, i.e. using words, and do not think about certainty in terms of −5 to 5 or whatever scale has been chosen. Statistical analysis rarely helps, as all this shows is what happens on the average, whereas what is needed is what happens in a particular case. Therefore the knowledge engineer is faced with quite a problem: how should he set up perhaps 1000 different certainty factors in a knowledge base? Imagine trying to set up a machine which had 1000 different control knobs, all of which interacted to a varying degree. In practice the knowledge engineer has to find the (hopefully few) factors which strongly influence the results, and tune those by experiment. The other values hardly matter. This is a long process which is difficult to validate. It also shows the ad hoc nature of certainty factors in practical systems.

It is now widely accepted that mathematical schemes are indeed ad hoc, and have little intrinsic meaning. The crudest scheme is about as effective as the most sophisticated. Software systems which use numerical certainty factors usually rely either on Bayes' theorem or on a simple, well behaved algorithm. Their purpose is to combine numerical measures in an expedient way, and nothing more.

8.6.5 Qualitative calculus

There is an extension to describing uncertainty in words (i.e. qualitatively) which has the potential to replace the use of certainty factors. This amounts to handling words on a scale, like one would numbers, hence the name 'qualitative calculus'.

To make the context clear, it is worth reviewing the main features of expressing uncertainty in words and in numbers. Words have the advantage of being explicit and understandable, and have the flexibility to handle different problem areas. They have the drawback that any interactions have to be specified in full (e.g. what is the result of combining 'probable' and 'a little unlikely'?), which is laborious and could consume much computer time. Numbers have the sole advantage that a single equation can always combine two numbers to give a result. On the other hand, the numbers are alien to users, and have little connection with reality. Qualitative calculus aims to retain the understandability and expressive power, whilst allowing the system to combine different certainties in a human-like way.

In a simple form of qualitative calculus, the knowledge engineer might specify a scale of certainty in terms of words, and also how these words were ordered. For example, in the salesman's scale mentioned above we might have:

already signed	(strongest)
next week	
next month	
never	(weakest)

This could be given the meaning 'if it can be shown that an order is already signed, then that takes precedence over other information which says it will be obtained next week'. The expert system has been given a miniscule understanding of what the terms 'already signed' and 'next week' mean, at least in this particular context. The expert system can use this to make more skilful use of the know-how in its knowledge base.

This interpretation of relevant words is actually part of the know-how about a topic, albeit one that is not usually recognised. Each such scheme would be tailored to a specific application, and possibly to a given part of that application. No single scheme could serve all purposes. This raises obvious difficulties of complexity and computing efficiency.

No commercial software has specific support for qualitative calculus, although some research systems would allow it relatively easily (e.g. Props-2 developed by John Fox and David Frost at the Imperial Cancer Research Fund). Considerable development work will be needed to find a convenient, intelligible, and efficient enough means of expressing this type of knowledge for use in commercial systems.

Part IV

Expert systems tools

9

Computer software

There are three distinct types of software tools available for building expert systems:

— the so-called 'AI programming languages',
— expert system 'shells', and
— knowledge engineering environments.

There are also a few applications available for purchase (see section 5.2).

Note that conventional programming languages such as Cobol, Fortran and Basic are not included. These languages only contain computer concepts (loops, branches, jumps, etc.), not human concepts. Therefore they cannot directly express expert knowledge. (A comparable problem might be to express a cooking recipe in music notation, a language which only contains musical concepts.) Digital Equipment Corporation spent tens of thousands of dollars on failed attempts to build an equipment configurer using conventional programming languages. They eventually succeeded using an expert system tool. You need not repeat that lesson.

9.1 AI LANGUAGES

These are computer programming languages which have specialised facilities for expert systems programming — for example in symbol handling and coping with dynamic data structures. Two languages dominate: Lisp and Prolog.

Lisp was developed in the 1960s and has been used for nearly all artificial intelligence research work in the USA. It is very much a programming language, and has a most unfamiliar syntax. Its greatest strength is the excellence of the supporting utilities which are used with it. These include top class graphics and a host of library software. However, the accretion of so many facilities on top of the base language has led to massive complexity. Experience in the USA shows that it requires six months' dedicated practice to become proficient in using the larger Lisp systems. Therefore the undoubted programming power is bought at a high price.

Prolog was developed much more recently, in Europe. It is a version of a logic language, in which the system builder provides a logical statement of the problem, and the Prolog system works out the answer. It does this using a powerful, built-in backward chaining mechanism and its own database (see chapter 6). The program is expressed in 'first-order predicate logic', a formal logic notation. (Philosophical mathematicians have defined many different logics, and of different orders, but a restricted first-order logic is the only form which has a practical implementation running on a computer.) In skilled hands, Prolog programs can be built in hours, which makes it very suitable for prototyping. However, it is hard to write efficient programs in Prolog. The language also suffers from almost a complete absence of supporting tools and utilities.

Both Lisp and Prolog are generally poor at most things that conventional languages are good at, for example file and database handling, communications and transaction processing. They are also unfamiliar to most programmers, which will affect the time required to get a project started. Highly accomplished programmers are required to make effective use of either Lisp or Prolog.

One other language must be mentioned, and that is OPS-5. Were it not for the fact that DEC's X/CON system (see appendix B) is written in OPS-5, then in our view it would be regarded as an oddity. OPS-5 is a rule-based programming language which includes a remarkably complex forward chaining inference engine. There is no backward chaining. It is not widely used outside DEC.

These languages just described are very suitable for expert systems work. They have many desirable facilities built in, and compared to conventional programmming languages the programs can be readily modified. However, the pressure from the market is to have products which run quickly on small computers and which can be used with other, conventionally written, packages and applications. Therefore product suppliers are increasingly moving their software into conventional languages such as C. This has the drawback that design changes become very much more difficult. However, provided that the design has stabilised, the loss of flexibility is seen as the price of improved speed, portability and integration.

9.2 EXPERT SYSTEM SHELLS

A 'shell' is expert systems jargon for a building tool. A shell is a ready-made expert system, except that it contains no knowledge. When a knowledge base about a particular topic is added, the result is an expert system. Some shells can even be used by experts to build the system themselves.

An expert system shell provides:

— A language in which to write the know-how which will make up the knowledge base (e.g. a language allowing for if–then rules, questions and facts). This language should be far more understandable than (say) Lisp or Prolog.

— Software tools for creating and refining the knowledge base (a means of inputting the know-how, an editor, display and browsing facilities, diagnostics, etc.).
— Software components for running the system (inference engine, user interface, etc., see chapter 6).

Shells are widely used in industry. In the past they have generally been used to build small- to medium-sized systems, but the pace of development is such that 1000+ rule systems are no longer unusual. Most shells have the virtue of being quick to learn, typically requiring only one week's training for a knowledge engineer to become proficient.

The great majority of commercial expert system shells are based on rules. Simplicity of use should be a key quality. There are a few shells which claim 'AI' features such as frames and object-oriented programming, but these features are sometimes more evident in the marketing than in the product. Such sophisticated features are better served by knowledge engineering environments (see below). A further complication is that some so-called expert system shells are little more than thinly disguised programming languages. Although they offer if–then rules, the inferencing is minimal. These are actually rule-based programming tools. Their power to express know-how is usually weak because the underlying concepts are oriented towards computers, not towards people.

Expert system shells allow expert systems to be built very quickly, and some are available to run on personal computers at very low cost (e.g. £1000/ $1500, or less if bought in quantity). This means that the hardware and software for a single user might cost as little as £2000/$3000. Expert system shells are deservedly popular, and the great majority of systems in the UK have been built using shells. However, all such products have their limitations, and it may be necessary to trial the software by implementing a small portion of an application during the feasibility stage.

9.3   KNOWLEDGE ENGINEERING ENVIRONMENTS

Environments are the 'Rolls Royce' of expert systems programming, and about as expensive to run! They provide a set of building blocks which aim to cater for the programmer's every need, and hence are sometimes known as 'toolkits'. Some of the building blocks represent man-years of development, for example graphics packages or frame handling systems. If a development project intends to tackle a high payoff problem which will require extensive, exploratory programming, then an environment may be worthwhile, since these products provide first-class support for writing large, complex programs.

The market is dominated by three products: KEE, ART, and Knowledge Craft. These all originate in the USA and are designed to run on workstations. Environments require programmers of the first rank, and are certainly not intended for use by experts or users. The experience is that about six months' full time effort is required to become productive.

9.4 CHOOSING SOFTWARE

A friend who practises traditional boat building once passed on a piece of his know-how which was so aptly expressed that it was hard to forget. His great interest was in collecting wooden pleasure boats — skiffs and other very English vessels — and restoring them to their former beauty. He once explained the importance of using copper nails to attach the wooden planks which made up the hull. He said 'use a nail if you can, a bolt where you should, and a screw when you must.' The expert systems equivalent for choosing software is:

> Use a shell if you can,
> an environment where you should,
> and an AI language when you must.

The reasoning is simple. If your system can be implemented using a shell, then this will certainly be the most cost-effective choice. (Mainframe shells may be an exception; they are expensive.) If extensive, special developments will be needed then a knowledge engineering environment will provide the best support. If attempting specialised developments on a minimum capital budget, then an AI language it must be; you should expect a large investment in time.

It is no accident that expert system shells dominate the market, probably by a factor of three or four to one (by numbers of installations worldwide). If we were to exclude publicly or corporately funded research, then the ratio might be doubled. It is strongly recommended that all inexperienced teams should develop their early applications using a shell. This will allow them to develop their knowledge engineering skills without going through a protracted period of programming to build some software tools.

Starting an inexperienced team using an AI language or a knowledge engineering environment will waste both time and money. Whilst it is easy to produce some sort of result using (say) Prolog, it is much more difficult to produce robust and widely applicable software which can be trusted to run commercially important applications. This latter activity requires skill, experience, and strong management. The required qualities are those of product developers, not of expert systems specialists. However, all too often, line managers have been persuaded that the technical team should write their own software tools. This is undoubtedly a stimulating challenge for the technicians, but it is an indulgence. Business objectives will be better served by using a shell for the first six months as an absolute minimum. Both the technical team and the management will then be better placed to make an informed decision on the appropriate technical approach. If the decision is then to fund a programme of software tool development, then at least it will be soundly based.

The typical features of expert system shells, AI programming languages and knowledge engineering environments are summarised in fig. 9.1. Features have only been attributed to a class of software tool if the facilities

	shells	AI languages	KE environments
understandable know-how	•		
access by the expert	•		
development by non-programmers	•		
attractive user interface	•		•
sophisticated graphics			•
low initial cost	•	•	
runs on standard hardware	•	•	
fast development	•		•
handles large systems	•	•	•
programming flexibility		•	•
uses nets, frames etc			•
extensive support tools			•
easy interfacing	•	•	•

Fig. 9.1 — Gross features of software tools. Note that there is great variation between different products in the same category (see text).

are generally good or the desired quality can be readily achieved. If a particular feature is often missing in software systems of that type, or it is difficult to achieve, then it has not been attributed. Fig. 9.1 is purely intended to highlight the principal merits of each type of tool. Of necessity it contains some gross generalisations and does not reflect the strengths and weaknesses of individual software products. For example, the better expert system shells have facilities to rival some knowledge engineering environments.

Having decided on the class of software to be used, the available products can be surveyed. The issues are much the same as for any purchase, i.e. does it do what you want, is it of good quality, and are the costs acceptable?

Does it do what you want?

- Can the expert understand the know–how which is in the knowledge base? (Knowledge engineers can put up with some gobbledegook, but not experts.)
- Will the system be intelligible to users? (Ask for a demonstration.)
- Can the know-how for your application be conveniently expressed? (It may be necessary to do a trial to find out for sure.)
- Are there good facilities for setting up and developing knowledge bases? (It is very important that these should be highly productive. Try for yourself.)
- Will the software cope with reasonably large systems, still with good response time? (Ask to see a large one.)
- Does the software run on existing computers or does it require special hardware? (See chapter 10.)

- Does the software provide any special features which you require (e.g. database access, videodisc, etc.)?

Is it of good quality?

- Is there an established body of existing users and/or applications?
- Is the software readily available? (Obscure sources provide obscure lines of support.)
- Is the software reliable? If not, look elsewhere. (Ask other users. There may be a User Group.)
- Does the supplier enhance and develop the product? Does the software support future trends such as graphics? (You may want to use it for some time.)
- Are knowledge bases compatible across different machines and different versions of the software? (You may want to transfer your systems in the future.)
- Does the supplier provide effective maintenance and support, including a 'hot line'?
- Does the supplier offer training and consultancy services?
- Are the supplier's staff competent and helpful?
- Is the supplier organisation stable and financially sound?
- Can applications be purchased? (This is indicative of commitment by others, and useful for your own learning.)

Are the costs acceptable? Consider the costs of:

- The development software, and a maintenance agreement.
- Computer hardware, its accommodation and maintenance, and someone to be a system controller if needed.
- Knowledge engineering training, and possibly programming training if appropriate.
- Consultancy support, if this is being used.
- The likely future costs of delivering expert system applications to users.

Needless to say, at the outset there will be no basis for comparison. The problem is much the same as a householder might face if he had to personally choose a new central heating system, even though he had only a layman's knowledge of domestic heating. Where should he start? The usual solution is to spend a short while gathering whatever background information can be found, and then going to see a few products. Most people do the same for expert systems. It is worth making one or two visits to exhibitions, since a variety of products can be seen in a short space of time. Conferences, business acquaintances, and periodicals can also help (see appendix C).

If starting from scratch, the first project will usually be carried out using an expert system shell running on a personal computer. This is an economical and productive way of gaining experience. (There is no substitute for experience as a means of gaining skills in knowledge engineering.) If two or three shells are candidates for purchase, then acquire them all and give each a week of intensive use. A thorough investigation would also include the supplier's product training course as a fast way of gaining proficiency. The choice of product should then be self-evident, although management must take the lead. The choice must be the tool which will best suit the business applications, not one which contains the most interesting technical features.

Trying mainframe expert system shells or knowledge engineering environments is more difficult because of the expense of the software, the possible need for special hardware, and the extensive training which is required. Short term rental may be available, although a six month period should be allowed to seriously evaluate such complex products. Alternatively, the supplier may be able to offer access to the software at one of their own sites or at a customer site. Here again it will be necessary to budget for a substantial period of evaluation. The best source of information on these arrangements is obviously the software supplier involved.

In our experience, companies select expert system software by one of the following methods:

— retaining an outside consultant,
— appointing an in-house sponsor to oversee the selection, or
— choosing the cheapest course of action.

Appointing an in-house sponsor is clearly the best of these, especially if he has a business requirement which might be met by an expert system. This should drive the selection towards an assessment of overall value to the organisation. Retaining a consultant has obvious merit, provided that they have practical experience and are carefully briefed. Choosing the cheapest course of action can actually be quite expensive, since under this regime the investment of staff time is usually ignored. Furthermore, if initial cost is the only criterion then the most suitable software for the task is unlikely to be selected. The resulting difficulties can hinder the take-up of expert systems throughout the organisation, since the first project is usually seen as a demonstration of potential.

Our recommendation is that the software should be chosen by an in-house sponsor, possibly after some experiments with an expert system shell.

10

Computer hardware

10.1 HARDWARE REQUIREMENTS

In the early days of expert systems, research work was usually done on mainframe computers at Universities. These were the only available source of substantial computer power. Work on mainframes subsequently migrated to specialised 'workstations', and these are still the preferred vehicle for research. In business, most expert systems are run on normal data processing machines, principally personal computers.

Hardware is only important in that a project will need enough computer power to run the software which is to be used. This may not be a popular message with hardware manufacturers, but it is the truth. In an ideal world, the choice of hardware would simply be dictated by the choice of software. However, most pilot projects will be obliged to use existing equipment, and therefore will be constrained to use software which runs on an existing machine. Fig. 10.1 shows which types of computer are most often used for

	Personal computer	Mini computer	Work-station	Mainframe
Expert system shells	●	●		○
Lisp and Prolog	○	●	●	
Knowledge eng. env.			●	

Key: ● principal usage ○ minor usage

Fig. 10.1 — Typical hardware requirements.

the different types of software described in chapter 9. Whatever the machine used for development, there is strong pressure from business to use standard commercial machines for delivering expert systems to users. This means that nearly all expert systems are planned to be delivered to users via personal computers or mainframe terminals.

10.2 MAINFRAMES

Mainframes are corporate data processing machines as supplied by IBM, ICL, Honeywell, Unisys and others. Nowadays they are only infrequently used for expert system development because of the heavy overheads of interactive computing, and the high cost and restricted range of software. IBM could change this picture with its expert system shell known as the Expert Systems Environment (ESE), but its uptake has been slow. No doubt this is partly explained by its high price (approximately £30,000 for each of the two components at the time of writing). ICL also has an expert system shell and AI language products. Very few third-party software products have yet been implemented for mainframes.

Mainframes should be cost effective for delivering corporate expert systems to many users who already have a terminal installed. We predict that as large corporations move to deploy their expert systems in the field, there will be a rash of software products to allow expert systems to be run on mainframes. The bulk of expert systems development (as opposed to running by users) will remain on personal computers and workstations.

10.3 MINICOMPUTERS

Minicomputers are medium-size computers which are often used to provide interactive computing, typified by DEC's VAX range. These can be very powerful, with large memories and substantial storage. There are large numbers of minicomputers installed, particularly in technical, production, and engineering departments. Developers may be able to beg or borrow time on an existing machine, although this is hardly satisfactory for more than initial experiments.

Minicomputers are very suitable for running expert system shells or Prolog programs. They have the advantage over personal computers of providing a multi-user service. Lisp is rarely run on minicomputers because the implementations available are usually fairly basic. Running a fully featured Lisp system, as used on workstations, would require the full capacity of most minicomputers for just one user.

10.4 WORKSTATIONS

A workstation is a single-user minicomputer. This means that the machine provides a substantial amount of computer power dedicated to that individual, much more than would be provided by a mainframe or minicomputer service. Some workstations are specially constructed to run Lisp efficiently, such as those sold by Symbolics and Xerox. Others have been derived from general purpose machines by providing them with expert systems software, e.g. the products offered by Sun and Apollo. These have other applications in computer aided design and distributed computing.

Workstations invariably have sophisticated graphics, since this is a major selling point. They also have the processing power required to run the elaborate user interfaces of knowledge engineering environments. Technicians love them. Accountants are less keen because of typical costs in the range £15,000 to £80,000 to buy the first machine, plus software. Prices are coming down, but workstations are still a very expensive means of delivering expert systems to end users. In the future we expect to see all workstation vendors offering delivery to users via personal computers.

10.5   PERSONAL COMPUTERS

Personal computers are an integral part of modern management, and will need no introduction. They are typified by the all-pervasive IBM PC and its developments. Most business expert systems are developed on personal computers because they provide enough processing power to run expert system shells and are easy to obtain. Lisp and Prolog can be used on personal computers, but generally only for small applications. (Unless written with great skill, Lisp and Prolog tend to use a lot of processing power and memory space.) Typical costs of between £500 and £5000 per user also mean that personal computers are the first choice for delivering an expert system, irrespective of the machine used for development.

10.6   CHOOSING HARDWARE

It has already been stated that the choice of hardware should be dictated by the choice of software. For an experienced project team this is absolutely true, although the costs of buying or renting a machine, its accommodation, and its maintenance are all part of the required funding. Exceptional items such as purchasing a workstation must be anticipated when the business case is being prepared. The sponsor may need considerable persuasion to purchase such a specialist machine, since the investment may have to be written off on this one project.

Inexperienced teams are in a different position. Typically, they will be under pressure to adopt modest initial goals (rightly so) and to minimise capital outlay. It has already been strongly recommended (in section 9.4) that such teams should begin with an expert system shell. If a computer has to be purchased, then a personal computer (or two, or three) is the only choice.

Depending on how an organisation allocates its costs, the lowest budget solution may be to use an existing personal computer or a share in a minicomputer. However, it is obviously short-sighted to commit substantial human resources to a project and then be constrained by existing equipment. Therefore it is important to secure sufficient access to these resources. It would be most exceptional to find a mainframe service already equipped with expert systems development software, so this is not usually an option.

10.7   FUTURE DEVELOPMENTS

Technology is improving the cost/performance of personal computers faster than any other type. Modern personal computers may not be specialised for running expert systems software, but they have such raw power that large systems can still be run with very acceptable response times.

Personal computers based on Intel's 80386 processor have sounded the death knell of workstations as delivery vehicles for expert systems. They have as much processing power as the entry-level workstations, and will surely become standard equipment for widespread delivery of expert systems to users.

Workstations will be confined to the upper end of the market, running the most elaborate knowledge engineering environments and using graphical interfaces. Their processing power will be increased 10 or 100 times by miniaturisation of their processors (i.e. implemented with VLSI technology rather than the current LSI). However, similar processing abilities could be provided on personal computers via add-on boards, and if history is anything to go by then these boards will be available within months of the components reaching the market. Texas Instruments' recent development of a shoebox-size Lisp processor also points the way towards integration of workstation capabilities into other computers.

Mainframes will become increasingly important as delivery vehicles because they are already being accessed by many potential users of expert systems. It will certainly increase the acceptability of expert systems if they are presented as an integral part of the users' current tasks. The expert system could be run on the mainframe itself, or on a personal computer acting as the terminal. In the latter case, the mainframe would take the role of communications centre, data provider, and holder of corporate knowledge bases.

Although mainframes have the power and capacity to run major expert systems, they are currently constrained by cost/performance and limited availability of software. A likely pattern for the future is development on personal computers and delivery via mainframes.

Part V

Building effective systems

11

Overview

This chapter, and the one that follows, is devoted to the implementation of the expert system itself. The intention is to bring out the strategy and the principles here, and then to describe the techniques involved in chapter 12.

11.1 PERSONAL INVOLVEMENT

Building an expert system can be described as exhilarating, challenging, frustrating, tedious, exciting, and occasionally boring. Each of these emotions is sure to become evident at some time during the development of a system. What is most important is that the system builders will be experiencing these emotions, no matter how large or how small the system might be. It is a sign of their personal involvement, and the intellectual excitement of the work. These will be reflected both by the quality of the know-how and the way in which it is expressed in the system. Above all else, the expert system needs to come across as something appropriate, well thought out, and easy to use.

In order to build an expert system that is both effective and exciting for the users, the developers need to impart a certain underlying philosophy and psychology. That philosophy and psychology cannot be prescribed here, but it should in some way reflect what is personable and vital about the expertise. The ideal is to transfer something of the developers' own enthusiasm to the user. Without this background, the following descriptions of stages of work and techniques used could seem dry and impersonal. What we wish to alert you to is that expert systems *are* different in that they represent reasoning and thought, not just sophisticated manipulation of data, and there are correspondingly greater rewards for developers and users alike.

11.2 STAGES OF WORK

The development cycle of an expert system application has already been defined in section 4.4. This involves a progression from business aims, to setting objectives for the expert system, to implementing that system. This chapter focuses on the implementation. Implementation begins with the objectives which have been set, and ends with a review of the business impact.

There are four major activities to be carried out:

- Defining the system
- Acquiring and structuring the knowledge
- Building the components
- Refining the system

Defining the system

Defining the system means translating its aims into specific objectives and detailing what it will and will not do. It is important to be clear on the type of problem which will be tackled, and how the users will gain by using the system.

Acquiring and structuring the knowledge

This means obtaining expertise from the expert, recording it, and identifying the form of the system, i.e. the stages of problem solving and the functions carried out at each stage.

Building the components

Building involves using the computer software to prepare modules dealing with each aspect of the problem, and integrating these into a single, coherent system.

Refining the system

Refining the system entails developing the expert system from a state where it can solve problems into a form which is helpful to the users. This requires particular attention to the way in which the expert system solves problems (i.e. not just the results), the type and quality of information produced, and the facilities available to users.

These four activities are not carried out sequentially. For example, 'acquiring and structuring the knowledge' actually permeates every aspect of the work. Even when defining the system, it is necessary to explore how the expert operates and the demands which others make on him before one can identify a useful set of functions for the expert system to perform. The initial definition may well turn out to be incomplete or based on false premises. Additionally, some structuring can only be done effectively once building has begun, i.e. once some expertise has been implemented as rules and exercised on the computer. We have chosen to discuss these activities separately in the interests of clarity. However, the truth is that the development team actually have to deal with several activities in parallel, constantly re-assessing the aims of the system and the work to date. The output of any particular activity must be treated as the best current view, and not as being fixed.

The development work goes in many cycles, each cycle revising and extending what has gone before. The aim is that each cycle should lead to a slightly improved system. This is termed 'incremental development', since the system progresses via many small increments.

The cycles take place at all levels. At the business level, the progressive refinement of the system's objectives through cycles of implementation and evaluation has already been mentioned. Within the implementation, there is iteration around the four activities identified above: defining the system, acquiring and structuring the knowledge, building the components, and refining the system (fig. 11.1). For example, preparing the first prototype

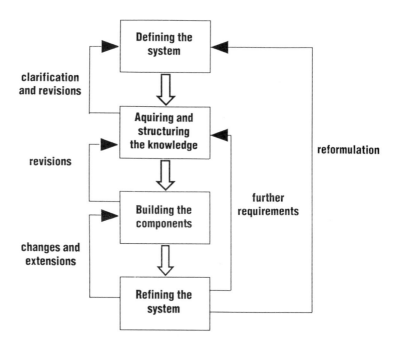

Fig. 11.1 — The implementation process.

may well lead to clarification of the system's definition, perhaps by firming up its scope or its potential audience. There is further iteration within these activities, for example as part of 'building the components' there are cycles of structuring the problem, structuring a task and building a task (fig. 11.2). At the lowest level there are yet more iterations during rule building (see section 12.5). The entire process is one of 'wheels within wheels', rotating on a time scale ranging from hours (rule writing) to months (application development).

The interdependence of different activities is particularly apparent when building the components of the expert system itself. It is usually self-evident that the initial structure identified for the problem is only an initial view:

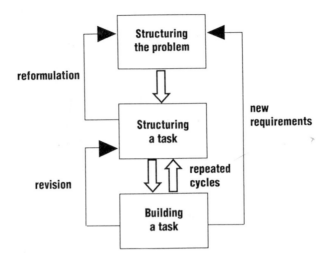

Fig. 11.2 — Building the components.

only time will tell to what extent it will remain useful. Structuring the component tasks inevitably leads to a reassessment of their functions and requirements, i.e. a re-assessment of the problem structure. Building the prototype knowledge base for the first topic will lead to a re-evaluation of both, and building further components will lead to yet more changes. Experience shows that even a medium-size application may undergo three or four major structural revisions, and many minor ones, before it sees field use.

These revisions are not to be feared, nor are they a sign of incompetence. Indeed, they illustrate one of an expert system's great strengths: the flexibility to respond to changes which are identified in the light of a system's *actual performance*. This means that early experience with the system can be incorporated into later versions. There is no requirement (or possibility!) to define the system fully in advance†.

11.3 PRINCIPLES

The guiding principles are:

- Start small, and grow
- Build the system incrementally
- Use the system itself as a prompt for the expert
- ● First make it work, and then refine it

---

† Note that this is the complete opposite of the situation with conventional programming (e.g. in Cobol, Fortran, or C) where the system must be completely specified in advance, and once built cannot be significantly changed.

- It is never too early to show the system to users

Start small, and grow:
Building should begin with the 'core' of the expert system, the know-how which is central to the problem. Subsequent development will build upon this core. The first, definitional, stage should seek to identify where this core lies.

Build the system incrementally:
Starting from the core, know-how should be added a few fragments at a time, exercising the system to verify the improvement. This means that the expert system is not implemented in a few large steps, but rather 'evolves' towards its final form. Specifically, the system is *not* implemented in stages of specify, design, implement and test as a conventional system would be. Building an expert system is much more interactive. The expert system will develop through frequent cycles of build, test, improve, and test again.

Use the system itself as a prompt for the expert:
The developing expert system is the best vehicle for discussing the task with the expert. Its mistakes and omissions are an irresistible prompt for more know-how. Therefore a great deal of the know-how needed for the system is acquired during sessions of exercising the system with the expert. Only the early sessions before a prototype is available need be carried out by abstract discussion.

First make it work, and then refine it:
The initial aim must be to make the expert system perform according to the expert's know-how. This takes priority over presentation or facilities, both of which can be developed later. As experience grows it will be easier to achieve a reasonable presentation at the first attempt, but the priorities remain the same. Refinement, i.e. turning the system from a working state into one which appeals to users, should be recognised as an activity in its own right.

It is never too early to show the system to users:
The development team should remember that if the potential users are disinclined to use the system — for ANY reason — then it will not be a business success. Representative users should be part of the team from the outset.

11.4   THE EXPERT'S APPRENTICE

The strategy of using the developing expert system itself as the main vehicle for knowledge acquisition and refinement is a cornerstone of our approach. The process is similar to forcibly teaching a human apprentice — if one could subject a human to such an intensive process of examination and improvement.

There is little alternative to beginning with unstructured discussions with the expert. By 'unstructured' we mean that the discussion cannot be planned in advance. As described in section 12.5, we recommend that knowledge engineers should provide focus by discussing particular cases, but this is simply to provide a prompt. However, as soon as a framework is established then discussion can be centred on specific tasks and specific objectives to be achieved. These focused discussions tend to produce a much greater quantity of detailed expertise, although knowledge engineers must still be sensitive to the broader issues. For example, there is always a need for the team to reflect on why an issue is important, or whether the details they are engrossed in actually matter at all. This requires a degree of 'standing back' from the details of the task. Therefore it would be naive to think that discussions must follow a strict agenda.

Once a prototype has been built, this serves as the focus of discussion. Being able to exercise the know-how is far more illuminating than discussing it on paper. An apparently plausible written statement of the know-how may be obviously wrong when it is applied to test cases. Initially the aim is to produce generally correct behaviour, using typical cases carried through to the end. As the system improves, attention may be focused on specific areas, perhaps using well known exceptions or cases which the expert had trouble with. Throughout this period the primary aim is to use the fledgling expert system to prompt the expert for further explanation and guidance. Later, the system will be tested by users when its further mistakes and shortcomings will yield a rich source of further prompts.

The benefits of this approach are:

- When the expert system makes a mistake or fails to take an action then it is glaringly obvious to the expert. This means that the rate of acquiring new know-how is very high.
- The know-how is obtained, and can be added to the system, while the context is still 'hot' in everyone's mind. This is very much better than analysis at a later stage, since it avoids the risk of the knowledge engineer misrepresenting what is said.
- There is a much better chance of capturing the expert's general principles of working. A helpful expert will tend to give an explanation in broader terms than just the specific instance being tried. Proficient experts are able to identify the fundamental component which is missing, rather than just identifying a 'fix' for the immediate symptoms. These generic rules are arguably the most powerful pieces of know-how in an expert system. They are certainly the hardest to identify. Exercising the system is unequalled as a method for bringing them to light.
- The expert is led into providing an explanation related to achieving better solutions and/or better understanding for the user. This provides a very user-oriented system — exactly what is being sought.

By allowing easy modifications, expert systems can 'grow' in step with the increasing understanding of what the users require, and how the expert would provide it. This greatly improves the chances of having a system which is genuinely useful to the users. An expert system may be the first computer program which actually helps the users in their work!

Additionally, expert systems have the flexibility to follow changes in working practices as they occur. Because the know-how in the system can be read and understood, future developments are simply an extension of the refinement stages of the project. Long-term maintenance is actually long-term development. Unlike a conventional program, the performance of an expert system should *improve* as it matures.

11.5   USE OF EXPERT TIME

It will be apparent that this approach requires the expert and the knowledge engineer to work closely together for much of the time. During structuring, there is no choice: the expert and the knowledge engineer must work closely together to create the maps (see section 12.4). However, once rule building starts there is greater flexibility. The options for constructing the first prototype are as follows:

(1) Implement the rules during the session with the expert, starting as soon as an adequate map of the first task has been produced. This leads to excellent expression of the know-how , but requires the expert to be present throughout.

(2) Exercise the prototype system with the knowledge engineer making comprehensive notes (which can usefully be supplemented by tape recording). The knowledge engineer will then build the next increment using these notes. This is a commonly adopted approach.

(3) Have the knowledge engineer build the first prototype after a few sessions with the expert and a potential user. The intention is to provide an effective prompt for the expert even though the structure may not be settled. This can only be done by an experienced knowledge engineering team with an adequate background knowledge of the problem, so that their prototype is not too implausible or too simplistic to be useful. It has the advantage of making very good use of expert time.

Building the rules with the expert present leads to excellent expression of the know-how, and reduces errors of interpretation by the knowledge engineer. However it is obviously expensive on expert time. Once the expert has confidence in the knowledge engineer, then only the fundamental rules need be implemented during the session with notes on how the details are to be handled. The knowledge engineer can then be entrusted with the task of making the rules work together, and the next session with the expert will begin with testing. This is our preferred method of working. Using this accelerated method, the quality of the know-how expressed in the system will certainly suffer, leading to more time being required for refining, but that is the price of much reduced involvement by the expert. The ratio of expert time to knowledge engineer time can be reduced from the preferred level of about 1:2 to as little as 1:10. It is important that the knowledge engineer should have informal access to the expert for checking on details and points which have not been fully understood — and there will be many of these. Issues which seem clear when in conversation with the expert often seem ambiguous when they come to be defined in the form of rules. Either telephone contact or being located in a nearby office is usually sufficient.

We are against the 'smash and grab' approach whereby the knowledge engineer interviews the expert for perhaps one or two hours, and then spends several days implementing the rules. This can certainly be done, but much of the inspiration will necessarily come from the knowledge engineer, not from the expert.

11.6 DEVELOPMENT STYLE

In section 4.4 it was emphasised that there are important differences between demonstrating benefits for management and establishing feasibility via a pilot system. It follows that the development team must be clear as to the type of system which must be delivered, and the corresponding style of working.

To avoid constant qualification, chapter 12 describes the building of an expert system as if there were only one style. In reality, different aspects will be given a different emphasis because of the difference in objectives (fig. 11.3).

We can identify three separate styles of system:

— management demonstration,
— pilot for assessment,
— full system.

In a management demonstration the requirement is to show skilful performance on a specific problem, where solving that problem has clear business benefits. Presentation is very important since management may expect to make a decision based only on brief demonstrations. This implies careful attention to phrasing of messages, spelling, use of graphics, colour, etc. There are also aspects of building a relationship with the expert, learning about the subject, and following interesting avenues to see where they lead. However, the demonstration need only cover a narrow set of cases to achieve its purpose. Once an overall picture has been gained then attention can be focused on just one or two aspects. If we think of the whole problem

	Management demonstration	Technical pilot	Full system
Principal purpose	demonstrate benefits, gain support	test feasibility, assess user requirements	deliverable system
Business relevance	self evident	established beforehand	established by pilot
Presentation	'glossy'	important but not critical	polished
Dialogue	polished	understandable	polished
Scope	one slice	key areas	full
Completeness	unimportant	fair	good
Problem-solving	highly specific	broad	broad
User facilities	indicated	prototyped	delivered

Fig. 11.3 — Purpose and approach, showing the emphasis given to different aspects.

area is a cake, then the demonstrator need only be a small slice — but it must taste good!

A successful pilot will serve as the basis for developing the full system. It is a test bed for technical issues and user requirements. It needs to be much more complete than a demonstrator since it will be exercised on many different cases, although known omissions are acceptable. The general style of working is aggressive: the development team will be testing their ideas and exploring different avenues in some depth. There is incentive to work fast and to investigate any idea which seems important to the overall problem. Explanations, help and report facilities can be kept to a minimum: a one line summary is often sufficient. Although secondary, presentation cannot be ignored since the system is to be reviewed by users. It is surprising how much apparent value is lost by clumsy wording or mis-spelling. However, presentation as such takes second place to the user facilities which must be prototyped and evaluated.

When developing a full system, the approach is much more measured. The pilot will have established an overall structure and the essential facilities. Therefore the work is more planned and more thorough. Much more attention should be paid to completeness, for example taking care to include eventualities which could safely be ignored when prototyping. Lines of reasoning are developed until they are exhausted, or judged to be sufficiently detailed for the required purpose. Presentation and dialogue are obviously important, and they are dealt with as a distinct activity once the system is working satisfactorily. There will also be a requirement for comprehensive help and explanation, tutoring on the use of the system, supporting documentation, and so forth.

In summary, the same techniques are used to build the three styles of system but in different amounts. For a management demonstration, initial investigation gives way to a tight focus and a polished appearance. For a pilot system, development is exploratory, doing enough on each aspect of the problem to establish the way forward and to gauge users' reactions. For a full system, the approach is methodical, aiming to achieve what should by now be well established objectives.

11.7 SPIDER DIAGRAMS

When exploring the structure of an expert's decision making, there is a need to record his ideas in a simple, sharable way. We use a diagram known as a 'map', drawn as a 'spider diagram'. These are the principal means of recording and discussing the structure of the expert system.

Spider diagrams are so useful that it is surprising that they are not more widely used. They are also called 'spray diagrams', 'concept maps' and 'mind maps'. Buzan (1982) gives a highly readable account of their use and some associated psychological theory. They are a high level means of representing knowledge in a way which is independent of the choice of expert system software†.

Spider diagrams are drawings which show the key ideas (written in as short phrases) and the relationships between them (lines connecting the ideas). An example is given in fig. 11.4. Spider diagrams are a powerful method of organising ones thoughts and making them visible to others.

Just three conventions define the construction of a spider diagram:

— The highest level concept is drawn in the centre, with lower level, more detailed concepts being drawn radiating outwards. The reason for doing this is delightfully simple. There is more room the further out you go!
— There is an implicit sequence starting at ten o'clock and going round clockwise to end at eight o'clock. This is arbitrary, but widely used.
— Each map is complete in itself and fits onto a single sheet of paper. If there is more detail than can conveniently be drawn on the first sheet, then one item from the edge is placed in the middle of a new sheet and 'exploded' into a more detailed map. This means that everything on a given map is at roughly the same level of detail.

It is important to appreciate that a spider diagram is not a specification of the expert system, nor is it intended to be. Its prime purpose is communica-

† A business consultant has a technique for establishing credibility which involves giving presentations at high speed and laden with technical jargon. He refers to the technique as ATN, standing for 'Amaze The Natives'. It wins him far more business than it deserves. He would doubtless refer to spider diagrams as a 'tool-independent intermediate knowledge representation paradigm'.

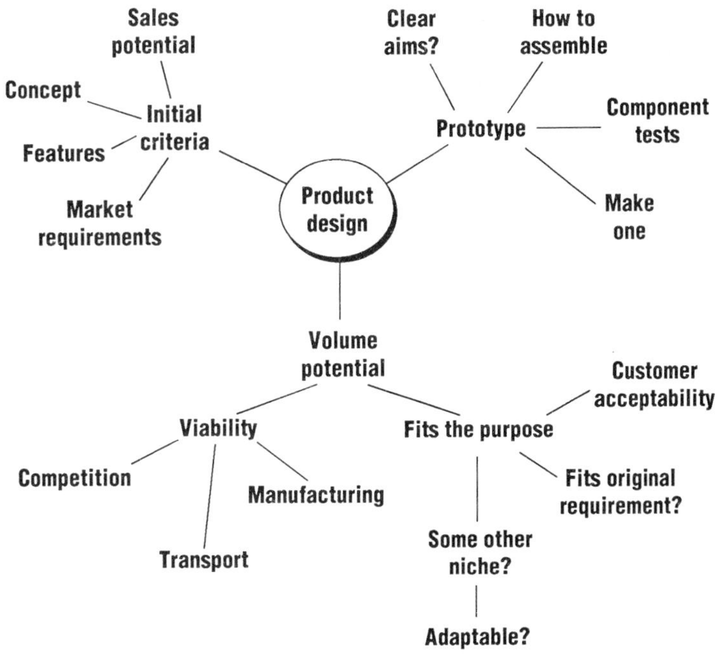

Fig. 11.4 — A spider diagram.

tion. The diagram is a form of summarised notes, expressing the development team's emerging understanding of the problem. Initially it is used for communication between the team members, including the expert, and later with those who will maintain and develop the system.

The spider diagram will not contain sufficient information to define the rules. Experienced knowledge engineers can (and do) write rules directly from the spider diagram, but they are using the map only as a prompt and a guide. It must be supplemented with know-how about how the concepts on the diagram interact with one another. The spider diagram shows 'what', but not 'how'.

A spider diagram is definitely *not* a flowchart. A spider diagram shows which ideas are important, and how they relate together for purposes of solving the problem. A flow of control is implied by the clockwise sequence, but that is not the main function. If a flowchart already exists (e.g. for fault finding), then it will still be necessary to work with the expert to prepare a map. The two forms are not interchangeable.

Spider diagrams get their power from being large, and from being graphical. This means that the whole map can be viewed at once, and closely related ideas are physically close together. Being able to visualise the whole structure helps to place any one item in context, and it is surprisingly easy to recall the relationship of ideas according to their proximity (or distance apart) on the diagram.

Artistic tendencies can be indulged to the full. Shape, colour and size can all be used to indicate associations or differences. Sheets of flipchart paper are often used, and these can be pinned to the wall so that several are on view at once. Normal writing paper (A4 or foolscap) is not large enough for working in a group. We have standardised on working in soft pencil on the largest size paper which can be readily photocopied. Coloured ink is fun, but cannot be altered — and there will be many alterations.

At present there is a shortage of software packages for handling spider diagrams on the computer. Large drawings can certainly be produced, and plotters can provide excellent quality output. However, the diagrams will be updated hundreds of times during the project, so that ease of updating is a crucial requirement. For example, a cluster of ideas may be disconnected from the centre and re-attached elsewhere, or a completely new concept may be introduced in the middle of an existing link. An appropriate software tool would support such activities as single operations, preferably working on a graphical image of the diagram. Automatic adjustment of the layout would be an added bonus. Such ease of updating can be found in 'outlining' packages intended for authors and journalists, but these are oriented towards text, not graphics. Conversely, drawing packages require considerable manual work to make changes. We still find that working on paper is the most effective method.

12

Building the system

In section 3.2 it was stated that know-how was hardly ever written down. This chapter attempts to be 'the exception which proves the rule'. It describes methods which we have found very successful for building expert system. The methods are based on experience and have been found to work in practice, but are not guaranteed to be effective in all possible cases. Many of the guidelines are heuristics and can only be expressed in the form:

> if you recognise this particular situation
> then you might try this corresponding tactic

Other experts and knowledge engineers should adapt our guidelines to suit their own requirements.

There are two pre-requisites for the methods described here:

(1) the aim should be to capture the know-how of a cooperative expert, and
(2) the software being used must allow the expert to understand the know-how which is in the system. If the knowledge engineer has to translate, this will act as a barrier.

The central philosophy of this method is that the expert system is 'grown' out of the expert's own words. 'Grown' because a first, crude prototype is built at the earliest opportunity, and this is expanded by prompting the expert for corrections and additions. 'Out of the expert's own words' because the system directly represents the expert's know-how *in the way that he would say it*, for example when instructing a junior.

The stages of work have already been identified in section 11.2. For the purpose of detailed discussion the stages of building have been expanded into more detail, as follows:

— Preparation
— Defining the system
— Acquiring the knowledge
— Structuring the knowledge
— Building a knowledge base
— System integration

— Testing
— Refinement for use

12.1   PREPARATION

Preparation is a combination of 'people factors' and project management requirements. Since the senior knowledge engineer is often the technical manager as well, it falls to him to ensure that the necessary preparation has been carried out whether or not he has been specifically required to do so. In any event, it will be the knowledge engineers who have to compensate for any weaknesses in preparation, so these tasks are best tackled at the outset. The responsible person should check that:

— all the knowledge engineers have a sufficient background knowledge,
— suitable experts have been identified,
— one expert has agreed to be the lead expert for the first prototype,
— a knowledge engineer has confirmed (by discussion) that the expertise of the lead expert is appropriate and covers a sufficient range of tasks,
— the lead expert has been recruited, i.e. briefed about the project and encouraged or intrigued into wanting to participate,
— it is clear what purpose the system is to serve, and for whom,
— initial objectives for the system have been prepared, and discussed with a representative sample of users,
— management, experts and users have given their commitment to the prototype,
— any necessary hardware or software has been procured, and
— a suitable venue has been arranged as a workplace.

Diligent preparation will pay dividends throughout the project. An enthusiastic team working well together can make quite remarkable progress. This is particularly true if one is used to the pace of a conventional software project. Conversely, hasty preparation can lead to poor communication and a lack of direction. In such cases the pace will be wearisomely slow and the quality of the resulting system will suffer. There is also the possibility that even if the work is sound, the lack of direction might mean that the system will not fulfill its users expectations.

12.2   DEFINING THE SYSTEM

The broad objectives for the expert system will already have been set by agreement with management (see section 4.4). However, these will usually need further interpretation and clarification before they can be used to guide the day-to-day project work. Therefore a primary task is to define the system more closely.

The main concern for the technical team is to define what the system will and will not do, i.e. its scope and limitations. The initial draft should be discussed with users and management to make absolutely certain that the development team's aims are consistent with the end result being sought. This statement of scope and limitations can be thought of as the definition of the system's requirements. It is an essential part of the expert system's prospectus (see section 15.2), which is the key management document for the project.

The requirements may well be modified during the subsequent stages — after all, they were written from a position of ignorance! If the requirements change significantly (e.g. if it becomes necessary to severely limit the scope) then it will be necessary to confer with management and users again.

12.3   ACQUIRING THE KNOWLEDGE

Acquiring the knowledge means obtaining knowledge from an expert for use in the expert system. It is the point at which the expert and the knowledge engineer first come together to begin work on a knowledge base.

Know-how cannot be acquired in isolation: it can only be done in the context of how it will be used. This means that the processes of acquiring and structuring the know-how are inextricably linked. The knowledge engineer must first establish the general structure of the task being tackled so that the know-how can be placed in its proper context. Structure is to an expert system what chapters and paragraphs are to a book. It provides form, and allows related material to work together. Imagine trying to read this book if the paragraphs were in random order. The same information would be present, but it would be in a useless form.

A sound structure will also reflect the expert's tacit knowledge of the problem, those concepts and principles which have 'soaked through the skin' by long association. Just viewing the problem in an appropriate manner can go half-way to solving it. Therefore the expert's assessment of how to partition the problem should be treated with some respect — even if he cannot provide logical justification.

Therefore the early stages of knowledge acquisition are mainly about acquiring an overall structure. The purpose is to obtain 'the big picture', which we call the map of the problem. This means that the knowledge engineer must actively pursue the broad issues, and must not become immersed in the detailed know-how for the time being. It would be a daunting task to attempt to 'refine out' the key issues from among a mass of details. Therefore it is vital to tap the expert's appreciation of his speciality as a whole. Indeed this broad appreciation is one of the notable distinctions between a newcomer and an experienced expert. As the project progresses, and the structure is clarified, attention will move to a more detailed level. This involves mapping the tasks, and finally to implementing the detailed know-how.

As stated in section 7.1, obtaining know-how is not difficult. In fact, the opposite is true. Given that an expert is enthusiastic to see the expert system succeed, know-how is usually forthcoming in such quantity that it is hard for the knowledge engineer to cope with the flood. Most experts thoroughly enjoy discussing their speciality with an interested and responsive listener. This can be true even when the person concerned is normally thought of as being reserved. The key is the expert's motivation to see the system succeed, which is why we place such emphasis on 'recruiting' the expert to the project (section 13.3.3).

So, obtaining know-how is not a problem in itself. The real difficulties lie in organising the know-how into a useful form, i.e. in structuring. Structuring is discussed in the following sections.   .

We suspect that the commonly held difficulties of knowledge acquisition arise from either or both of two sources:

(1) the task is being discussed with the wrong expert, or
(2) the expert's pronouncements do not fit with what the knowledge engineer is hoping to hear.

Using our approach, it is axiomatic that:

(1) A suitable expert is one who solves the problem on a day to day basis (see section 13.3.1), and is motivated to help with the project.
(2) Knowledge engineers should believe that experts probably do solve problems in the way that they say. If this does not fit the knowledge engineer's ideas then those ideas will have to be changed.

There is no substitute for direct discussion with the expert. We regard the formal methods described in chapter 7 as supplements. The very word 'discussion' suggests a meeting between equals, with a two-way flow. Both the knowledge engineer and the expert are seeking a common viewpoint, and this can only be done interactively. By contrast, the description 'interviewing' fits with the idea of extracting knowledge from the expert, essentially a one-way flow.

12.4   STRUCTURING THE KNOWLEDGE

12.4.1   Basics of structuring

We have found that obtaining a good structure which the expert approves of is the hardest activity in knowledge engineering. It is the most nebulous of the building tasks, which is perhaps why it continues to cause difficulty at all levels of knowledge engineering. Experts provide know-how in whatever order it comes to mind. The purpose of structuring is to make sense of this stream of information, to identify the pieces which go together and the main functions involved. The knowledge engineer's contribution is to identify the structure which the expert appears to be using, make it visible as a spider diagram, and work with the expert to modify this picture until the expert is comfortable with it. Typically the first two or three days of a project are spent in alternating periods of intensive discussion with the expert, and consolidation of what has been learnt. This is a gruelling time for both parties.

The output of structuring is a diagram of the main functions to be performed by the expert system, and the interdependencies between these functions. Detailed guidance about preparing structure diagrams is given in the following sections.

The most direct means of obtaining a structure is to ask the expert. For example, 'Can you tell me in broad terms how you would approach this?'. If published reports are to be taken literally, many teams neglect this most obvious step. It is true that the ensuing narrative by the expert is unlikely to yield a coherent, well formed structure straight away. The experience is that very few experts have such a clear picture in their mind. (This says much for the power of the human brain in being able to apply loosely structured knowledge without apparent effort. Unfortunately, computers have more stringent requirements.) However, almost all experts will say something in response to such a question, and this is the place to start.

It is mainly up to the knowledge engineer to identify the structure from what the expert says. This relies on the everyday human ability to understand the essence of what is being said by another person. It is as trivial, or as wonderful, as that. It can be compared with the task of identifying someone's occupation if you overhear their conversation on a bus. From the flow of words, there is an unconscious process of picking out phrases and noting their implications. Meanwhile, the conscious mind is making guesses as to the general type of occupation, reinforcing or abandoning these guesses as further clues arrive. Similarly, the knowledge engineer will be making conjectures about the structure of the know-how, noting promising ideas and discarding those which seem inappropriate. Like the listener on the bus, the knowledge engineer will not know if the structure is plausible until he shows it to the expert.

It is important that the knowledge engineer should make the emerging structure *visible*; unvoiced thoughts cannot be shared or reviewed. This is the purpose of mapping as described below. Once a structure is visible, the expert may recognise it at once, or more likely will suggest amendments. The process of identifying the structure will then have begun.

Structures are even more volatile than most of the documents produced for an expert system. The expert will be trying to form a mental picture at the same time as the knowledge engineer, so the initial efforts will only be tentative. It is also likely that the expert has never seen such a structure before. Indeed, this high level picture of his decision making can be a welcome contribution to the expert's own understanding.

The expert's views can be altered by the discipline of explaining them, and he may change his mind. This is a valuable process: the expert is being prompted into new insights. Knowledge engineers simply have to accept the possibility of the expert changing his view, and investigate why the change is needed. What knowledge engineers must *not* do is to accuse the expert of being inconsistent, for example by referring to recordings of previous interviews. Referring back is fine — it is the 'accusation' which damages the spirit of cooperation. It may well be seen as the knowledge engineer attempting to score a petty victory over the expert by catching him out. The truth might be quite different — experts have been known to give simplified explanations to help the knowledge engineer to understand.

Sometimes it is possible to get good initial structures from staff who are accustomed to giving training. Training schools are generally best avoided, since full-time trainers are remote from the day-to-day practicalities. However, those staff who are good at teaching new recruits are usually able to explain the basics clearly. This can be of great assistance to the knowledge engineer, even if such a teacher does not have the full depth of know-how which will be needed later.

There are informal methods which can occasionally help with structuring. 'Concept sorting' can be used to group like ideas together, and thus establish an overall organisation. In a simple form of concept sorting, the ideas of interest are written on separate cards. The expert is then asked to divide them into groups and to explain what they have in common. Note that the groupings often depend strongly on the current problem being examined. Such methods are best used as a means of overcoming a temporary difficulty, and must not become an end in themselves.

An example may illustrate the point. One of us was approached with a classification of an expert's knowledge about mathematical simulation†, and asked to implement it in an expert system shell. This was at an international conference, and the request was from a student on an associated workshop. (There seemed to be an element of 'trying out the professionals'!) The classification was a hierarchy of simulation types, and some particular qualities of each type. The hierarchy had been derived by tape recording a two hour interview with an expert, transcribing the text, editing the text to pick out key phrases, transferring these phrases onto cards, and asking the expert to sort the cards into a hierarchy. The hierarchy could be implemented in an expert system in several ways, none of them difficult, but what was it to be used for? The student did not know. Without knowing the purpose, the knowledge itself was of little practical use. So there was little to be gained by putting it onto the computer. We regard this as a clear example of the knowledge engineers being a slave to their methods.

> 'Methodologies are for the guidance of wise men
> and the obedience of fools'

To complete the story, the student also volunteered that the very first point that the expert had made was missing from the hierarchy. This key point was that mathematical simulations were easy to build, but very difficult to validate. Hence their predictions should not be accepted lightly. The expert had 'stressed this time and time again'. It was a fundamental part of his know-how. However, since there was no place for it in the knowledge engineer's hierarchy, it was not recorded. Had the knowledge engineer been

† A mathematical simulation is a way of modelling the real world on a computer, usually to forecast what might happen in future. Mathematical simulations are used for modelling the national economy, future sales, the behaviour of bridges, the weather, etc.

mentally attuned to recognising practical skill when it was offered, such a point would have been seized upon. The obvious follow up is along the lines of 'When would you decide that a simulation was worth doing?'. We suspect that the resulting material to go into the expert system would have been quite different.

12.4.2 Mapping the problem

Mapping the structure of the problem is a method of acquiring knowledge and structuring it in one process. It is described in some detail because it highlights many practical tips.

'Mapping' means literally drawing a map of the problem as a spider diagram. Its purpose is to identify the key tasks within the problem, and how they relate to one another. The type of knowledge being acquired is descriptive rather than operational, i.e. it concerns how ideas relate to one another rather than how the reasoning operates. This descriptive structure will be the framework underpinning the operational knowledge which will eventually form the bulk of the knowledge base.

Maps are the basic working documents of the project. There are two levels: mapping the problem to identify the constituent tasks (described here), and mapping each of the tasks (section 12.4.3).

Ideally a map of the whole problem would be obtained before moving on to examine any of the tasks in detail. Later, the tasks would be implemented by mapping and then building each of them in turn. In reality. the two processes are interleaved with each other and with building (as discussed in section 11.2). Therefore a typical progression might be:

— draft a map of the problem,
— map some tasks,
— build part,
— review the mess!
— revise the maps,
     and so on.

Mapping begins with mapping the whole problem. The map of the problem shows the division into separate phases (fig. 12.1). Nearly all problems can be divided into a number of phases which occur in a well understood sequence, and are essentially independent. This makes the building easier and greatly facilitates testing. There is a truism that 'big problems get easier if they are split into little problems'. It is certainly true of expert systems.

The division into phases is subjective, and relies to a large extent on what seems obvious to the expert. The knowledge engineer contributes by helping the expert to categorise different issues and to identify which distinctions are important. The intention should be to choose phases which help the user to understand the problem solving process as it unfolds. This means that each phase should deal with a particular aspect, and some milestone should have been achieved at the end of it. The experience is that

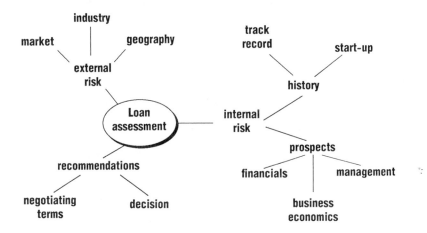

Fig. 12.1 — A map of a problem.

dividing a problem into only two parts is hardly useful for the user. Half the problem often seems as complex to him as the whole. Conversely, having too many phases makes it difficult for the user to appreciate the contribution each makes to the whole process. If many phases are used, the user's attention will be narrowed to the current phase only. Their focus of attention will shift from one phase to the next, but will tend to ignore the wider implications (of course, this can be used as a deliberate ploy). Therefore the maximum number of phases is usually restricted to six or seven†. During building, it may turn out to be convenient to sub-divide the phases, but this does not affect the higher level structure.

Mapping begins with a discussion between the senior knowledge engineer and the expert about how the expert typically goes about solving the problem. This will usually be the first technical session on the project. Note that if the expert is doubtful as to the eventual value of the expert system, or feels threatened, then overcoming these concerns takes complete priority. Any thought of obtaining a structure should be abandoned in favour of recruiting the expert back into the team. It can be useful to experiment with a few rules which handle just a simple case in order to explore the structure. This approach has the incidental benefit of allowing the expert to see his own know-how in action.

Mapping the problem is definitely a task for the most experienced knowledge engineer, and should be conducted on a one-to-one basis with the lead expert. Other experts (or managers) should not be present. To avoid repeating what often amounts to a detailed briefing, any other knowledge engineers on the project should be included in the meeting, but should act as observers and occasional contributors. They must not insist on directing the discussion. The senior knowledge engineer will be trying to

† Like all heuristics, this one fails sometimes. Trust in your own judgement.

determine a structure while the discussion is in progress, and it is a serious interference if he also has to control a public debate. Correspondingly, the senior knowledge engineer has an obligation to make the emerging structure visible to all. This should be done using spider diagrams (see below). These diagrams are the method of forming a collective view for all the parties present.

There is an obvious problem about how to begin. We recommend discussing how the expert would tackle a typical problem. If the expert has difficulty visualising a typical problem, then the knowledge engineer should ask about what happened yesterday, or what happens most often, or what are the classic cases. Perhaps surprisingly, senior experts who are no longer required to solve everyday problems may have difficulty in citing routine cases. We now recognise this as a signal that this particular expert may only be familiar with difficult cases. This suggests that the knowledge engineer may need to contact more junior staff to establish the typical problems experienced by the eventual users.

Some knowledge engineers prefer to start with exceptional cases as a means of keeping the expert interested. We prefer to start with typical cases since the expert will be very confident on these examples, and tends to relax more quickly. Typical cases are also a better means of illustrating the basic truths of the subject. Also, these discussions take place right at the beginning of the project when sustaining interest should not be a problem. (See section 14.4 for an insider's view of the expert's motivation.)

Some gentle role-playing by the knowledge engineer often helps to get over any initial awkwardness:

> 'OK, let's suppose that you are about to go on holiday for two weeks, and I am going to handle your enquiries for you. Unfortunately I have very little experience, and there are only ten minutes before you have to leave. What would you tell me to do?'

This is more subtle than it may seem. The unreasonableness of the request can help to create an easy atmosphere — and the 'instant advice' is often surprisingly potent. Faced with the ten minute constraint, there is no time for detailed explanation. The expert has to fall back on simply stated, widely effective rules of thumb. This is exactly what the knowledge engineer is looking for as a starting point. The fact that complications are ignored for the moment is all to the good: filling out the details of rules already identified is relatively straightforward. Furthermore, the expert may well produce know-how about what *not* to do, which is equally valuable.

This kind of interview is always unstructured. The knowledge engineer has yet to identify the right questions, and the expert does not know what sort of information the knowledge engineer is seeking. (Take heart — both of these improve rapidly!) So the session proceeds as a discussion or informal briefing, with plenty of open questions from the knowledge engineer and ample opportunity for the expert to talk. The only control needed from the knowledge engineer is to try and keep the expert on the main issues and avoid lengthy digressions into detail.

These discussions take place during the first few days of a project. Sessions should be planned to last about two hours, with either one or two sessions a day. During the initial work, less than an hour with the expert is usually too little to make significant progress. (Later, 'little and often' access is best.) At the other limit, most knowledge engineers lose efficiency after about four hours because they need time for assimilation. In contrast to some reports, we have found that the knowledge engineer invariably weakens before the expert!

In many ways knowledge engineering is an exercise in rapid learning, and new concepts need time to become familiar. It is essential that the knowledge engineers do take the necessary time out for assimilation. This often involves discussion between themselves, re-drawing of maps for clarity, and identification of points which have not been understood. They must not simply record the sessions and press on, expecting to extract what they need later. What they should be doing is building the scaffolding for the building to come, and there is little point in collecting more scaffold poles if the existing ones are in a tangled heap. The existing ones must first be assembled into a framework. Only then will it be apparent where more are needed, and where some are missing.

During the discussions, the knowledge engineer's task is to pick out that which is relevant and record it on the spot. When mapping the whole problem, the key points are:

— What are the principal activities or phases which are used to solve the problem?
— How are these separate parts used? In what circumstances? Is it always like that?
— Can the activities be grouped into essentially separate tasks?

As already stated, it is rare to find an expert who already has a clear picture of the structure of his own decision making. It is up to the knowledge engineer to bring out the major features by observing the process. The sensation is one of 'groping in the fog', seeking out a form which should be there but which will only be apparent when it is found. This is taxing for the knowledge engineer, who must assimilate the information and build a mental picture of the expert's decision making process while keeping the broad objectives in view and managing the conversation with the expert. The purpose of drawing a map is to provide a vehicle for noting whatever structure has been identified so far, and to act as a framework for adding further pieces.

Most experts will be unfamiliar with spider diagrams, but the representation is so obvious that they will soon become involved. The expert should be encouraged to add to or modify the map themselves (have pencils and erasers to hand). There is an important psychological point here: the map should be a joint production, and not the property of the knowledge engineer. For this reason, a single, large piece of paper which can be laid on the desk and worked on by both parties is considerably better than the knowledge engineer's notepad.

The knowledge engineer should use the spider diagram as the means of discussing his emerging view of the structure with the expert. This means that the expert and the knowledge engineer are working together to build up a joint picture of the main tasks. Happily, experts often have an intuitive feel for a good structure once it is found.

The initial aim should be to construct a map of the major tasks involved in solving the problem. This is the map of the whole problem. Each task should be annotated with what it does, what are the main issues within it, what type of information it requires as input, and what contribution it makes from the user's point of view. The same diagram can also be used to show the interdependencies between tasks, although these may not become clear until later.

Since the whole team will be learning about the problem as the building work progresses, the initial structures will rarely be correct. Mapping the tasks will often show that the map of the problem must be revised. This is not too important. Extra tasks can be added, and old ones deleted or subdivided relatively easily. This means that there is little point in trying to achieve a perfect map before moving on. The law of diminishing returns applies. It is much better to start detailed mapping and building as soon as a workable map for the problem has been prepared. Once the first section has been built, both the expert and the knowledge engineer will have a better grasp of the problem and subsequent mapping and building will proceed that much more effectively.

Mapping the problem often requires a few days' intensive effort by the whole team. An initial structure can usually be established within the first day, with the following day or two being spent reviewing, modifying, and elaborating this outline.

12.4.3   Mapping the tasks
Once the whole problem has been mapped satisfactorily, attention can be turned to the individual tasks. The order in which they are tackled is rarely important. Where there is doubt, we recommend starting with the most central task, i.e. one on which several others depend. Frequently this central task will follow some kind of preamble (e.g. localising the area of interest) and will precede any analysis of the outcome. If the expert has a particular preference, then it is usually best to follow that.

Mapping of the individual tasks follows the pattern of mapping the whole problem, except that it is easier. The map of the problem obtained earlier provides a specific context, and the discussion can focus on one task at a time. This exercise is less of a struggle than mapping the whole problem because experts usually perform better the more specific the problem they are set. The result of mapping each task is a spider diagram just for that task illustrating the key ideas and how they are related (see fig. 12.2).

Mapping the tasks is done at a sufficient level of detail that experts are

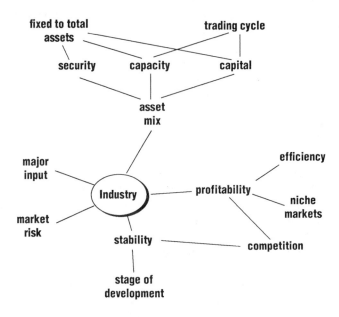

Fig. 12.2 — A map of a task.

usually confident about its detailed structure. Details are part of their everyday routine, whereas bigger issues require reflection. Nevertheless, task-level maps must still be thought of as 'the best current view'. Once the map appears to be satisfactory, then the team should move on to writing the rules. We advise against any prolonged period of 'dry running' the map to validate it. It is much more effective to experiment with some rules representing simple cases. This will quickly reveal gross errors and serve to build confidence.

12.5   BUILDING A KNOWLEDGE BASE

Building a knowledge base means implementing a task which has been mapped. As already emphasised, building should begin as soon as one or two tasks have been mapped. Building makes a definite contribution to subsequent maps and to improving the existing ones. Attempting to map all of the tasks before starting to build is both unnecessary and undesirable.

The completed expert system might reflect the problem structure by having a knowledge base for each task, or there might be a single, large knowledge base. The choice will probably be dictated by the software being used. In either case, we strongly recommend that the system should be built in a modular fashion. This is the only course which offers even a hope of adequately testing the system (see section 12.7).

Building a knowledge base proceeds as many cycles of:

— obtaining some rules,
— making them work, and
— validating and extending the know-how, thereby obtaining more rules.

Initially the intention is simply to make the expert system work, i.e. to ask the expected questions, to produce output in the right order, and to reach appropriate conclusions. As the system improves, more attention can be given to the expression of the rules, wording of questions, presentation of output and so forth.

This is the innermost cycle of the many cycles involved in expert system building (see section 11.2). The major inputs are the map of the task and plenty of know-how from the expert. Provided that the software allows it, each cycle might take only an hour or so and will result in a few more pieces of know-how being added to the knowledge base. After many cycles, the end result of building is a working knowledge base which will form one section of the completed expert system.

12.5.1   How to begin

The basic method of developing a knowledge base is for an expert to comment on a partially built version, and to include those comments in the next version (see below). However, first you have to begin! This section suggests how to reach that first, primitive knowledge base which will be the launching point for further development.

The first steps in building a knowledge base should be devoted to establishing those rules which relate the principal ideas together. The map of the task which has already been prepared shows the main ideas, and how they are related. Since the highest level idea is at the centre of the map, then that is the place to start. These first rules should relate the central idea to its immediate neighbours, since these have been mapped as the factors on which it depends. Discuss with the expert what there is to know about the central idea. For example, in the map shown in fig. 12.2 you would usually begin by discussing which conclusions about the industry would be useful, and how these were affected by the major input, asset mix, profitability, etc.

If the expert is not readily forthcoming, then there is a top-down method which is laborious, but usually works†. Proceed as follows:

— Ask the expert what outcomes he is expecting for the central idea. Make a list of them.
— Choose one of these outcomes; any one will do.
— Ask the expert when that outcome would occur (i.e. under what circumstances).
— Use the map as a guide. The necessary conditions should all be found connected directly to the central idea. If not, modify the map.
— Record what the expert says in the form of rules (either on paper, or better directly into the expert system).

---

† This analysis maps directly onto a backward chained reasoning structure; see section 6.3.

Do not be too concerned about completeness or absolute precision, for example listing every conceivable outcome at the first step. There are thousands of extensions and improvements to come, and it is important to make headway. A brisk pace is also much more exciting for all concerned, and will yield a much better harvest of know-how.

Similarly, do not be led off into a discussion about issues at the edge of the map, such as details of the questions which the expert would ask. It is quite common for an expert to lead off with a detailed procedure, listing which questions he would ask and in what order. This is not what is needed, and the knowledge engineer may need to steer the discussion. A question which the expert would ask is simply the end result of his reasoning. What is needed in the expert system is the know-how which leads to that question being asked. Therefore it is much better to focus on an end result and centre the discussion around that. This will eventually lead to the questions which have to be asked, but they will then be seen as a step in the reasoning and not as a starting point.

At the same time the knowledge engineer should be sensitive as to whether a digression is actually important.

> if the expert appears to be straying off the map
> then the map might be wrong

If the expert is tongue-tied, then a gambit which has never failed us yet goes as follows:

> 'Forget the diagram for a moment. Just tell me what you would do, and we'll worry about putting it down afterwards.'

The expert will sit back in his chair and give you a summary of what he wants to say, in his own words. WRITE IT DOWN — immediately, exactly as it was said. The way it was described will often be close to the final form which is used in the knowledge base, such is the power of spoken expertise. Very often the problem will have been that the expert was struggling to find the right words for a complete yet concise statement. Once freed from having to deliver a 'specification' (a self-imposed restriction), the words come tumbling out. The phrasing which conveys meaning to the knowledge engineer will probably suit users too. If the description needs further elaboration or closer definition, then no matter, that can be the subject of further rules. And rule building will have started.

Once there are sufficient rules for the central idea, which is when the builders cannot think of any more for the moment, then attention is shifted to the first of the subordinate ideas. These are the ideas on the map which are directly connected to the central idea. The first in sequence will conventionally be found at 10 o'clock on the map. Rules have already been written to deal with the central idea, and the same process can be repeated here.

One can choose to work clockwise around the central idea, progressively moving outwards towards the more detailed ideas at the edge of the map (fig. 12.3). In graphical terms, this means covering an expanding circle around the central idea. Rather than doing this, we recommend dealing with the map in segments.Having written at least one rule for the central idea, a single subordinate idea is followed all the way to the edge of the map. Narrowing the view in this way means that only a few items have to be considered at any time, which makes the work considerably easier.

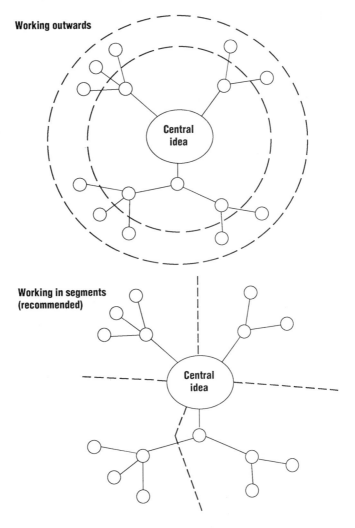

Fig. 12.3 — Using a map.

When rules are being written at a detailed level, it may be that the information required will be obtained by asking the user rather than being deduced from other rules. In this case a question should be written. Alternatively, the item may be a fact (a conclusion which is always true).

At this stage all data should come from questions or facts, even if they will later be supplied by other programs. This is to avoid having to wait for links to those other programs to be developed (see section 12.6).

If the rules for a segment of the map are still not complete after (say) an hour, then we recommend pausing to test what has been written so far. Putting in many detailed rules before exercising them may lead to wasted effort if the same mistake has been made many times over!

The top priority is to get the prototype knowledge base running. Two devices are particularly useful for reaching this objective quickly:

- Start by implementing just the positive rules, i.e. those where all the necessary conditions are true and a positive result follows. For example, when purchasing some equipment:

  > if the budget has been approved
  >   and the equipment fulfills the specification
  >   and the paperwork has been completed
  > then the order can be placed

  There may be three other rules like this where one of the conditions is not true, and either remedial action or deeper investigation will be needed. Using only positive rules, the knowledge base will run but will only reach a conclusion if all the replies to the questions are positive. This is hardly robust, but it is a beginning!
- If a particular topic appears to need substantial detailed work, then temporarily replace the entire topic with a single question or fact. This parallels the way that a single idea on a map can stand for a whole complex of reasoning contained on a more detailed map. For example, in the rule above, there might be many rules concerned with 'the equipment fulfills the specification', but for present purposes it can be replaced by a question such as:

  > 'Does the equipment fulfill the specification?'

  In the fullness of time, this question will be replaced by rules which supply the know-how needed to make the decision. However, having the question allows the knowledge base to be run before those rules are implemented.

It is preferable to enter the rules directly into the computer software being used. Preparing the rules longhand is a waste of time. The better expert system shells provide some assistance for adding rules, although other systems require their rules to be prepared separately using a text editor or word processor. Time permitting, the expert can comment on the phrasing of the rules as they are typed in.

12.5.2 Making the rules work
Experience will soon show how much of the knowledge base should be implemented before it is tested. This is a matter of individual preference, but

approximately twenty rules is a guide. Fewer than ten rules and the correctness should be self-evident; more than (say) thirty rules and the number of possible cases becomes too great to test any reasonable fraction of them. The size of each fragment should be kept small so that each piece can be tested as it is built.

The knowledge engineer should run a few consultations to check for logical errors. It will help the expert if the system always presents a conclusion. (A conclusion amounting to 'don't know' is acceptable provided that this is expected.) Where necessary, the knowledge engineer should make changes to the rules so that they function correctly, with corresponding updates to the map of the task.

The expert need not be involved in this testing. A knowledge engineer who is familiar with the software will have done most of this logical checking by eye as the rules were being entered. He will have been relating the rules to the map of the task, and checking for correspondence. Nevertheless, test runs are always worthwhile to estabish confidence in the work so far.

The knowledge engineer should also add rules to produce a summary of key results and data at the end of the consultation. This will be a great help to the expert.

12.5.3   Adding control

Most of the know-how which will have been gathered so far will be concerned with reasoning about the problem, i.e. how to interpret questions and reach conclusions. However, it is also necessary to know when and how to apply these reasoning rules. This can be thought of as making a knowledgeable system into a skilful one.

Deficiencies in control will be all too apparent. The system might still reach correct conclusions, but the route taken will be quite different from the way in which an expert would work. This makes it very difficult for the user to appreciate the expertise which is being used, and the expert system will appear to be acting erratically.

The missing component is a knowledge of when to apply particular pieces of expertise. It is know-how about using know-how. In the knowledge base, this appears as rules about using rules. Such rules are called control rules, or meta-rules ('meta-knowledge'). Control rules are not directly concerned with processing data or reaching conclusions, but are responsible for controlling the activities of the other rules.

Simple forms of control provide for topics to be explored in a particular order, and groups of questions on the same topic to be asked together. (It is very disconcerting for users if the focus of questioning keeps changing — they need to be able to follow what is going on.) Control rules can also be used for such purposes as localising the area of interest before investigating any particular topic in depth. Otherwise, the expert system might explore the first possibility in depth even though an expert would have known that it was fruitless. Most control rules use forward chaining — they respond when familiar situations occur.

Experts have know-how about when and when not to take different courses of action, and this is the source of control knowledge. For example, in a system to suggest personal investments there might be the following reasoning rule:

> if the client already has an emergency fund
>   and is willing to accept some risk
> then stocks and shares are a possibility

This is considered to be reasoning because it uses data (about an emergency fund and the acceptable level of risk) to produce a conclusion (about a possible investment). The same system might contain the following control rule:

> if the client is aged over 50
> then investigate pension arrangements
> before speculative investments

This is control because it does not directly produce a conclusion. Instead, it directs the inference engine in its use of other rules, in this case to examine pension arrangements before considering any more speculative ventures.

In reality, all expert systems software would require this control rule to be expressed in a more computer-oriented style. The knowledge engineer must use his computer skills to add control rules which reflect the expert's intent. The example given above depends on the reader's ability to interpret the rule as a single sentence. Computers are very poor at extracting meaning from sentences, and the control might have to be expressed explicitly using two rules:

> if the client is aged over 50
> then *investigate* pension arrangements

> if *finished investigating* pension arrangements
> and there are still funds to invest
> then *investigate* speculative investments

Where the words in italics are interpreted by the expert system software as control actions rather than as names used in the knowledge base. An element of computer programming is being introduced here, specifying how the computer should perform its task not just what the task is. This is inevitable in all current systems and is one reaon why experts find it difficult to build systems unaided. (Even these rules are expressed in a far more understandable way than most software systems would allow).

Note also the need to specify that speculative investments are only of interest if there are funds remaining to invest after pension arrangements have been dealt with. If this condition were not present, then the speculative investments would always be investigated, even if all the funds had been allocated to a pension. No human would make this mistake. It is a small example of the expert system's lack of common sense.

Experts rarely make a mental distinction between reasoning and control. Humans seem to be able to operate at different levels of generality without conscious effort. However, knowledge engineers have to be sensitive to the difference between reasoning and control because in an expert system the distinction has to be made explicitly. A skilful knowledge engineer will have been identifying and recording control know-how as the rules were being collected. It might be details of the order in which things should be done, or under what circumstances a particular feature becomes important. Very often such information is volunteered by the expert, or given as a casual aside, so the knowledge engineer must be alert.

As a point of interest, experts are intrigued to discover their own methods of control. Often their expertise has been gained by assimilating many examples of successful problem solving, i.e. many particular cases of reasoning. From these they have been able to distil more general rules, and with real expertise comes the ability to select and apply those rules which are relevant. Knowing what is relevant is the hallmark of an expert. Lesser experts may be familiar with just as many cases, but may lack the ability to focus on the important issues so reliably or so quickly. One manifestation is the inexperienced man's tendency to 'dive in' and take hasty action without appreciating all the circumstances. Therefore the knowledge engineer should be at pains to discuss the control aspects with the expert. It is not something which the knowledge engineer should regard as a technical activity of no direct interest to the expert.

12.5.4 Validating and extending the knowledge base

The next stage is to establish the validity of the know-how which has been implemented, i.e. to validate that it is effective in solving problems. Attention should still be focused on a small area of expertise at any time, perhaps only on one section of a task. The two aspects of:

— having a clear context, plus
— the expert observing the system's actual behaviour

are important features for acquiring further knowledge. Although the process is approached as validation, many modifications and extensions can be expected. Therefore validation and improvement are synonymous.

The expert system should be run to exercise the know-how which has been added, preferably on examples of the expert's choosing. Gross errors will be readily apparent — the system will either take a wrong action, reach a wrong conclusion or fail to reach a conclusion at all. If this happens, the system's reasoning should be examined, and the expert should be asked to suggest the necessary alteration or addition. Experts are extremely good at identifying a system's mistakes in this way, although it may take a little reflection to determine the required change in the know-how. The expert system's abilities to justify its attempted line of reasoning, and to explain how it reached conclusions, are obviously essential.

Working in such a specific context makes a great contribution. A small, clearly defined topic is being worked on, the team have been concentrating on implementing it, and now a test case is misbehaving. The expert is being subjected to very strong prompting, which makes it easy for him to recall relevant expertise.

The required alteration should be made immediately, and the test re-run to verify that it is an improvement. Test cases are then continued until the expert and the knowledge engineer are satisfied. Changes should be made on the map of the task as soon as they are identified in the system. If this is not done the map will have to be re-drawn from scratch with reference to the modified knowledge base. Like a road map, a map of the task which is too out of date is not only unhelpful, but is actually misleading. Validating the result of half a day's rule building can easily take a further day, during which time many improvements and extensions will be made.

Several types of error are commonly found during validation:

— The expert system fails to reach a conclusion, even though it asks the expected questions. This is an obvious sign of a shortage of know-how — the system has no rules to deal with the case being presented. If the expert believes that the existing rules should have covered this case, then the expert should be asked to check the reasoning at the point just before the system gives up.

— The system stops unexpectedly, before asking all the questions it should. This probably means that a detailed condition has failed, and the expected chain of reasoning has collapsed. The knowledge engineer should identity the reasoning being tried just before the system stops, and explore what was expected to happen immediately afterwards.

— The expert system jumps to a wrong conclusion, or perhaps deduces several results when there should only be one. This means that rules are being applied when they should not be. The usual reason is that the context for a rule has not been defined sufficiently, i.e. its conditions do not fully specify when it should be applied. In human conversation, much of the context is assumed, but in an expert system the context must be specified in full. The conditions of every rule must specify exactly when it can be applied†. If no context is specified, then the software will operate as if that rule applied in all circumstances.

— The expert system asks questions to which it should already have the answer. This is often the result of the same idea being expressed in more than one way. For example the expressions 'relations' and 'family members' may have been used for the same purpose. Since the expert has no understanding of meanings, the different expressions are assumed to be quite separate ideas.

† This does not mean that rules should have a huge number of conditions. For example, a condition such as 'if considering a takeover bid' states a very specific context in just one line.

— The expert system tackles problems the wrong way, i.e. it follows lines of reasoning which are plausible but which are inappropriate for this particular case. This is a symptom of a lack of control, a lack of know-how about how to apply the know-how (see section 12.5.3). The expert should be asked to say which features of the case are significant, and how this affects the required approach. Know-how should then be added to the expert system about how to tackle the problem under differing circumstances. An experienced knowledge engineer will have probed the expert for this information as the system was being built, but testing the whole knowledge base invariably shows up deficiencies of some sort.

This is also the time to review the system with other experts ('peer validation') and user representatives. The reviewing experts' contribution is to verify and correct the existing know-how, and to extend it into areas where the lead expert is not confident. The user representative will be able to advise on the suitability and acceptability of the system. If they have reservations about the system's eventual usefulness then strenuous efforts must be made to fulfill their actual requirements. (See also section 12.8 for comments on reviewing.)

12.5.5 Initial refinement

It would not be human to exercise the system for validation purposes without noticing clumsy phrases, grammatical errors, missing words, poor screen layout and other such aspects of presentation. This applies both to the rules and to the dialogue with the user. Although individually small, these faults have a disproportionate effect on a user's appreciation of the system. It is like speaking to someone who slurs his words: not crucial, but very noticeable. Corrections can be made at a convenient moment during the validation.

Any substantial changes to user interface should be left till later when the whole system is refined with potential users.

During refinement, as during validation, it is important to realise that a more precisely worded rule is not necessarily a better rule. Ultimate precision typically involves long, complex phrases and many conditions in order to establish a rigorously accuate meaning. By making them hard to understand, this may in fact *reduce* the utility of the rules. For example:

> if the rules are simple
> then people can understand them

is likely to be more useful than:

> if the rules specify details of the context
> and each rule contains many conditions
> (unless the rule expresses a procedure
> in which case having many conditions is more acceptable)
> and use pedantic rather than understandable wording
> then the know-how is concealed by the words
> and the utility of the rules is reduced

Therefore the precision with which rules are expressed should be appropriate for their intended use.

'Knowledge engineers know that truth is approximate.'

Legal phraseology is just one example of where understandability has been abandoned in the interests of supposed precision. The result is that most of us will not understand the statutes. Expert systems cannot afford to follow the same path.

12.6 SYSTEM INTEGRATION

There are two aspects to integration:

- integration of the different tasks which have been constructed, and
- integration of the expert system with other computer programs such as links to a database.

12.6.1 Integration of the different tasks

In general the building work will have produced a number of knowledge bases which will be used singly or in cooperation in the completed expert system. Integrating these components requires the same activities as already described in section 12.5.4, but on a broader scale. The interactions to be tested are not between rules, but between knowledge bases. The same approach can be adopted: the knowledge engineer checks the functions, and the expert verifies the reasoning.

Consistency across the system is obviously essential, for example using the same names where the same idea occurs in different knowledge bases. This arises naturally if the maps are kept up to date with the actual names used in the knowledge bases.

A useful technique is to implement a controlling knowledge base which we call a 'parent'. The knowledge it contains is not about the problem to be solved, but about the expert system itself. Its principal function is to control the 'child' knowledge bases which make up the system, for example by conducting the initial dialogue with the user and transferring control to whichever knowledge base is required. This means that the bulk of the rules required for control at the system level can be contained in one knowledge base, which is a great convenience for maintenance.

A 'parent' knowledge base has become a standard feature of systems built by the authors. A fully developed parent knowledge base might contain:

- a tutorial on how to use the keyboard and how to use the expert system software,

- a tutorial about the application itself (what it can do, how it might be used, who might benefit from using it, etc.),
- introductory questions to gather routine information and to identify the type of session required, and
- control rules to perform initialisation and to pass control to the correct knowledge base.

12.6.2   Integration with other programs

It may also be required to integrate the expert system with existing computer-based systems. For example, data about pay scales may already be available from a corporate database, the state of a production process may be directly measurable from sensors, or customer complaints may actually be due to a known problem which has already been recorded. It will obviously be convenient for the users if this information can be fetched automatically, rather than the user having to type it in or perform a manual check. Whilst a stand-alone system is acceptable during development, lack of integration will not be tolerated for routine use. This will undoubtedly be identified by the user reviewers at the refinement stage (see section 12.8).

Integration with other computer systems may involve considerable development effort. It should be left to this late stage because of the financial commitment involved in developing conventional software. Such facilities as connections to an external database, perhaps held on a remote mainframe, will require a substantial software effort. The data processing department must be involved as this is their province. Additionally, since conventional software lacks an expert system's ability to respond to changes, it is prudent to wait until the requirements for external data are fixed before committing to a specification. It may be tempting to start work earlier to avoid delaying the expert system's delivery, but changes which are identified after work has begun on the conventional components may cause the programmers as much work as starting afresh. A useful compromise is to implement primitive external connections which serve the user's purposes during the building and refinement stages. For example, instead of connecting to a remote mainframe, it may be possible to made do with a subset of the data held in local file. The temporary facilities can be replaced with properly implemented versions before the system goes live.

12.7   TESTING

The aim of testing is to ensure, as far as possible, that the system is complete and always works as expected. The validation already undertaken was to verify that the system contained appropriate expertise. A compromise has to be struck between testing as the system is being built (desirable, but prey to later modifications) and testing as a whole (necessary, but a lost cause).

We recommend a definite testing period to ensure that this tedious task is carried out thoroughly. The expert system will already have been tested in considerable depth while it was being built. It remains to ensure that the full system works as desired. This corresponds to system testing in conventional computing, and is carried out for the same reasons. There are two important points to be faced while testing:

(1) It is not possible to test that the system works in every case.
(2) Even if the system did work in every case, then it might still produce wrong answers.

Firstly, it is not possible to test every case. This is easy to demonstrate. Suppose we have a modest knowledge base containing twenty-five questions. (Live knowledge bases may contain a hundred or more questions and many conclusions, but this case will suffice to illustrate the point.) Let us further suppose that each question has four possible replies. Then, if every possible combination of answers is to be tested then the number of tests is:

$$4^{25} \text{ (i.e. 4 multiplied by itself 25 times)}$$

If these could be checked at the rate of one combination every 10 seconds, which includes deciding if the result is correct or not, then the testing time would be:

$$4^{25} \times 10 \text{ secs}$$

Since there are about 30 million seconds in a year (3×10^7), the testing time is:

$$(4^{25} \times 10)/(3 \times 10^7) \text{ years}$$

or about

$$300 \text{ million years}$$

which is appreciably longer than mankind has been walking the Earth!

Even a trivial knowledge base of only ten yes/no questions would take nearly three hours to check on the same basis. Some unfortunate person would also have to verify the thousand-odd results so produced.

This is the 'combinatorial explosion' known to mathematicians. When independent choices are combined, the total number of combinations explodes as the number of choices increases. Since real-world problems usually involve a large number of choices, this means that it is not possible to test every possible situation.

The same is true for conventional computer programs of course: one cannot prove that they will always work. The best that can be done is thorough validation. At least with an expert system, an error of omission will result in 'don't know', which is easy to detect, rather than a wrong answer.

Secondly, it has to be accepted that testing the whole system can only show that the system operates and reaches conclusions. It does not prove that the system is correct. Since the know-how is an expression of rules of thumb, the rules will certainly fail if used outside their context. Some of them may even be wrong! In the latter case the expert system may reach an entirely logical, wrong answer. This is why the expert must be the one to validate the know-how. He is the only one who can say if the system's behaviour is correct to the best of his knowledge.

These two aspects of the combinatorial problem and the nature of know-how relate to the separate activities of checking that the expert system works, and of validating the know-how. The former is the responsibility of the knowledge engineer, and the latter the responsibility of the expert. Given that exhaustive testing is impractical, both aspects can only be addressed using the implementors' knowledge of the task itself.

The main weapon is to exploit the structure inherent in the know-how. The aim is to reduce a big problem to many small ones, each of which can be conquered in isolation. This is why such emphasis was placed on validating the individual tasks as they were built. As soon as an aggregation of small functions (sub-tasks) amounts to a larger task, then this can be tested in the same way. However, given that there is confidence in the sub-tasks, it should only be necessary to test that the sub-tasks work together correctly. Here, the maps which show the expert's view of how the components should work together are essential. In their own work the authors follow a policy of systematically re-testing every sub-task and complete task in turn, using the maps as a guide.

The knowledge engineers should accumulate a set of test cases which have been verified by the expert for use in routine testing. Regrettably, expert systems lag well behind conventional software when it comes to facilities for running large scale tests. It usually has to be done by hand.

Despite the best efforts of knowledge engineers, the most effective form of testing is to let users loose on the system. Users will exercise the expert system in ways that the builder did not expect, and will not have tested. Therefore refinement with users (see below) also has a testing function.

12.8   REFINEMENT FOR USE

Refinement is essentially a protracted period of review and validation, where the objective is to validate the applicability of the know-how and its suitability for the intended users. All expert systems require refining before they are fit for widespread use. The purpose of refining is to develop the system from a working state into a form which is both attractive and useful to the users.

The system should already have been exercised by interested experts and sample users. Therefore the reviews during refinement should not produce too many shocks. However, if major shortcomings are revealed or if a major change of direction is required then the team has no alternative but to re-enter the building phase. If necessary, the system's basic objectives must be revised; there is little point in blindly continuing if the outcome is known to be wrong. The purpose of inviting early reviews (section 12.5.4) is precisely to avoid such a major reworking of the system.

Refinement begins as soon as the expert system is complete enough for a management demonstration. A sample of interested users should be invited to exercise the system to see if it really addresses their requirements. Does it help with the real problems? Does it go far enough, or into too much detail? Can the users provide the level of information being asked for? Would it really help in practice? It is vital that these questions are addressed before too much effort is committed to building the system.

Users have a habit of suggesting changes and new requirements which are obvious in hindsight, but which had not been anticipated by the builders. Experienced knowledge engineers come to expect this.

Additionally, the system should be reviewed by other experts in the field. They may be subject to the same fears, misinformation or scepticism as the lead expert, and will need a certain amount of recruiting themselves (see section 13.3.3). The best approach may be from the lead expert, especially if he is pleased with what has been achieved. It would be thoughtful of the knowledge engineer to prepare the lead expert for the inevitable criticisms. Input from the reviewing experts can be included in the system in the same way as extra input from the lead expert.

The main contribution sought from outside experts is to validate the know-how. (See also section 13.3.5 on using multiple experts.) They should be specifically asked to check that:

— the overall approach being taken is correct,
— the know-how being used for each task is correct, and
— the functions which have been provided in the expert system reflect user's actual problems.

The circle of user reviewers should then be widened to include those who have not been involved with the project before. Their key contribution is to test the usability of the system. Hopefully their main requirements will have been anticipated by this stage. However, such users will be much less tolerant of any inconveniences or shortcomings in the presentation than reviewers who have contributed to the development. The comments being sought from users are:

— Does the system address the decisions they are called upon to make and the problems which they encounter?
— Are the questions expressed in a clear and unambiguous manner?
— Where should additional help and explanation be provided?
— Was it easy to follow what the system was doing?
— Was the know-how presented in easily understood form?
— Where jargon was used, was it familiar?
— Were the reports, summaries and other output clearly understandable?

The one, crucial question which should be asked of every user is:

'If this expert system were available for you whenever you wanted, would you choose it use it?'

Any doubts or hesitations which the users have should be fully explored. The crux of this question is whether the expert system actually provides sufficient benefit for the user to make the effort to use it.

The experience is that users seeing the expert system for the first time react only to the information on the screen. This means that they are excellent critics of presentation and facilities, but seldom comment on deeper issues such as the general approach. They may feel a degree of intimidation — after all, the system was built by an acknowledged expert — so frank criticism should be invited. The knowledge engineer must encourage this by reacting positively to the user's first suggestions, whatever their significance. Once the user sees that his contributions are valued, he will be encouraged to provide more. It is crucially important that the knowledge engineer does not defend or excuse the expert system, however tempting this may be, since this will stifle further comments.

The authors are in the habit of allowing almost any interested party to test systems which they have built. This is the best means we know of exercising the system in unexpected ways. The one house rule which has served us well is:

> 'You may criticise absolutely anything,
> provided that you also suggest how it may be improved.'

13

Being a knowledge engineer

This section gives detailed guidance on how a knowledge engineer should approach his task, emphasising the demands on his own skills and behaviour.

There are three parties directly involved in building an expert system: the expert, the knowledge engineer, and the user. It seems obvious that the quality of the expert system should depend primarily on the accomplishments of the expert. However, at present there is an acute shortage of experienced knowledge engineers. Therefore the success of expert systems within an organisation may depend more on having competent knowledge engineers than on having access to any particular expert.

13.1 GENERAL APPROACH

The role of a knowledge engineer is to help experts to describe their know-how, and to present the know-how in a form which is attractive and useful to the users. 'To help the expert' is a crucial phrase here. Knowledge engineering is a cooperative process, a journey of discovery taken by the expert and the knowledge engineer. We feel very strongly that their meetings should be discussions, not interviews. The two parties should be seeking a joint view of the expertise which the expert uses in solving the problem in hand. All too often one reads descriptions of a knowledge engineer 'extracting' knowledge from an expert. Extraction should be left to dentists.

Furthermore, building an expert system is not an opportunity for the knowledge engineer to design a computer program which seems to behave like the expert. The knowledge engineer's function is to discover the expertise which the expert already uses, and to implement that. The knowledge engineer is *not* at liberty to create his own design. This may seem like an obvious statement, but conventional computing requires that computer professionals should do just that: the user states the end result he thinks he wants, and the systems analyst decides how to achieve it. Too many expert systems have been approached in this way, with the programmers deciding how the job will be done, but they have lost contact with the expert knowledge. The end result is like having the know-how in a foreign language. How much better to have the know-how in one's own language. Not only will the expert then identify with it, but users will also be able to gain from it.

So the knowledge engineer's task is to work with the expert to identify know-how, and to make that know-how work on a computer. The measure of success is whether users like it.

13.2 PREPARATION

13.2.1 Finding knowledge engineers

There can be quite unnecessary anguish over finding knowledge engineers. True, there are very few experienced staff in the marketplace, but knowledge engineering is not magic. With judicious use of experienced help, there is no reason why existing staff should not develop into skilful knowledge engineers. Since building expert systems based on know-how rarely requires any deep knowledge of artificial intelligence, personal qualities are much more important than technical qualifications.

Promising knowledge engineers might be found in many quarters. There are no formal tests: the qualities being sought must be judged subjectively. An ideal candidate would be, inter alia:

- generally positive about life, with an ability to express themselves verbally and in writing. Expert systems rely heavily on communication in words and graphics, and the quality of expression will have a big effect on the value which users derive from it.
- keen to try knowledge engineering. This is important. The work requires persistence, so knowledge engineers have to enjoy what they do if they are to sustain commitment.
- reasonably bright, which implies that they might be performing well in their existing role.
- personally secure and able to establish a relationship of mutual regard with experts.
- interested in the experiences and knowledge of others for its own sake. Such people often show a general receptiveness for new ideas and new methods.
- able to thrive on suggestions from others, i.e. criticism! Defensiveness has no place here.
- proficient in using the chosen computer hardware and software. The level of technical skill required depends heavily on the type of software tool being used.

Knowledge engineers should not:

- require a degree in artificial intelligence or cognitive psychology.
- be experts themselves (or think that they are experts).
- be difficult to like.

Professional knowledge engineers tend to be verbal, curious, and the type of people who pick up what is said to them at the first time of telling. Maturity is definitely an asset, although one which is not always related to age. Nevertheless, many knowledge engineers are at least in their thirties. Some of the most successful knowledge engineers have previously become skilled in another professional field (other than computer programming). This seems to bring an appreciation of the value of know-how, something which is notably lacking among a proportion of new graduates. It also promotes empathy with experts and makes it natural to treat experts as equals.

Industry and business experience are much more important than computer skills. Indeed, we have seen several accomplished systems analysts having great difficulty in shaking off their ingrained methods, most of which are not suitable for knowledge engineering. (In fairness, software engineers must marvel at the way that wheels are being re-invented for expert systems!) Broad experience in industry is a distinct advantage when the knowledge engineer is called upon to tackle a new problem in that industry. This always involves acquiring an appreciation of the concepts, something which comes with time and cannot be learnt in a few days. For example, a strong engineering background would be inappropriate for a project in finance, and vice versa.

13.2.2 Training knowledge engineers

There is little formal training available in knowledge engineering. Most product suppliers offer effective training for their own products, but these courses seldom cover the broader issues. Some academic institutions offer secondments, but the methods taught are usually concerned with artificial intelligence programming rather than delivering business systems.

We recommend a period of practical training, preferably in close contact with experienced knowledge engineers. The training philosophy is 'learning by doing'. This requires trainees to be taught the use of an expert system shell, and learning the techniques of knowledge engineering while building actual systems. The steps are:

— getting to know the software,
— using a sample application as an exemplar,
— building a system using the trainee's own subject expertise, and then
— building a system based on someone else's expertise.

The trainee should begin with reasonable computer literacy (i.e. familiarity with the computer itself, its operating system, and standard business packages). The strategy is then to provide them with a sequence of progressively more responsible tasks, leading to a junior role on a live project:

(1) Allow the trainee a few days for background reading, especially periodicals, plus a visit to a major exhibition if at all possible (see appendix C). This will expose them to current trends, some applications, and a range of software tools.
(2) Provide them with an expert system shell on a personal computer. The

choice of product is best made by someone experienced: the better the software is able to express know-how, the more useful it will be.

(3) Send them on the supplier's training course on how to use the software. (If there is no course then do not buy the software — no matter what the supplier says.)

(4) Ask them to build one or two 'toy' systems with just a few rules to consolidate the training course. This should only take a few days. The systems can be on any subject, but it is best if the trainee is given clear objectives to achieve.

(5) Give the trainee a copy of the highest quality application which has been built or can be purchased. Let them explore how it works and discover the different techniques which have been used. If the application is of sufficient quality, it will also illustrate the power of well expressed know-how. As understanding grows, they should be encouraged to explore further applications.

(6) Set them the task of modifying this example application in some way. This might be to add an extra function or to modify an existing function. The trainee should be expected to obtain the additional know-how to go into the system for himself. The work should be reviewed by an experienced knowledge engineer, and the task expanded to provide sufficient challenge.

(7) Ask them to build a modest system from scratch. The trainee should serve as his own expert here. Almost any topic will do: hobbies or special interests are often used as subjects. The trainee should be allowed sufficient time to make a good job of this, perhaps several weeks. There is a strong motivation to show off one's own expertise in a good light, hence the suggestion that the trainee should be his own expert. If a group is being trained, then there is the alternative possibility of them serving as experts for each other. This will need to be controlled by a supervisor.

It is important that the developing system should be seen by the trainee's peers, not hidden away until perfect. They will usually not shrink from suggesting improvements! Additionally, an experienced knowledge engineer may be able to suggest a better approach — but not until the trainee has tried his own first. This self-inflicted education will make the trainee appreciate the difficulty of identifying just what is at the core of a particular problem, and what is involved in expressing it so that others can understand.

(8) Give them a small system of their own to build where the knowledge is already documented. This might be part of a larger undertaking, or a small system in its own right. For example, they might be asked to assemble a prototype system from written documentation. A fair number of prototypes begin in this way.

(9) Ideally, the trainee should be allowed to go back and re-assess his earlier efforts. This is very constructive, and is not the luxury it may seem.

Using a sample application will avoid the budding knowledge engineer having to invent his own style. We have seen some truly incomprehensible systems written by people who have learnt in isolation. They are forced to invent methods which seem obvious to their more experienced colleagues, which is both tedious and frustrating.

Expecting trainees to build systems at a very early stage does them no harm at all. If the manager of knowledge engineering schedules six months familiarisation, then it will take six months. Trainees following the scheme above can be expected to begin contributing to projects after a month. By that time they should be effective rule-writers, and can concentrate on learning knowledge engineering. They should be able to implement modules for themselves after (perhaps) three months, and should be fully fledged members of the team before six months are out. There is an analogy with learning to drive a car. It takes a few weeks to learn to control the vehicle, which is when you start learning how to be a safe driver. However, like driving, one never finishes learning about knowledge engineering.

Knowledge engineering skills will be acquired much faster if the trainees can 'rub shoulders' with their more experienced colleagues. This is clearly the most effective way of sharing their know-how. For this reason a knowledge engineering group should always be accommodated together, certainly if there are six people or less. If no experienced help is available within the organisation, then a consultant could be retained for (say) one day a week.

When the trainee first joins a project he should accompany an experienced knowledge engineer during the structuring of a task (see section 12.4). The trainee should then work with the expert to implement the detailed know-how within this structure. As his ability increases, he can be given progressively more responsibility.

13.2.3   Preparation for a project

Knowledge engineers must be well briefed at the beginning of a project. The aim is that they should acquire the background knowledge which practitioners in the field take for granted. If the expert system is intended for a lay audience, it is valuable for the knowledge engineer to record the difficulties and misconceptions which he had to overcome during his own learning — they are so easily forgotten. Some of the most troublesome problems with an expert system arise because of a conceptual gap between the developers and the users, and these early obstacles are vital indicators.

The knowledge engineer must become familiar with the main ideas and the jargon used in the field. Background reading can be useful, particularly if there is a training manual. Any material which is given to trainee experts should be read. Relevant documents should be scanned quickly to identify important issues. (Buzan (1982) gives useful ideas for quickly extracting the important topics from books and papers.) Best of all is a briefing by someone familiar with the field. A greater understanding can be achieved in one afternoon with a person than in a week spent with books. The person will contribute fewer facts, but more insights. Such a briefing need not be given by the expert. Indeed, it can be an advantage to speak to someone who knows less of the intricacies, and might better remember what it was like to be a novice. A junior who has the expert's confidence should be a good choice.

The most effective way of learning is, of course, by doing. Therefore the knowledge engineer can be asked to try the task himself, provided that he will not be a hazard to life or property. The knowledge engineer should be asked to carry out the same tasks as the eventual users of the system. Naturally, he will fare badly and will be slow, but there are few better ways of instilling a little sympathy for the users' problems!

13.3 WORKING WITH EXPERTS

13.3.1 Finding experts

Whether formally required to do so or not, it is the knowledge engineer's responsibility to ensure that a suitable expert participates in the project. This involves locating suitable candidates (described here) and identifying one with suitable know-how (section 13.3.2). Note that we strongly recommend beginning with a single, lead expert (see section 13.3.5).

When looking for experts, the key point is that:

experts are not always found where you expect them.

The people with know-how are those who are responsible for making decisions on a day-to-day basis. Frequently, such people are not recognised as being the company authority on anything. In an office, the expert on administration is probably one of the secretaries. In a factory, the expert on efficient loading of vehicles may well be found in the loading bay. Managers and designers usually know what *should* happen, but may not have the field experience of solving user's problems which leads to know-how.

The main qualities to seek in experts are that they should be:

- Authoritative,
  recognised by their colleagues as making good decisions.
- Reasonably articulate,
  so that they can describe their methods and rules of thumb.
- Enthusiastic,
  one volunteer is worth a dozen conscripts.
- Available,
  so that they can give sufficient time to the project.

'Local' experts are often a good choice to work with, rather than the company guru. These are people who are known to be effective by their colleagues, but may not be known to corporate management. Pressure on their time should be less, and the expert system team can always refer to the recognised authority to clarify points and to review the work. Local experts often have an excellent grasp of the practical issues, even if they lack the expert's depth of understanding. The latter may be hard to use in an expert system anyway. Asking their associates is a good way of locating local experts. Ask 'When there is a problem, who do you call on for help?'.

Occasionally there is a problem with the expert system's sponsors or the user management. They may have retained the services of a recognised authority to serve as the lead expert. This person might be in charge of directing the company's policy or researching new developments, perhaps working in a professorial role. Despite being highly skilled, it may transpire that he does not have the kind of practical expertise which is needed for the expert system. For example, a director of an insurance company is unlikely to be a suitable expert for a system about underwriting life insurance. His skill is concerned with running a company. A problem can arise because neither the management nor the expert might appreciate being told that the expert is not suitable.†

A solution is to turn to someone more junior, the person who actually makes the decisions on a day-to-day basis. Naturally the knowledge engineer will still be looking for first class skills, but of the practical kind rather than the supervisory or theoretical kind. Management can usually be persuaded that this will make much better use of the senior expert's time. The bulk of the system can then be built with the junior expert, and the senior expert (the authority) can be involved as reviewer. This is most satisfactory for the project, and has worked well on many occasions. The knowledge engineer has access to the expertise he needs, the senior expert can still make an essential contribution, and no one's pride is threatened.

13.3.2   Identifying real know-how

Having found a likely lead expert, the knowledge engineers must discuss the problem with the expert and decide if his know-how is indeed suitable. 'Suitable' means sufficient in quantity, sufficient in quality, and appropriate for the system being built. It is essential that the senior knowledge engineer should be the final arbiter of who is to be the lead expert. Having discussed the problem with several possible experts, he will know who has the most appropriate breadth, and level, of expertise. In our experience it can take three or four attempts before a suitable person is found. The insights provided by the previous candidates allow a judgement to be made of where the relevant expertise lies.

Other people's assessments of who are the experts cannot be accepted unquestioningly. A project for a major retailer illustrated this clearly. The application concerned controlling the stocks held by retail stores, an area where even minor improvements have a high payoff. The knowledge engineers had begun work on the project but were having great difficulty in building the system. They were working with two experts, the Sales Director and the Finance Director.

---

† This is, of course, a generalisation. We have met several distinguished experts who have themselves identified that one of their juniors had more relevant knowledge.

The Sales Director's key heuristic about stock was:

> if the stock levels are high
> and there is a wide range of goods
> then people will buy more

So the Sales Director was in favour of stocking the stores to their maximum with a wide range of items.

The Finance Director's main concerns about stock were the costs involved:

> if the stock levels are high
> then stockholding costs are increased

> if there is a wide range of goods
> then items may become obsolete

Therefore his expertise was about minimising the total inventory and eliminating slow-moving lines.

Who was the real expert? Neither of these people! What the knowledge engineers had overlooked was that neither of these directors actually made the day-to-day decisions about what, and how much, to deliver to each store. The simple question 'Who actually makes the decisions about stock?' provided the immediate answer 'the Stock Manager'. Voila! There was the most likely expert.† The Stock Manager was clearly not as skilled as either of the Directors in their respective specialities. But he did have the key skill of balancing the attractions of well filled shelves against the need to contain the investment in stock. This is the essence of skilful stock management.

Finding an expert with a sound and practical knowledge is so important that it is worth being persistent to locate him. The knowledge engineer has to begin by meeting a number of possible experts. These meetings are a mental juggling act which require the knowledge engineer to perform several tasks simultaneously:

- give the expert sufficient background about expert systems so that he can understand the broad objectives, and what the value of the system could be for potential users;
- be conscious of the expert's possible fears (see section 13.3.3) and make the effort to overcome them;
- transfer sufficient enthusiasm about the undertaking to secure the expert's interest;
- decide if the expert has the right scope and depth of expertise to fulfil the expert system's aims (or at least enough to make a start);
- make sure that the two can successfully work together at a personal level;
- ensure that the expert can express himself sufficiently clearly for the

---

† A knowledge engineer on the project was unreceptive to this suggestion, even though he had been bemoaning the difficulty of knowledge acquisition. 'But he (the Stock Manager) is not an expert' he protested. He was wrong.

knowledge engineer to cope with (more skilful knowledge engineers make fewer demands on the expert),

and at the same time conduct a coherent and brisk interview with an expert who is probably a busy man.

The outcome should be either an initial commitment from the expert, or a mutual agreement not to proceed. The need for tact should be obvious if the knowledge engineer decides not to continue. The same expert may still make a valuable contribution by supplementing the expertise of others, or by reviewing what has been achieved.

There is always some uncertainty as to whether the right expert has been chosen. During the initial interview, the knowledge engineer should begin to explore the expert's know-how in order to form a view. This amounts to some preparatory design work on the system using the techniques described in chapter 12. Fortunately, although expertise is hard to judge from external appearances, it is easy enough to recognise in someone you are talking to. Strong signs of real know-how are:

- the expert having confidence in his own ability to cope with whatever problems may occur (one has to be aware of ill-founded confidence of course);
- demonstrable skill in solving real problems;
- an ability to provide explanation on many levels, e.g. to describe the broad issues before going into detail;
- a knowledge of what is *not* relevant to a problem, or skilful use of *negative* information — these are particularly good indicators;
- an unanxious admission of what the expert does not know — real experts do not have to defend their self-esteem;
- the expert's peers having a good opinion of his decision making;
- others choosing to consult this expert with their difficulties — knowledge engineers should be aware of the unofficial channels of help and advice.

Conversely, there are warning signs either of lack of know-how or an unwillingness to participate:

- the expert and the knowledge engineer are unable to strike up reasonable communication;
- the expert chooses not to answer direct questions.
- the expert persists in returning the conversation to the details of his day-to-day work;
- the expert is unwilling (or unable) to discuss what really goes on, as opposed to what is officially approved;
- the expert is anxious to impress the knowledge engineer with his importance to the organisation, or his depth of knowledge;
- the expert seeks to find reasons why the system will not be useful in practice;
- the expert is unwilling to commit to at least an initial experiment.

The warning signs have to be treated more cautiously than the signs of strength. For example, many experts have a fund of anecdotes which illustrate particular situations or exceptions. These are not to be ignored, as they often hint at valuable rules. However, making useful points via anecdotes is very different from an inability to see above a sea of details. The knowledge engineer must also recognise that in a preliminary meeting, the expert will have little idea of what is a useful way of expressing himself and what is not.

13.3.3   Recruiting an expert
The knowledge engineer should actively 'recruit' an expert he plans to work with. This usually has to be done during the initial meeting: there may be only a few minutes to secure the expert's personal commitment. Management can instruct an expert to cooperate, but that is not enough. His willing commitment is essential. The purpose of recruiting is to stimulate the expert's interest sufficiently to make him *want* to be involved. If this can be achieved, many 'difficulties' have a habit of melting away. There are two particularly effective ploys.

Firstly, show the expert an example of an expert system working. This is by far the quickest way of conveying the type of system being considered. Its special features of explicit knowledge and explanation should always be demonstrated. The application should be chosen so that it relates to the expert's own interests in some way. Applications from unrelated fields are usually of much less interest.

Secondly, demonstrate that a small fragment of the expert's own knowledge can be put into an expert system and run. If time (or enthusiasm) is short, this can be done in the space of the first half hour. Naturally, the knowledge engineer must have the necessary skill and software tools to do such an on the spot demonstration. Seeing their own know-how running on a computer is exciting for an expert. If it fails to intrigue them, then the knowledge engineer should seriously consider why this is so. It may well be that the expert has personal reservations which have yet to be uncovered.

The knowledge engineer should be sensitive to an expert's possible doubts. After all, once his knowledge is in the computer, will he be out of a job? (The answer, of course, is no.) Questions which often trouble an expert are:

- Will this affect my status, even my job security?
  An expert system cannot replace people. What it can do is to allow the more routine tasks to be done by less skilled staff. Experience shows that a successful expert system will in fact enhance the status of the expert.
- What am I being asked to do?
  A certain 'fear of the unknown' is to be expected. The expert will simply be asked to talk about his daily decisions: what he really does, not what might be written in a manual. If the expert wants to be involved in details of the building, then so much the better.

- Will I need to learn how to use the computer?
  No. But there is no reason why not if that is what the expert would like. Familiarity with rule writing will help the expert to express himself in a way which is convenient for the knowledge engineer, and may be a prelude to the expert making his own modifications.
- How do I know this will be worth my effort?
  i.e. Will the system be useful, and can it be built successfully? The business potential should have been identified already (see chapter 4). It is important that the expert should believe in its value. The best way of establishing if the system will be successful is to build a small piece of it. The whole team will then be able to judge for themselves. Using the methods of know-how programming, this feasibility stage can be as short as one or two weeks. The expert is being asked to give it a try.

13.3.4 Handling the expert

As a discipline which deals with empirical knowledge, it seems fitting to present advice about knowledge engineering as empirical guidelines. The following guidelines for knowledge engineers have been found to be very useful in practical situations.

Know your jargon

The knowledge engineer should be familiar with the normal jargon shared by experts and users. This is necessary if he is to discuss issues freely with the expert. Note that a dictionary of terms is not enough: the knowledge engineer needs some grasp of their significance as well.

Don't be your own expert

It is hard, though not impossible, for one person to build an expert system unaided (see section 7.3). There is considerable difficulty in clarifying one's own decision making by working in isolation, and the quality of the resulting system will suffer. Additionally, knowledge engineers who believe they are also application experts are a nuisance. They tend to compete with the expert.

Establish mutual respect

The relationship between expert and knowledge engineer has to be one of mutual confidence and trust. Each party should recognise the essential role of the other. Regrettably, some treatises on knowledge engineering encourage the view that the expert is present to do the knowledge engineer's bidding. This attitude is quite wrong. The knowledge engineer must make the expert feel that he (the expert) is in charge of the knowledge, and this relationship must be established at the initial meetings.

Be undisturbed

The telephone is a great disturbance to thought. Meetings should be held where interruptions will be minimal, off-site if necessary. The expert may need to arrange an alternative contact while he is working on the system.

Within this constraint, meetings are best held wherever the expert is likely to feel relaxed and has access to any equipment or supplementary information that might be needed. There is a psychological advantage in holding meetings on the expert's territory rather than on the knowledge engineer's.

Work in a context
The knowledge engineer should always know what he wishes to achieve during a meeting — and should agree this with the expert during the first few minutes. This will help to guide the discussion and make the best use of time. At an early stage the objectives will be broad, such as 'establish the main functions and overall structure'. Later, this may progress to 'refine the section on legal liabilities', and later still to details such as 'run tests using every exception during the last month'. As a rule, the more specific the context the easier it is to identify many, small pieces of know-how. It remains important to reflect on bigger issues.

Use gentle methods
Interviewing an expert should not be an interrogation. The discussion has to be flexible, since the knowledge engineer should be seeking to clarify the expert's own understanding. Furthermore, the knowledge engineer should not impose his own techniques on the expert unless the expert also finds them relevant. Adherence to an inappropriate method once led to a memorable comment from an observer. 'You could see the glint of desperation in (the expert's) eyes as he realised that nothing of what he was saying was sinking in'. Such a beleaguered expert is likely to opt out as soon as politeness allows.

Avoid interrupting the expert
In general, experts should be allowed to talk on a topic as long as they wish, even if the knowledge engineer feels it is a digression. The fact that the expert thinks it relevant, or illustrative, is sufficient to warrant attention. Changing the topic is the clearest of conversational signals that the listener is not interested. Typically the information being provided is too detailed to be of immediate use to the knowledge engineer, but it can be noted for later inclusion. Obviously, digressions of more than a few minutes can waste considerable time and must be limited. The knowledge engineer should wait for a suitable pause and gently steer the expert back to the main area of interest.

Listen
Knowledge engineers have to be conscious of *why* things are said, as well as *what* is said. The implications of a statement are often very important to its expression in an expert system: why is this piece of know-how being used now, and why have others not been used? Experience suggests that many technically trained people are very good at evaluating the words they hear, but poor at recognising that which is not said out loud. This ability to

appreciate the unspoken content has been described as 'active listening' and it is an important skill for knowledge engineers.

Feed back your own understanding
As well as capturing know-how, the knowledge engineer must capture its context: when and how it is applied. The context is usually assumed, hence the importance of active listening as described above. When there appears to be a pattern or a structure emerging, the knowledge engineer should always describe this to the expert to check that it fits with the expert's understanding. This clarification of half-formed ideas is a key contribution from the knowledge engineer, and can be of great help to the expert in rationalising his own views.

However, it is entirely inappropriate for the knowledge engineer to constantly intervene with requests for clarification like 'Do you mean that …'. Few things are more tedious to the expert. They also effectively interrupt his train of thought. A thoughtful knowledge engineer will note such points and return to them when the expert has finished his current explanation.

Expect the expert to reconsider
The process of knowledge engineering involves considerable effort for an expert. Possibly for the first time in their lives, they are being asked to clarify how they take decisions, and to set it down in unambiguous terms. Fudge and cover-up do not survive. The expert is required to delve into areas of his own skill which are rarely tested. As a result, it often happens that when an expert sees his own know-how running in an expert system, he realises that it is not quite right, or perhaps it is not expressed correctly. Therefore it is predictable that the expert will appear to change his mind. This is not a product of confusion, but is the expert in the throes of climbing to a better understanding.

Never underestimate experience
It has happened that an unusually articulate and thoughtful expert has been able to give a simple and clear description of what he does. 'Nothing to it really' thinks the knowledge engineer, and goes off to implement the system. The result is painfully naive. The moral is that if it seems simple, that probably means that the expert has simplified it for you. To echo Mayor Koch of New York:

> 'For every complex problem, there is a solution which is
> simple, economical, and wrong.'

Most practical problems have a wealth of detailed know-how associated with them.

Nothing is ever 'by the way'
Skilled knowledge engineers are very alert for throwaway remarks by the

expert. They may be introduced by 'everybody knows that' or 'by the way'. The truth is that everybody does not know, and it is never 'by the way'. Such remarks usually contain basic know-how which has not yet come out in the discussion, but which the expert thinks is relevant. This occurrence is so common that we call it 'the door knob effect'. Hand on door, about to leave the room, a thought occurs to the expert: 'by the way ...'!

Make a point of changing the pace of the discussion
Throwaway remarks such as those just described often occur at moments of relaxation, such as coffee breaks or at the end of a session. The brief relaxation seems to allow thoughts to surface which may have been suppressed while the expert was concentrating. It can be helpful to deliberately change the pace about every twenty minutes or so if a break has not arisen naturally. Even a trivial diversion will do: a change of topic, a joke, getting up and walking around, a cup of coffee, etc.

Ask for a copy of any written material
If the expert refers to any written document, note, table, diagram, etc., then ask for a copy of it, and find out when it might be used. Informal notes pinned up in the workplace are particularly valuable! Documents are nearly always of some use, if only for filling in details. They may also suggest issues which have not previously been raised, so a quick scan at the time is worthwhile.

Have sympathy for the expert's own problems
Knowledge engineering is sufficiently taxing that it is easy for the knowledge engineer to be fully absorbed in his own role. This is particularly true during the early stages of a project, which is also a difficult time for the expert (see section 14.4). An empathic knowledge engineer can provide valuable counselling, and so help to smooth out the peaks and troughs in the expert's motivation.

13.3.5   Working with multiple experts
There is normally more than one expert with respect to a particular application. While it may be valuable to let them feel involved in some way, they certainly cannot all be involved all of the time.

We strongly recommend beginning with only one expert, the one we have referred to as the 'lead' expert. He will be the main source of know-how up to the point of having a good, working prototype. The prototype will then serve as the basis of discussion with other experts. This procedure is far more productive than attempting to form a joint view while the prototype is being built. If there is a choice of suitable experts, we would select the most articulate and the most interested to be the pioneer. Naturally, whoever is chosen should have the respect of his peers: this must be confirmed with his colleagues, his juniors and his management.

Later in the project, other experts can be involved to enrich the rules which have already been obtained, and to check the correctness and consistency of the solutions proposed. Additionally, they can often contribute expertise which extends the scope of the existing system, or improves on topics which were only covered weakly. It is only to be expected that different experts will have a different mix of skills.

It has happened that the scope of a project falls between the specific skills of various experts, so that each of them will make a small contribution. This implies that the problem is currently handled badly — often by relatively inexperienced staff attempting to liaise with the experts concerned. It then becomes very important for the knowledge engineer to locate a 'general practitioner', someone with experience of solving past problems even if they do not have detailed know-how. The general practitioner can provide the right approach to the problem, which is a pre-requisite for making good use of the various expert's contributions. If such a general practitioner cannot be found then the effort to build a prototype can increase two- or three-fold.

A recent project illustrates how several experts can each provide complementary know-how. The task was to help small businesses to make good use of their first computer, and the lead expert was a director of a computer systems company. She worked with the development team to build prototypes of each module in the expert system. The system was later reviewed by five other experts:

— a systems expert from a management consultancy,
— a consultant to government who advised small businesses,
— a highly experienced system implementor and business consultant,
— a training consultant, and lastly
— a specialist in 'open learning' methods.

These others made valuable contributions concerning the computer aspects, typical business problems, and the effective deployment of training. This is about as many experts as could be accommodated during the course of a four month project. There is no point inviting experts to participate if their input will not be used.

We had expected many more conflicts of opinion than actually occurred. This is not a unique finding when tackling business problems — the reality of solving practical problems tends to expose unworkable decisions very quickly. Therefore the experts were generally in agreement on the basic issues. Some apparent differences of view were resolved by the experts themselves: 'I had never thought of it like that!'. Each of the experts seemed to gain a little from having to question their own views, which did much to secure their interest. One expert even asked for the loan of a portable computer so that he could continue the review in the evening. This was a clear sign that the expert had found a strong personal interest in making the system better. Expert systems can be like that.

Differences between experts were generally those of emphasis. These were usually resolved by rephrasing, and were not contentious. As suggested above, the principal differences lay in their particular areas of interest. One expert would set great store on 'polishing' topics which another expert considered secondary. This resulted in a considerable roundness and breadth to the system. It is worth remarking that the prototype system built with the lead expert was a very effective tool for prompting these other experts. Therefore the reviews proceeded very efficiently, with minimal time spent in preparing or recruiting the other experts and an excellent rate of progress.

There are occasions when experts disagree. We have found that 90% of the time this is due to differing assumptions about the context. When this occurs, the knowledge engineer may have to explore the basis of the disagreement in great depth. If it is traced to differing assumptions, then the differences can be made explicit in the rules and the problem is resolved. However, when experts of equal authority disagree on the correct action when faced with *exactly* the same circumstances, then an arbitrator may have to be consulted. The company guru can be called upon here. We know of no method of resolving outright differences of view, for example as found in economics.

In the final analysis, it may be that there really is more than one solution. One such case happened when a group of medical practitioners assembled to record their know-how about a series of medical complaints. The results were remarkable. This was not formal medicine, but represented what doctors actually did when confronted with a patient. Among other memorable rules, it contained one such as this:

> if . . .
> then treatment is antibiotics according to Doctor D
> and treatment is painkillers according to Doctor R

The two doctors were each confident that their treatment was correct, and their colleagues were divided as to who was right.

When two different solutions are equally valid, then the real know-how may be more subtle. For example, the key issue may be that a decision is made quickly!

13.4   TRICKS OF THE TRADE

This section is based on questions which are repeatedly asked of consultants.

Question: How do you get knowledge from an expert who cannot say what he does?
Answer: Decide what the problem really is.

Truly inarticulate experts are very rare. Some people have 'a colleague who knows of one', but we have never met one. Does the expert communicate his expertise to anyone else? An expert who does not communicate at all will be obvious on first meeting. If the expert does not have the necessary know-how then do what you can during the meeting and identify who to speak to next. Most experts will freely admit their limitations outside their own speciality.

Is the problem caused by the expert not knowing what is wanted? Has the project been clearly defined, and has he been shown a working system?

Alternatively, it may be that the expert has really been describing his know-how all along — the knowledge engineer is simply not used to recognising know-how. Some people with a strong technical background want the expert to describe some well defined mechanism. Know-how is not like that.

If the problem is that the expert does not *want* to participate in the project then try to intrigue them, perhaps by showing an example of their own know-how in action. Discuss what impact the system will have on the expert's work and status. The expert may well have unspoken fears which must be resolved first. Experts cannot be conscripted into building an expert system, so this issue must be tackled head-on.

Question: How do you deal with an expert who says 'I just look at the problem and decide'.
Answer: Probe more deeply.

This response probably means that the expert is very familiar with the know-how and no longer needs to apply it consciously. Try prompting with slightly different examples. When you hit upon examples which lead to different action from the expert, probe the reasons for the differences. Do not be too insistent, and give the expert time to think. This may require a considerable effort from both the expert and the knowledge engineer. In compensation they will have the exciting experience of identifying unwritten know-how.

Question: How do you go about determining the initial structure of a problem when you cannot see what it should be?
Answer: There is no set procedure. But there are rules of thumb!

Try the following:

(1) Break the task into phases and take them one at a time.
(2) Ask the expert to talk you through a typical case, a simple case, today's case, or any other case the expert thinks is illustrative.
(3) Pick out what seem to be the key points as you go, and record them as notes. Just jot things down to begin with, and decide what is important as you go along.
(4) Record the connections between the main ideas you have noted as the expert is talking, preferably using a spider diagram (see section 11.7).

You should now have an untidy map of the task. Do not be concerned that it is not correct — at this stage it would be remarkable if it were correct. Feed your understanding back to the expert. If the expert has not responded to the drawing then replay it in words — remember not to impose your methods. See if your picture makes any sense to him. This method will give you a base to start from.

Question: What should I do if there is still no apparent structure after
          talking to the expert?
Answer: Try the 'jigsaw approach'.

Begin by brainstorming around the problem, recording anything and everything which might be a rule ('spread all the jigsaw pieces out'). Capture rules
in any order, about any type of case, and by any means you like. Start with
whatever the expert first discusses. Now, look for any idea which seems to
occur in several places, and group those rules together ('find all the edge
pieces'). You can either do this on paper, using a word processor, or by
writing each rule on a card. Modify the rules as you go so that the same
phrase is used to describe a given idea wherever it occurs. Sift through the
rules to group them under common headings, or else assign them to 'don't
recognise these'. These groupings under common headings then reflect an
initial structure: draw it as a spider diagram ('assemble the edges'). This will
serve as a framework. Start work on any interesting grouping by identifying
the desired outcome and focusing on how that will be attained ('start work
on the most obvious object').

Question: How can I maintain the interest of the user managers?
Answer: Involve them in the development of the system itself.

    Management demonstrations are rarely wasted, although they have to
be polished to be effective. Managers who have authorised expenditure are
usually very interested to see what is being produced. Their interest can be
harnessed to help improve the system: they should have a clear view of
which functions are directly helpful to the business and which are secondary.
The project team should take care to reflect the management concerns, both
for the success of the end product and because no computer development
will ever have responded to them before!
    A word of warning: perhaps for the first time, managers will be able to
see how their operation really functions. Previously they could continue
with their own vision of what was going on. With an expert system, they can
actually interrogate it, try their own cases, and see how it performs. Once
they understand how it really works, it is not unknown for them to want to
change what happens in practice! This occurs when the activities on the
ground do not reflect the management's intentions, an all too common
occurrence. Correcting the situation should be beneficial for the organisation, but the knowledge engineers may need to ask for an extended budget
to cover the extra work which will be generated.

Question: What do you do if the expert and the knowledge engineer find it
          impossible to work together?
Answer: DEC used to say 'Shoot the knowledge engineer!'.

    This should be correct, since the expert's know-how is essential. In
practice the answer depends on which of the two is the easier to replace.

Question: What is the biggest barrier to starting an expert system project?
Answer: (i) Management awareness of the vital role that know-how plays
           in the organisation, and hence the benefits that expert systems
           can bring, and
           (ii) user's awareness of how that know-how can be brought to
           their aid using expert systems.

Note that technical issues are not a barrier. The technology which is
currently available is far ahead of industry's ability to exploit it.

Enthusiasts should take care to propose projects which will stimulate the
interest of management and be viewed as useful by users. However compel-
ling the need, the project will still have to compete for funds (see chapter 4).
Some technically oriented groups do not seem to appreciate the importance
of a well executed management demonstrator. It must be relevant, it must
look good, and it must be well presented.

14

Being an expert

This chapter is devoted to the experience of developing an expert system, from the expert's point of view. Although the chapter draws on personal experiences and views of just one member of the expert system development team, there are some general lessons, and heuristics, for potential experts and knowledge engineers alike.

The views expressed here are very much those of the expert. Some of the points have already been discussed in chapter 13, but from quite a different viewpoint.

14.1 THE REQUIREMENTS OF A SUITABLE EXPERT

All expert systems depend on the suitability and cooperation of an expert. The importance of selecting a suitable expert cannot be understated. If the chosen one 'is volunteered' and does not volunteer himself, this is often a bad beginning. We believe that, regardless of the type of application, the most important requirements are:

- True expertise.
  First and foremost, the potential expert must have real expertise in the problem being tackled. This means that he can provide practical solutions to complex problems. Experts are people who have extensive experience in the problem area (the 'domain'), and who can thus approach problems both effectively and efficiently. True expertise manifests itself in speedy and accurate assessment of problems, know-how about effective solutions, and pragmatic proposals for their implementation. (See also section 14.3.)
- Willingness to part with, or share their expertise.
  It is important that the expert is happy to share his expertise. Should the expert fear that his job might be de-skilled, he is unlikely to be forthcoming when clarifying or justifying the problem solving approach being adopted. An appropriate expert for an expert system development should be someone who takes pleasure from imparting their knowledge to others. This view will stimulate empathy with the users, and result in a more expansive approach. A 'stingy' expert will build a like expert system.

- An ability to share knowledge.
  It is important not only that the expert wishes to share his knowledge, but also that he is able to to do so. This is where an experienced knowledge engineer can be enormously helpful. Some experts are naturally good at setting out or articulating their knowledge, whilst others are just not communicative by nature.

  The knowledge engineer is often the best person to establish the suitability of the potential expert. The knowledge engineer usually holds several interviews with different experts in the field to establish who is most suitable for the challenging task ahead.
- Patience and tenacity.
  Building an expert system will call for considerable reserves of patience and tenacity. Most experts, if they are correctly classified as such, are tenacious. This will probably have made a large contribution to their achieving the status of experts in the first place. Expert systems place a considerable demand on the expert to be introspective, which is not always easy to sustain. Tenacity also implies an ability to persevere until the goal is reached, i.e. a determination to achieve results. This may well be tested when other business priorities intrude into the time allocated for working on the expert system.

  Patience is required for many reasons. The expert will be asked to spend a considerable amount of time with a knowledge engineer who may have no experience in the field whatsoever. Therefore he may need to explain the basic issues which dominate his subject, and the factors which really matter. These are topics which any of the expert's co-workers would take for granted. Furthermore, the expert will need a lot of patience with himself — not least when he discovers that his expertise is not as thorough or as well founded as he might have believed!

  People often lose sight of the overall objectives of any system once they are embroiled in the detailed work. This is equally true of expert systems. This results in added stress on the whole development team and thus requires increased dedication and purpose.
- The ability to accept contest.
  The expert must be able to deal with criticism and constructive feedback about his views and ideas. If an expert believes that he is beyond changing or expanding his views, then he is not suitable to work on an expert system. Few thinking people would publicly admit to having rigid views, but private beliefs can be different from the public stance.

  Experts must also 'move with the times'. This means that they need to be open minded, and positively responsive to change and adaptation. If this is not so, then not only will the expert build a 'narrow minded' system, but the long-term development of the system will be at risk. The implication of this is that the expert should be graced with a degree of humility.
- Confidence.
  If an expert is not confident, the stresses and strains of building an expert system can be quite damaging. Above all, it requires a belief in one's own

problem-solving abilities and methods, a belief in one's personal rules of thumb. If this belief is ill founded, the knowledge engineer and the users will rapidly find this out. An expert who is involved in building a pilot system (i.e. the first venture into a new area) should be generally positive about life and work as well as confident of his own speciality.

- Credibility
  It is very important, especially with regard to 'customer' acceptance of the system, that the expert is held to be credible. This means that the expert will have established himself as a competent 'consultant' to whom others are willing to refer complex queries. (Although this consultant role may or may not be formally recognised.) This test of referral should on the one hand eliminate self-confessed experts with unrealistic confidence, or on the other hand serve to reinforce user acceptance. If the expert does not have the confidence of the user community then he cannot be considered an expert for the purposes of the expert system. Experts are only of value if they are perceived as being able to provide value.
- Enthusiasm.
  An expert should be enthusiastic about what he does. If not, then it is questionable whether he is really an expert at all. If you do not enjoy an activity, then seldom will you do it very well. In the authors' experience there is no question that building an expert system demands considerable reserves of enthusiasm. This is not only because of it being a new endeavour, but also because the building can be a very trying process. The extent of enthusiasm will affect the motivation of the expert which is all important to the success of the system. (The expert's motivation is discussed below in section 14.4).

Where can one find an expert who is such a paragon of virtue? Naturally, few people will have all these qualities in full measure. When choosing the main expert to participate in a practical, commercial expert system project there will have to be compromises. The areas in which compromise is least acceptable are:

— the expert's true expertise,
— his willingness to share knowledge,
— credibility with potential users, and
— patience and tenacity.

This may still seem to call for a remarkable person. Contrary to what one might think, experts of this nature do exist, and in greater numbers than are usually thought. Discovery of these people who have such value to the organisation will depend largely on the organisation's culture and the extent to which the existing infrastructure allows experts to express themselves. An inhibited, narrow minded organisation is unlikely to foster outward going, entrepreneurial experts who have pragmatic yet dynamic expertise.

14.2   FINDING A SUITABLE EXPERT

The individuals who have the qualities needed by an expert should stand out in an organisation, but do not always do so. Such people are often 'behind the scenes experts' who actually keep the machinery of the organisation running. It could be Sam in the stores who actually makes the production scheduling decisions but is never accredited for this; it could be Sally in the administration department who in fact manages the office; it could be Stephanie in the back office who knows how to process contract documents most effectively, and thus avoids the bottlenecks which exist. These are all people who might be suitable for expert systems building. They usually have a great deal of practical know-how developed over years of experience which gives them exceptional problem solving abilities in their particular domain.

Finding these people is a challenge both for management and the knowledge engineer. The primary requirement is a clear understanding of the role that such people play, and a recognition of the value of their know-how. Then all it takes is a little time and persistence.

14.3   THE EXPERT AND THE KNOWLEDGE ENGINEER

It is essential that the expert and the knowledge engineer are able to establish a rapport. This will soon become evident after a few sessions of working with one another in the initial sketching out of the system. This rapport requires a mutual respect and a consensus on for what needs to be achieved, and thus willingly giving and taking throughout the development process.

It will readily become apparent to both parties whether they can or cannot work together effectively. The expert will soon understand whether the knowledge engineer has the mental agility to follow his or her reasoning, and the knowledge engineer will soon be in a position to evaluate the qualities of the expert — that is if the knowledge engineer is any good!

In this expert's opinion there are certain clear characteristics that a good knowledge engineer is usually endowed with. Experience is the greatest teacher and naturally an experienced knowledge engineer will far outperform one who is inexperienced. So, leaving experience aside, a good knowledge engineer (from the expert's viewpoint) is one who is:

— personally self secure,
— mature in outlook,
— empathic by nature,
— very enthusiastic,
— intelligent,
— tenacious, and
— achievement oriented.

It would seem that one is looking for another virtuoso. This is not necessarily true, as all personal qualities are relative! It is irrefutable that developing expert systems requires different types and combinations of skills to the development of conventional systems. This is largely due to the unique ingredient of expert systems, which is knowledge. Knowledge engineers are obliged to operate in the real world, the expert's world of awkward problems and practical constraints. They may not confine themselves to the realm of the computer. Handling knowledge as a new, marketable, commercial commodity is also the new challenge facing management and organisations.

In this expert's personal experience, the requirement that the knowledge engineer should be intelligent and empathic is held to be fundamental. Intelligence is particularly required so that the knowledge engineer can in some way follow the expert's reasoning in an area which may be totally foreign territory. He must also recognise the importance of what the expert is trying to impart, and when it contains relevant expertise and when it does not. The tendency to stumble on important know-how by way of casual remarks is all too common a phenomenon (the 'door-knob effect', section 13.4).

An intelligent and empathic knowledge engineer can also play a large part in sustaining the motivation of the expert and ensuring that the reality of the predetermined objectives is kept in sight. Knowledge engineering sessions do go 'flat', and a joint commitment and enthusiasm is needed if the project is to remain enjoyable.

While the power and usefulness of the expert system is mainly dependent on the talents of the expert, the *apparent* quality of the expertise and its presentation are largely due to the knowledge engineer.

14.4 MOTIVATING THE EXPERT

The importance of the expert's motivation and interest in building the expert system cannot be over emphasised. If the expert's interest is lost, then the system is doomed to being second-rate. Therefore it is important that those who embark on an expert system project should understand what the project will entail for the expert.

14.4.1 Motivation

Different experts have different sources of motivation. For the purpose of developing expert systems, it is preferable for the expert to be internally motivated. 'Internally motivated' means that he is less dependent on external recognition to achieve motivation, but relies on an internal need for achievement to provide the necessary drive. An internally motivated person usually has greater tenacity and confidence than one who is dependent on external recognition and acclaim.

It follows that the more extrovert and outspoken experts are not necessarily the best experts for our purposes. It is the experts who have many of the qualities already outlined, and the ability and staying power to persevere throughout the expert system's development, that one wants to involve in this new and exciting task.

Motivating experts to participate in a project will depend on:

— the manner in which the concept is introduced to them,
— the commitment of senior management,
— their own internal motivation, self-confidence, and the recognition already awarded to them as an expert,
— their general disposition towards information technology, and
— their willingness to learn, explore, and to seek new horizons.

Perhaps surprisingly, know-how experts reside in the organisation in many unexplored corners (see section 13.3.1). It is often these hitherto unrecognised experts who are happy to participate in experiments and new projects.

14.4.2 The Expert Transition Curve

Fig. 14.1 sets out the 'Expert Transition Curve'. This is a guide to the changes in motivation that an expert often experiences over time. The knowledge engineer can play an important role in smoothing out the curve, i.e. in reducing the drama of peaks and troughs. He can also reduce the overall time taken to develop the system, which places less of a demand on the expert's staying power. The system being developed might be a pilot or a full system; the effects are much the same.

The shape of the curve indicates the state of motivation that the expert experiences through different stages of the project. The extent of the peaks and troughs and their duration, will be affected by:

— the expert's expectations, largely influenced by how he perceives expert systems,
— the support of management throughout the project,
— his own confidence and overall ability,
— the skills of the knowledge engineer,
— the understanding of the objectives set and the manner in which these are to be achieved, and
— feedback from potential users of the system.

The stages of the curve are as follows.

Stage 1 — trepidation

Most experts, no matter how confident, experience a degree of doubt before starting to build an expert system. Part of this trepidation will naturally be with respect to how they see themselves, and how this new challenge will influence the way in which others see them. There will also be uncertainty because of not knowing what to expect. Trepidation is usually experienced as a mixture of fear and excitement. It is considered to be a healthy emotion, especially before tackling something new and unknown. Most experts go through this phase, the only difference being in its degree.

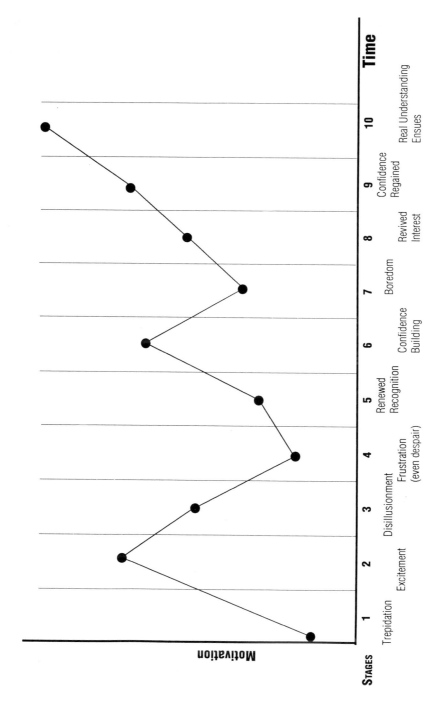

Fig. 14.1 — The Expert Transition Curve.

Stage 2 — excitement

During this stage motivation soars. The expert has a clear view of the objectives set, and the first few paces that he takes seem to bring those objectives immeasurably nearer. The goals of the project may seem to be almost within grasp without undue effort. The expert acquires a feel for the technology, and can marvel at the ingenuity of his own thought processes. This feeling is heightened as the first rules are played back and the power of an expert system begins to emerge. There is nothing like learning by doing.

Stage 3 — disillusionment

Now the initial excitement has worn off. The enormous rate of progress experienced initially has slackened. The problem of huge numbers of different combinations may have presented itself as an apparently insurmountable obstacle. The expert starts to become weary of articulating everything in the form of rules. He starts having difficulty in explaining some of the more intangible or subtle reasoning processes, even though he is sure that he could solve the problem concerned. The system's objectives become blurred and structuring difficulties may occur.

Stage 4 — frustration (even despair)

Frustration sets in. The nadir is usually reached during this stage: motivation hits rock bottom. Possibly the original structure was wrong or needs substantial revision. The expert's knowledge can seem rather superficial. The expert may start to wonder whether the application selected was an appropriate one after all, or whether it will be worth the slog of making it work.

To compound the problem, managers and users begin to press for a demonstration. They are keen to see signs of progress.

Team work is critical at this point. If the negative feelings are not discussed and plans laid for the way forward, then the expert may even drop out. The knowledge engineer has a crucial role to play here. His empathy and awareness of the stresses on the expert will make a great contribution to sustaining both parties. There are two actions which will help:

— The expert should resist becoming too excited during the euphoria of the early successes, and perhaps building his expectations too high. There is hard work to come!
— Simply being aware that others also go through a low point can do much to prevent it having a major impact. Firm plans for the way forward are important.

Stage 5 — renewed recognition

Something positive happens that reinstates the expert, the objectives, and the expert system. This could be a combination of many factors, not least the rapport and respect which the expert and the knowledge engineer share. It could be that the system takes a step forward, and the problems of the previous stage are seen as transitory. It could be that the expert reaffirms his belief in the potential value of the system. The expert shakes off his antipathy and renews his efforts. There is revived recognition of what the objectives should be, and of the opportunities and the constraints related to expert system development.

Stage 6 — confidence building
As a consequence of stage 5 and the renewed progress, confidence grows again and there is a renewed sense of achievement.

Stage 7 — boredom
The excitement and the frustration are over. Now comes the grind of getting the system to work and overcoming the technological constraints on what can be done as opposed to what the expert wishes to see achieved. Boredom can set in. Fine tuning, which usually takes a substantial effort, can seem pernickety.

Stage 8 — revived interest
The back is broken. The systems works over a wide range of problems, albeit with many unfinished aspects still. There is something worthwhile to show. The system becomes a focal point for demonstrations and the real sophistication is about to proceed.

In our experience there is a threshold which systems go through, beyond which they are obviously valuable in themselves. They reach the point where users cannot escape the impression that here is a substantial body of useful know-how, more than they could easily acquire by themselves. By contrast, even just before the threshold the system may not be impressive. The transition is mainly to do with the know-how content rather than its presentation. Once this threshold is reached, the expert system will have acquired its own momentum, and will be its own justification for the expert's attention.

Stage 9 — enthusiasm and real understanding
The expert feels that the marathon is all but over. He feels a master of this skilful tool which he has produced, nurtured, loved, and even hated. The reality of how he can relate to an expert system is unique to each expert. Next time he is likely to be better prepared, to start differently, and above all to have more realistic expectations.

There are several important reasons for highlighting the expert transition curve. Not all experts will go through all of these experiences, and obviously their reactions will be as varied as the individuals concerned. However, discussion with other experts and knowledge engineers would seem to indicate that the curve represents a common pattern. The main tasks facing both the expert and the knowledge engineer are those of diminishing the overall time to build the system, keeping the average motivation level as high as possible, and not allowing the expert to become so disillusioned as to abandon the project altogether.

Let us consider each of those likely to be involved in an expert systems project individually:

Experts
Potential experts need to realise that developing an expert system is not all

plain sailing. It can be a demanding time. It may help to realise that they might go through these stages, and that they will emerge if they persevere. Being prepared is half way to overcoming the obstacles.

Knowledge engineers

Knowledge engineers would do well to recognise what the expert might be going through. Their task is not just facilitate the delivery of know-how, but also to assist and counsel the expert through the stages of the project. The empathy of the knowledge engineer is vital to the performance of the expert.

Users

Users must be sufficiently informed about the capabilities of expert systems to have realistic expectations of what it can deliver, and how they might use it. Additionally, they should be prepared for the fact that the prototype versions of the system will be far from a finished product. User support can be akin to an intravenous dose of vitamins to the experts concerned — it gives a real boost. Their support, advice, and help will raise the whole level of the motivation curve.

Management

Management must also be sufficiently informed to have realistic expectations of what the system will do. In our experience, management expectations often swing like a pendulum from well below what is possible to gross overambition. This needs to be curbed.

It is also important that management should understand some of the stresses being faced by the expert. All too often, management will apply pressure, act negatively, or worst of all downgrade the priority of the project, while being completely oblivious to what might be happening within the expert. Instead, management should endeavour to enhance motivation by uniting experts, knowledge engineers, users and management in a combined endeavour.

15

Managing the project

This chapter describes the aspects of an expert system project which are of particular concern to the project manager. There are obvious connections with the technical stages described in the preceding chapters.

15.1   PROJECT STAGES

The project management stages of an expert system are as follows:

(1) define the application,
(2) obtain commitment to the system,
(3) assemble the team,
(4) confirm the feasibility,
(5) secure management approval,
(6) build the system,
(7) hand the system over to users.

The stages are the same whether the expert system is a pilot or a full application, although a certain informality is often accepted on pilot projects. (See section 4.4.3 for a description of the pilot/full system development cycle.) However, it is prudent to encourage good practice in the development team for all projects, and a disciplined pilot project will certainly make the full implementation easier.

It will normally be the case that there is no existing corporate culture of expert systems. Hence it is assumed that the project definition and a paper assessment of feasibility must both be done before management will authorise a pilot project. This contrasts with the technical view whereby feasibility is established by the pilot project itself.

The project manager is responsible for supervising the project stages and ensuring that *all* the necessary actions are taken. Since the eventual success of the system will depend on its overall value to the organisation, he must also ensure that the business objectives are always in view. Technical achievement is not enough.

The project manager may also be the man best placed to determine if an expert system is actually the most *appropriate* solution to the problem being presented. An enthusiasm for expert systems needs to be tempered by objective judgement. This point was demonstrated by a recent feasibility study at a plant for mass-producing car engines. The assembly line required precision components which were finished on grinding machines. These machines had to be adjusted very often to maintain the accuracy of the parts being produced. Because the machines could be out of service for several hours each day, the lack of components was holding up the production lines — a cardinal sin in a plant such as this. Worse still, unacceptable parts were sometimes assembled into engines and then had to be replaced (at considerable cost) during subsequent inspection. An expert system to help diagnose faults and identify adjustments seemed a good proposition. However, it turned out that the grinding machines were being used beyond their real capabilities. The solution was to run the machines more slowly and to work extra hours, when the adjustment problems disappeared. An expert system would have helped to reduce the symptoms, but would not have solved the problem.

15.2 DEFINING THE APPLICATION

A written statement of the system's objectives is an important tool for the project team to maintain its focus and direction. The statement should include:

— The role the system is to play, i.e. what function is it expected to perform, and what benefits are being sought by the sponsoring organisation.
— Its scope and limitations, including what it will *not* do. This defines the specific topics which will be addressed. If the system is a pilot, it should be made clear how the scope of the pilot relates to the full system.
— Its target audience, including any significant variations which are expected for different types of users.
— What the users are expected to gain from a session: what information and/or understanding they will have at the end of the session which they did not have at the beginning. This is a powerful question which should be asked repeatedly throughout the project.
— What prior experience or knowledge is required of the users, and what information (type and level) the users will be expected to provide.

This statement of objectives should obviously be discussed with management and potential users. Ideally, the potential users should have provided the main input. Identifying the objectives in an unambiguous form is an excellent means of ensuring that neither management nor users have unrealistic expectations of what the expert system will do.

The statement of objectives is also the basis for an initial assessment of feasibility (see section 4.5). This should be carried out by an experienced knowledge engineer, who should also be able to suggest improvements and to anticipate difficulties. This is a valuable contribution and may save the development team much wasted effort.

It would be inappropriate to insist that users and management should 'sign off' the system's objectives as being final and unalterable (as is the practice in conventional software development). It would also be foolish of the development team to want this! The requirements are *expected* to evolve as the team members gain experience and prototypes become available for review. This means that the final objectives will be confirmed by the users based on their experience with a working system, which is a much more fruitful approach.

15.3   OBTAINING COMMITMENT TO THE SYSTEM

If the objectives are promising and the initial assessment is that the project is feasible, then the project manager must obtain commitment from:

- Management — by approving the necessary budget, and the secondment of the staff involved. The 'opportunity cost' involved in committing expert time must be accepted (see section 4.7).
- Experts — at least one to act as the lead expert, and others to act as reviewers and to supplement the lead expert's know-how where necessary (see section 15.4).
- Users — to provide guidance on the system's desired capabilities, and to review its performance and presentation.

It is inviting failure to begin serious work on the project without this commitment. Informal arrangements can easily be upset by other demands. During exploratory projects there can also be a risk if the source of funding and the eventual user department are different, for example when the project is funded from a research and development budget. The project manager may then find that even though he has fully achieved his technical objectives, the expert system may not be well received in business terms. Therefore he needs to be aware of the organisational politics and the motives of the different interest groups.

15.4   ASSEMBLING THE TEAM

The strength of a project is set before it ever begins — by involving *all* the necessary people. The following roles must all· be filled, although not necessarily by different people:

A sponsor
... who is usually the head of the department which will use the system. Obviously the system should contribute to his business goals, and he should monitor its objectives and its overall progress. The sponsor is normally the source of funding. Provided that the sponsor is genuinely committed, he will also be a valuable champion within the organisation in the event of

competition for resources or unexpected difficulties. Such commitment derives from the expert system making a genuine contribution to business success.

A project manager
... who reports to the sponsor, and is responsible for day-to-day progress. The project manager will need a sound appreciation of expert systems if he is to actively direct the project.

One or more experts
... of course.

One or more system builders
... the knowledge engineers, to work with the experts to build the system. On a small project the senior knowledge engineer often serves as the project manager as well.

Some cooperative users
... to keep the project focused on providing what users actually need, and to ensure that the system is understandable. They should include key representatives of each class of user, for example product sales, administration, and third-party distributors. Towards the end of the project, the system should be exposed to users who have not been involved before to simulate field conditions. Those users who have been involved in the project from an early stage are likely to be over-tolerant of its failings.

A system owner
... someone from among the users who will be responsible for maintenance, distribution, gathering feedback, and keeping the system up-to-date after the project team has disbanded. One of the local experts (see section 13.3.1) is a suitable alternative to a user. The lead expert is not recommended since he is too closely identified with the know-how in the system. The lead expert may have difficulty being objective about suggested changes, or else users may assume that this will be the case. Either of these will be damaging to long-term progress.

The sponsor can initiate a project with just a knowledge engineer to carry out the initial investigation. The knowledge engineer will make contact with experts and users at a very early stage. The future system owner need not be identified until the decision to build a full system has been taken; he must then become part of the team.

It will be apparent that the minimum staffing is just one knowledge engineer working with a single expert. More typically, a small development team might consist of:

— A lead expert
— Two supplementary experts
— A consultant knowledge engineer/project manager

— A knowledge engineer/software specialist
— Three, representative users

A possible distribution of effort is shown in fig. 15.1. This is by no means

Phase	Week number	Man-days effort				
		Consultant knowledge engineer	Knowledge engineer	Lead expert	Other expert	Users
Investigation and structuring	1–2	8	10	5	—	1
Building and testing	3–8	8	30	8	4	4
Refinement and evaluation	9–13	8	25	5	2	7
Totals		24	65	18	6	12

Fig. 15.1 — Project staffing levels. This shows how effort might be used on an intensive, three month project using an expert system shell. It is intended purely as an illustration — the variability is very great. Any software development (e.g. link to a database) would extend the effort and the timescale.

definitive, but is intended to show typical trends. It is cost effective to have only one knowledge engineer involved in any one module of the expert system, hence the small teams used. We have found that both the quality and the rate of progress are worse if two or more knowledge engineers share the detailed work on a single module. If any task is too large to be allocated to an individual then strenuous efforts should be made to subdivide it. Each knowledge engineer should then be given clear responsibility for distinct components of the total system. It will be necessary to have good communication within the team, and any interdependencies between modules must be thoroughly documented. It is likely that some editing will be needed at system integration time to achieve a consistent style between the different sections.

15.5   CONFIRMING THE FEASIBILITY

The only method of establishing feasibility with confidence is to perform the initial design work. In the first instance, an experienced knowledge engineer will be able to give an opinion as to the feasibility, and give some indication of the difficulty. However, the true feasibility cannot be confirmed until the prototype is well advanced.

We strongly recommend that the system should be built in small, pre-defined stages. This is the principal means of containing the financial exposure at any time and monitoring the overall progress. The value of a pilot system as the first stage has already been emphasised (section 4.4). The aims of the pilot should be:

— to ensure that sufficient, relevant know-how exists and is available to the project,
— to allow the users to evaluate the usefulness of such a system to them,
— to allow management to assess the likely business benefits, and
— to provide a basis for estimating the costs of a full implementation, and its likely scope.

If expert systems are new to an organisation, then the 'pilot' system will inevitably be used as a demonstration. This happens whatever the development team might choose to do or say. Therefore it is important that sufficient attention is given to polishing the rules and providing an attractive presentation on the screen. Section 11.6 identifies the different approaches required for a management demonstration (to demonstrate benefits) and a pilot system (to establish feasibility). If necessary the demonstrator should be tackled first, followed by the pilot.

Once the pilot system has been built, time should be invested in a formal review and reconsideration. Every project the authors have worked on has changed its objectives or scope to some extent. This is called learning from experience. The method of delivery to end users should also be finalised, as this will constrain the implementation. Factors such as cost, the users' normal patterns of work, existing equipment, and locations all have an influence.

The pilot system also provides a basis for estimating the likely costs of a full implementation. For reasons already described (section 4.6), the actual costs can only be estimated approximately, but a budgetary provision is obviously required. Provided that the pilot is truly representative of the full system, the simplest option is to estimate what fraction has been completed in the pilot and to multiply up. The team will have been on a learning curve during the prototyping phase, and so can be expected to progress faster in subsequent phases. However, the full system will have greater complexity, and will certainly absorb more testing time. Multiplying up makes the assumption that these two effects will cancel out. If in doubt, add 50%.

15.6   SECURING MANAGEMENT APPROVAL

Management now has to make a go/no-go decision for the next phase. For a full system, the project manager must secure the same commitments as for the pilot, but the investment is obviously greater. This should not be onerous as the pilot system should have demonstrated the potential benefits. If not, then these benefits must be evaluated first.

If the implementation is to be phased then there will be cycles of review, management approval, and build.

15.7   BUILDING THE SYSTEM

The expert system can then be built using the methods already described in chapter 12. The basic cycle is:

— build a prototype to the implementation team's satisfaction,
— review the system with users,
— refine the system in the light of users' comments to make it suitable for field use.

It may be necessary to integrate the system into the users' normal working environment (see section 12.6). The project manager may well have a better view of these requirements than a knowledge engineer, and the necessary management influence. For example, if some of the data which the expert system requires is available on an existing database, then arrangements must be made for connecting to that database. Alternatively, it may be desirable to integrate the expert system as part of a conventional system. In either case it will be necessary to liaise with the data processing department. They may well be the best placed to implement such links.

System integration may involve substantial components written in conventional programming languages (e.g. for database access or communications handling). These can be tackled with the normal methods of data processing.

15.8   INVOLVING USERS

A cautionary tale:

A US company was making coated paper products at their UK plant, supplying customers throughout Europe. There was fierce competition both on price and quality from alternative suppliers in the USA and Japan.

One machine in the production process was particularly important. It had been purpose built to cut wide rolls of paper into narrow ones, and to chop the strips to length. Cutting paper cleanly and at high speed is a particularly awkward feat, and the machine required careful setting up and constant tending. The company correctly identified this as a good prospect for an expert system, to help the maintenance fitters identify the right adjustments first time. This would improve the availability of the cutting machine, thereby improving the capacity of the plant as a whole.

Work began with the existing flow diagrams showing how to locate faults. These had been prepared by the cutting machine's supplier. However, the team soon realised that the man who really knew what to do was the supervising engineer. It was he who was summoned from his bed at 4 a.m. when the machine demanded attention. An expert system was built with his help, and gently introduced into service. The project team avoided the mistake of imposing its use, thoughtfully making it available for any fitter who wanted to try it.

Only a few did. The rest made an effort to demonstrate its shortcomings, for example by presenting it with what they knew to be 'one-off' faults, and scorned its slightest error.

The fitters who ran the machine 24 hours a day perceived the expert system as being a device to tell them what to do, in a field where they felt that they themselves were the real experts. There was also a suspicion that the company was using it to spy on them, and/or to replace them (neither was true). The Trade Union also intervened.

All was well in the end, but only after much conciliation and a year's delay. It turned out that the fitters were indeed the real experts on a host of details which the supervisor did not know. The system was all the better for being partly the users' creation, and they began to be interested in it.

There is only one answer to the question 'When should users be involved in an expert system project?', and that answer is 'As soon as possible'. Failing to involve users is second only to failing to involve management in achieving disappointment at the end of the project. It costs little to discuss the system requirements with a sample of users as soon as the requirements are drafted. Naturally, they will have difficulty in envisaging the reality of what is being proposed, but at the very least a discussion should cause the users to consider what contribution the system might make. A demonstration of an existing system of the same type is usually the best way of conveying the 'flavour' of what an expert system is like. Its role as an assistant, not as a replacement, should be clearly explained and not merely stated.

Additionally, there is the need to brief users before introducing any form of new technology. How much better it is to have them participate, rather than the system being offered as a fait accompli.

15.9   HANDING THE SYSTEM OVER TO USERS

Handing the system over to users is largely a matter of common sense management, but there are tasks specifically concerned with expert systems. Most importantly, the development team may have to 'sell' the idea of expert systems. This involves giving briefings and demonstrations to anyone who might come into contact with the system, including potential users and all the way up their management line. If this is not done then they will assume that the expert system is a data processing system, like all the computer applications they have known before. If users and management are to obtain real benefits then they need to appreciate that expert systems are a different way of using computers, and that they can provide know-how, not just data.

Potential users may also need training in the use of the system, not to overcome difficulties in use but rather to encourage them to explore it. (If the system *is* difficult to use, then back to the drawing board!) Expert systems are most fun when users can experiment with cases of their own choosing, and they need sufficient confidence with the software to do this. (Fun is important — it encourages learning.) The experience is that many users are somewhat intimidated by the data processing systems they are required to use. They have learnt to stay out of trouble by only doing what is known to work. Expert systems are quite different: the know-how is there to be explored, stretched, and prodded. Therefore user training should concentrate on instilling this inquisitive, exploratory approach. The software should always be resilient enough to ensure that users cannot do any permanent damage.

It will also be necessary to organise the following:

— User documentation. A brief user guide should be prepared by the project team.
— A mechanism for distributing and updating copies of the system in the field. Management must decide whether the users are to be allowed to customise their systems or not.
— Any necessary security arrangements to protect confidential material.
— A line of support if the users have difficulty in using the system.
— Clear channels to the system owner for encouraging and collecting reactions from users, and refining the system accordingly.
— Continuing access to an expert to assist with future refinements and adjustments.

It is clearly important that users should have ready access to the expert system. The expert system is an aid to improving their performance, and if there is effort involved in using the system then the less motivated staff will not bother, and much of the potential benefit will be lost. Generally speaking:

if the problem occurs often
then immediate access to the system is essential

if the problem occurs rarely
then access to the system is non-critical
provided there is access when needed

if the expected payoff is high
then good access is worthwhile

For most applications, users should be within a few seconds walk of the expert system from wherever they are when they need the assistance. Placing a terminal in a recreation area may be an encouragement for training, but will be poor for operational use. Users will only tolerate great inconvenience to consult the expert system if they feel highly exposed when making their decision.

Imposition of any new technology on an organisation may lead to adverse reactions from the workforce. Expert systems can be particularly intimidating, especially to those who are unfamiliar with computers. The same care and attention is required as for introducing computerisation for the first time. Obvious steps include briefings for the workforce at an early stage, user involvement in the project, openness with union representatives, plus demonstrations and briefings by their managers. Fears of redundancy or de-skilling should be dealt with at the outset.

It may well be that professional and administrative staff will be more apprehensive than manual and craft workers. Those who work in a mechanised environment have had to adjust to a high degree of automation, and equipment such as robots and computer controlled machines are fairly commonplace. These people are more likely to accept an expert system as just another form of automated tool. However, consider the position for those who work with information. Although they may be making extensive use of computers for data processing, the data does not actually impinge on how they perform their tasks. The arrival of expert systems mean that, for the first time, computers can have a direct impact on their decision processes. They may feel threatened, and enlightened management will anticipate this and channel it productively. For example, can their concerns be harnessed to make the system more useful to them?

15.10   MAINTENANCE

Maintenance of an expert system is vital. Maintenance is actually ongoing development and refinement. If an expert system remains static then it will become ossified and will gradually fall into disuse. Its know-how will no longer be relevant, and users will cease to find it valuable.

We distinguish between maintenance of the knowledge base and fixing any problems with the underlying software. The former is the responsibility of the system owner and the expert, whereas the latter should be referred to the software supplier.

It follows that there must be ongoing access to an expert, since only he can identify the changes which are required in the system's know-how. This person need not be the lead expert, although a third party would need to become familiar with the detailed working of the system. Errors in the existing system and requests for new capabilities come via the system owner. He may need occasional access to knowledge engineering support if neither he nor the acting expert is able to update the system.

The errors which occur when a system is in use are similar to those found during validation and testing, and can be dealt with by the same methods (section 12.5). For example, over-simplified rules may cause the system to jump to premature conclusions. Additionally, there will be requirements for new facilities and increases of scope. For example, the system might be extended to accommodate a new class of user or a new product type. It is important that the whole system is considered when such major changes are undertaken, starting from its objectives and its overall structure. If ad hoc changes are made in any quantity then the system will quickly lose its clarity.

Experience with those few systems which have been in the field for several years shows that major restructuring will eventually become necessary. This happens when the original structure becomes too clumsy to accommodate current requirements, or a new function is sufficiently valuable to be worth major changes. This would be disastrous in a conventional system, which is why they have to be patched up until they collapse, but in an expert system restructuring means using the same know-how in a different way. Therefore the system can continue to grow in line with the demands of the users. When restructuring there is always a degree of reimplementation too, since the developers will have learnt how the system could be more effective.

15.11 PROJECT DISCIPLINES

Many of the project management disciplines are common to other types of project, although there are special considerations for change control, documentation, and management reporting.

15.11.1 Change control

Change control means managing the modifications to the system. Its purpose is to ensure that the expert system is always in a known state, and that the benefits of earlier testing are not thrown away by undisciplined changes. For example, it may be that the latest modifications have actually turned out to be undesirable, and it is necessary to revert to an earlier version.

Inappropriate use of change control is counterproductive. In the early stages of building, hundreds of changes may be made at one time and tracking these individually would be burdensome. An appropriate level of control is to 'freeze' versions which are known to be working to a given state, and use these as a basis for follow-on work. The sensible point to freeze a version is when a new sub-function has been implemented and satisfactorily tested. This might happen every few days.

Change control becomes more important as the system becomes more complex, and must be validated to a higher standard. Therefore change control should certainly be in place when user reviews are being undertaken.

For X/CON (a computer configuring system, see appendix B), DEC have implemented elaborate change control procedures. These are a model of good practice. They now sustain the integrity of a system which has grown twenty-fold over its ten year life, and which continues to evolve. At the same time, the products which X/CON configures change daily, and X/CON must be constantly modified to keep pace. DEC's solution is that whenever a rule is added or modified, then test data must also be supplied which will validate that change. The library of test cases is now vast, and versions of the system for release are routinely validated against this library. DEC's reward is an almost complete absence of configuring errors — the computer systems which X/CON fails to configure in full usually contain items which are not included in its knowledge base.

Regrettably, most expert systems software has very poor facilities for monitoring changes to knowledge bases. Software tools which allowed knowledge engineers to investigate changes between a modified knowledge base and earlier versions of that knowledge base would be welcome.

15.11.2 Documentation

Documentation is required both for maintenance purposes and for the users. The purpose of maintenance documentation is largely to preserve the working documents from the project, but there is an obvious need for these to be collated and tidied.

Maintenance of an expert system really means further refinement, and the documentation should reflect this. It should include:

- The system overview, defining the expert system's role, scope, and limitations (see section 15.2). It is best to set this out in terms of what the user can expect from the system. There should also be a statement of the system's authority, the source(s) of know-how used, and the extent of its validation. If there is any risk that the system might be regarded as having official or legal force when this does not apply, then this should be specifically disclaimed.
- A technical description, defining the key points of the design and the implementation. If particular strategies were tried and rejected during the building then it is important that these should be recorded here.
- The high-level map of the whole problem, showing the main tasks handled by the system and how they are related. If the system contains more than one module (which is usually the case) then the flow of control between them should be shown on the main map or on a flowchart made for the purpose. Where there are interfaces between knowledge base modules, or between knowledge base modules and external software, then these should be shown explicitly. Since the project team will have been amending and refining the high-level map as the building progressed, this document is simply the final version of the working map, possibly redrawn for clarity.
- Maps of the individual tasks. Once again, these are the working maps redrawn. It has been found to be very useful to annotate these maps with the *exact* names used in the knowledge bases — abbreviations or sloppy annotation can be very confusing to those who are unfamiliar with the system.
- An index of all items within a knowledge base which depend on actions outside that knowledge base. For example, a conclusion drawn in one knowledge base may depend on another conclusion having already been reached in another part of the system. During subsequent refining, it is easy to overlook such connections.
- A record of all the computer files used in the system, their purpose, and where they are used.
- The change control mechanism which should already be in place (section 15.10.1).
- Printed versions and back-up copies of all necessary software. This is

standard computer practice, but is often treated far too casually. The project team should always be in a position to recover from total loss of their equipment and their office premises by holding back-up software and copies of the design documents.

Notice that the trappings of conventional software documentation are missing, i.e. functional specifications, program specifications, etc. It is well known that these documents are rarely updated, and typically become completely irrelevant after three years. For an expert system, where the rate of change is many times greater, they would be lucky to last three months. The best specification of the know-how is the know-how itself. Provided that the know-how is expressed in highly intelligible form, there is little point in documenting a 'snapshot'.

However, the indices of interdependencies and messages lend themselves very well to conventional tools such as data dictionaries. In the past these have been little used because they tend to run in a mainframe data processing environment, which is not where expert systems work is usually carried out. Expert system builders and product developers should take heed of the many lessons from conventional software engineering here.

In addition to maintenance documentation, the team should prepare a guide for the users. This should consist of:

— An introductory brochure describing what the system can do for users, and who those users might be. There is a heavy responsibility on the authors to generate realistic expectations and not to over sell the system's capabilities.
— The system overview described above.
— A brief usage guide, including how to load and run the system and which keys to press. Even if this information is also available within the expert system itself (which we would recommend), users seem to appreciate it on paper as well.
— A note encouraging users to provide feedback on the system, saying why this is valuable and who they should contact with it (the system owner).

Some systems have included the facility to collect feedback within themselves, encouraging the users to comment while the experience is fresh in their minds. This has much to recommend it.

15.11.3 Management reporting
The main tool of management control of an expert system project is the use of incremental development. Each improvement in the system builds upon the work so far. The two measures of progress are:

— What functions the expert system performs. This can be used to measure progress against the total set of functions being tackled.
— How well the system performs those functions. This is a subjective assessment and is best made by the manager exercising the system for

himself. If the line manager finds it opaque or irrelevant, then the chances are that the users will too.

Managers should be cautioned that just because an expert system works, that does not mean that it is nearly finished. This is particularly true in the early stages when a first prototype may be running in only a few days. Even once the know-how is running and producing conclusions, there can be as much effort again in making the system presentable.

Note that counting the number of rules is not a good measure of progress. The initial rate of rule building is much higher than can be sustained. Also, the total number of rules may actually drop at several points during the project as the team identify simplifying themes, or more general ways of expressing an idea which had previously been fragmented.

Experience has shown that formal management reporting must follow the normal practice in that organisation. For example, this applies to the reports from the project manager to the sponsor, or from the sponsor to top management. For those outside the project, not conforming to conventional reporting may be perceived as not achieving anything. This means that the expert system measures must be interpreted in terms which are familiar to the recipients of the reports.

Part VI
Conclusions

16

Conclusions and recommendations

Numerous conclusions have been presented throughout this book. This chapter aims to summarise them and to indicate the way forward for business use of expert systems.

16.1 SUMMARIES

16.1.1 Principal conclusions

The main points for business are:

Hundreds of expert systems are in the late stages of development or already in service in industry and commerce. Typically these are relatively small, many of them running on personal computers.

The great potential of expert systems lies in the sharing of the expertise (know-how) which they contain. This means augmenting the abilities of the user, rather than providing intelligence in the computer.

The power of sharing know-how via expert systems is hard to appreciate until you have experienced it personally.

Very few successful expert systems are discussed in public. Therefore expert systems do not yet have an accepted record of success.

The correct organisational environment is a pre-requisite for success with expert systems.

The technology available to build expert systems is far ahead of the ability of most organisations to exploit it.

Intelligence, learning and understanding on the part of computers are as far away as ever.

While the power of an expert system is mainly dependent on the talents of the expert, its usefulness is strongly influenced by the knowledge engineer.

To develop an expert system, focus on developing the know-how not on developing the computer software.

A small expert system can be built for about the cost of one middle manager for a year.

Increasingly, the pressure on organisations is to look outwards rather than inwards, i.e. to expand market share and to exploit new markets. This they can only do by making best use of the corporate expertise — and expert systems are the most powerful tool available for amplifying that expertise. We believe that this is a matter of long-term survival.

It is not too soon to start.

16.1.2   Our approach to expert systems

The key points of our approach to expert systems can be summarised as follows.

Recognise the benefits and limitations of expert systems:

— Expert systems amplify an organisation's key asset: the decision making abilities of the staff.
— Expert systems do not replace people, they help people to perform better.
— An expert system is only as effective as the human expertise which it contains. No expert   no system.
— Practical problem-solving power is achieved by using an expert's know-how — the accumulated lessons of experience. Know-how is found in spoken advice, not in books or manuals.
— Like experts, expert systems can make mistakes.

Cultivate the growth of expert systems:

— Gain experience with non-strategic applications.
— Recognise the crucial role of demonstrations in gaining management support.
— Focus on delivering applications, not on developing the technology.
— Involve users and management throughout.
— Get user management to pay for the development. 'You don't value what you don't have to pay for.'

Identify profitable applications:

— Establish the business priorities and how they can best be achieved.
— Identify how expert systems could further these aims.
— Select promising applications according to technical feasibility.
— Use a pilot system to confirm feasibility and to verify the system's objectives.

Assemble a team. You will need:

— A management sponsor with a vested interest in the system's success.
— An expert who is recognised as making effective decisions, and is articulate, enthusiastic, and available. Real expertise means solving the problem in practice.
— An experienced knowledge engineer.
— Representative end users.

Develop the system incrementally:

— Gather knowledge by any means to begin with.
— Build a prototype at the first possible opportunity.
— Use the prototype as a prompt for further know-how.

— Pause after the pilot stage and review the system's value to the organisation and its users. Expect change.
— Grow the system incrementally by adding new tasks and refining existing ones.
— Test and validate as you go.

Monitor the business implications:

— Monitor against the original objectives.
— Confirm the benefits by testing with potential users.
— Be prepared to modify the system's objectives if this will further the business aims.

Introduce the system gently:

— Present the expert system as assistant, not overlord or spy. You cannot force the users to make better decisions.
— Easy access is important.
— The test of an expert system is whether the users find it sufficiently helpful to *want* to use it.

16.2   THE PRESENT POSITION

There are too few public examples of successful expert systems for the financial case for expert systems to be beyond doubt. There is an increasing number of claimed successes, but expert systems have yet to become a normal part of computer usage. Managers who adopt a conservative view will demand to see three established and profitable applications before agreeing to commit any funds for initial development. Such a demonstration is not realistic at present. The price of such a 'safety first' approach is that these organisations can only be followers, and never leaders in the marketplace. Those who wait for the future to happen will inevitably live in the past.

Secrecy is undoubtedly an obstacle. Organisations which are investing in expert systems, and see them as contributing to their competitive edge, are most reluctant to alert their competitors to their activities. The result is that even when an organisation is willing to discuss an application at its feasibility stage, a veil of silence may be drawn over it when serious development starts. For example, Unilever was highlighted in 1984 as being in the vanguard of expert systems use in the UK (d'Agapeyeff, 1984). In 1987, every one of their applications was being kept completely confidential. Secrecy is especially evident for financial systems and anything connected with business management. We believe that there are two reasons for this. The first is the immense rate of change, and the consequent uncertainty. The second is the sponsoring organisation's view of the potential gains to be derived from expert systems.

DEC's X/CON is a notable exception to the silence about expert systems (see section 4.6). It is currently saving its owners tens of millions of dollars annually. Its continued success over many years has led DEC to invest heavily in expert systems, to the point where expert systems are now indispensable to their operations. In the UK, ICL claims to have saved £1.5 million during 1986 using their own product configuring system, and also 'cured the seemingly endless headaches suffered by sales staff' (Haynes, 1986). It could be argued that both these companies have a vested interest in publicising their systems, since they both supply expert systems products. However, other computer manufacturers seem to be taking it a little more seriously, and are looking to their own arrangements for configuring customer orders. Recently, Westinghouse and American Express have also claimed million dollar savings with their own expert systems.

There is another, more far reaching effect of a publicised success: the acceptance of expert systems into the corporate culture. Nothing encourages confidence with expert systems like success with expert systems. The publicity given to these systems undoubtedly leads to wider exploitation within those companies. Organisations which maintain confidentiality may well be doing themselves a disservice. Similarly, if competitors simply respond by reproducing equivalent applications, then they will be undertaking no more than a catching-up exercise.

The broader picture of expert systems usage varies from country to country. In the USA, the waves of enthusiasm and major corporate investment in artificial intelligence seen in the early 1980s have been somewhat dissipated on the rocky shore of non-deliverable systems. A few of these ambitious projects will doubtless survive, especially where supported by the military. However, the promise of widespread 'machine intelligence' is now firmly in the 21st century. Many US corporations are having to reassess their enthusiasm for artificial intelligence.

In the UK, perhaps because of more limited funding and smaller computers, the trend in business expert systems has been towards less ambitious, but more achievable goals. The impression is of perhaps a hundred relatively small systems in routine use, with several hundred more under serious development. These are fulfilling the role of job assistants, handling a well defined fragment of a problem area. Typically they have been built by self-taught teams using expert system shells running on personal computers. The benefit being obtained is either to improve the performance of skilled but inexperienced staff (by passing on know-how), or to improve the effectiveness of experts (by automating common but well understood tasks). There is further activity in other European nations. Germany and the Scandinavian countries are substantial markets for expert system products, and France has a home-grown industry. A comparison of recent surveys of expert systems in the USA and Europe shows that, by aiming for more modest objectives, European companies are seeing the benefits of expert systems in a shorter timescale than their US counterparts (Hewitt and Sasson, 1985, Hewitt et al., 1986).

It is not clear if any of the attempts at 'intelligent' expert systems have reached the stage of being handed over to users for general use. By 'intelligent', we mean those that attempt to replace a human expert function or to perform a task which human experts cannot. This may change before 1990, with a handful coming into service. Most such systems have been developed by professional teams drawn from large government contractors, the major systems houses, and Universities. It is already clear that several such government funded projects will fall well short of their original objectives after five years work, and as many millions of pounds spent. Despite initial commitments to provide deliverable products, they have been conducted as research projects.

Expert systems have yet to become visible in everyday life. We know of no expert systems which are being offered for use by the general public without supervision. Where members of the public come into contact with an expert system, it is always via an intermediary who is already familiar with the system. This obviously eases the burden of making the system understandable to its users, especially when some might be intimidated by a keyboard. Speech input will be a great step forward, but that is a long way from being solved.

16.3 BUSINESS PROSPECTS

Expert systems have added a new dimension to the use of computers. Computer power can now be applied to tasks which require people to use their intelligence. Before expert systems, computers were confined to handling data. Manufacturing industry has had to come to terms with replacement of muscle with machinery, and later craft skills with automation. For those whose product is information, we have the analogy of clerks with labourers, and 'knowledge workers' with craftsmen. Knowledge workers and craftsmen are distinguished by their ability to transform their material, to add value to it, not just to handle it as clerks and labourers do. A large number of clerical tasks have already been replaced by data processing. Expert systems herald the automation phase for knowledge workers: 'power tools for the mind'. This group includes engineers, scientists, managers, technicians and many other professionals who are typically in the middle ranks of an organisation.

The practical realisation of this is that management and the professional and technical trades will increasingly be supported by capital investment in expert systems. In the past, capital investment in non-manufacturing areas has been very low, largely because the technology offered did not provide direct benefits. Expert systems provide a method whereby capital can be employed to increase the productivity of whole groups of workers who have previously had to rely on human capabilities alone.

For business, there is now an opportunity for all those who apply expertise to augment their own skills using expert systems. The pace of competition is such that expert systems will profit those organisations which make good use of them, and leave behind those which do not.

Expert systems could easily become commonplace in business within just a few years. There could be many thousands of expert system users by 1990, although organisational inertia will probably dictate a slower pace. It is a safe prediction that the number of expert systems in use will rise sharply, since so many are under active development. The usual vehicle will be a personal computer running an expert system shell. Prices of end-user systems will fall to a low level, in line with pricing for other high volume personal computer products such as spreadsheets and word processors. Prices for system building tools may remain higher, but they will have to offer productivity aids to justify their higher costs.

The first applications to be done in any numbers will be the simple ones with fairly obvious pay off. These are not necessarily the best topics to attack, but are the easiest to do. They include:

Fault diagnosis
Guides to regulations
Financial advisers
Archives of specialist know-how

Fault diagnosis is undoubtedly a neglected opportunity in manufacturing industry. All companies which ship complex products have a fault diagnosis problem. Even a small fault diagnosis system would help with maintenance, provide better facilities for the equipment users, and differentiate the equipment vendor. In addition there is vitally important know-how within a plant about how to run the manufacturing process efficiently and to maintain the plant itself. Fault diagnosis systems are usually straightforward to build, and at the very least can be used to screen requests for repairs to provide immediate fixes for well understood faults. Similar arguments apply to the other applications given above.

We expect that the number of packaged expert systems applications which are sold commercially will rise only slowly. There are three reasons for this:

know-how is often company-specific,
organisations tend to be jealous of their skills, and
management understanding will take time to develop.

Firstly, the fact that know-how is always specific to a context means that the skills of an expert in one organisation may not be transportable to another. Therefore the expert system may have greatly reduced value in a different environment. In addition, there are obvious commercial reasons for concealing know-how on pricing, competitive selling, and so forth. The likely outcome is the marketing of skeleton applications containing a basis of generally accepted know-how, which can be tailored to suit particular organisations.

Secondly, Western industrial thinking is to defend a technological advantage rather than to try and sell it to others at a profit. We jealously guard any competitive edge, whether real or potential. This has already been seen in the secrecy surrounding many expert system projects. Thirdly, the use of computers to promote human expertise is a novel activity. People are not yet accustomed to using their computers to obtain know-how. Managers do not yet see computers as a normal means of improving the quality of the decisions made by their staff. This understanding, and the corresponding willingness to use expert systems, will take time to develop.

The Japanese Fifth Generation Report clearly foresaw the possibility of packaged expert systems, i.e. knowledge being traded as a commodity (Moto-oka, 1982). Indeed, this feature led critics to suggest that the Japanese were intent on making knowledge-based industries their own, in the same way as they already dominated industries such as motorcycles, cameras and home electronics. The principle is very powerful: like technology, knowledge is of little value in itself, but can have a very high value because of what it enables you to do. The payoff comes when a company can apply its expertise to deliver its products faster, better featured, cheaper, or more attractive in some other way. Only a small advantage is needed to grab a large market share.

This 'knowledge war' is already being fought in the market for advanced semiconductors. Success goes to those who can produce fearsomely complex designs fast and reliably. We see this as a model for the future, for service providers as well as manufacturers. An organisation which can effectively deploy expert systems will have an in-built advantage.

One can speculate that the domestic market will eventually be very important, although it may be a generation before the necessary home computers become as commonplace as television sets. Individuals at home are in greater need of expert help than when they are at work, since at home there is no infrastructure of support services to call on. Applications such as financial advice, legal advice and first aid are self evident. These are skills which most individuals do not normally have the time, the ability or the funds to acquire for themselves. Access to such expertise would do much for their peace of mind — and the public is willing to pay for peace of mind. The biggest domestic applications will be those which affect people directly, such as health, fitness, diet, personal problems, and those relating to children. No concerned parent can fail to respond to the offer of authoritative advice about some injury or other problem with their child. We can expect all manner of other medical know-how to figure prominently. This raises important issues of involving established medical professionals in the development of such systems, but that deserves a fuller discussion than can be given here.

The volume of sales will be dictated by pricing. Experience with pre-recorded video tapes has shown that reducing the price by 75% can increase shipments twenty- to fifty-fold.

16.4   THE CHALLENGE TO BUSINESS

There is one major challenge to this rosy future for expert systems, and that is people's motivation to use them. Top management may not regard expert systems as sufficiently important to invest the company's time and money.

This will restrict the applications to being relatively small scale and few in number. As a result, the critical mass of applications which is needed to justify a corporate involvement in expert systems may not be reached.

Correspondingly, users may not be motivated to exploit the expert systems which are available to them. There is no doubt that users must invest some time and effort in an expert system if they are to gain from the know-how within. However, if the business climate is one of 'muddling along' then there will be no incentive to do so. The less interested users will take the course of least resistance, perhaps preferring a computer system which takes responsibility from them. Therefore it is essential that management should promote the *use* of expert systems (for example by rewarding self development), as well as their *availability*. This may seem obvious, but a remarkable number of companies claim to encourage self-development, whilst actually resisting it. Consider the reactions of some managers on discovering an employee reading a book, even though it might be relevant to that employee's work.

If expert systems are not used to promote the user's own know-how, then expert systems will be relegated to the role of just another form of computer programming. Such systems will be as alien to their users as conventional programs are today.

The success or failure of expert systems as a technology for amplifying the power of knowledge will depend on people's determination to take up this new tool, and use it to derive the benefits which undoubtedly exist. Like factory automation, expert systems will increase the gap between those organisations which make skilled use of technology and those which do not.

16.5 TECHNICAL PROSPECTS

16.5.1 Software

The fastest technical developments will occur on personal computers. Both the hardware and the software are developing faster than any other part of the market. New software products are appearing every month, and there is reason to believe that this will continue.

We expect to see expert system shells increase their share of the market even further. Their facilities will include many of the features of present-day knowledge engineering environments. Even the suppliers of today's knowledge engineering environments are aware that this could come about within a year. Therefore knowledge engineering environments will be obliged to retreat up market, catering for the most ambitious and the most complex of applications. The ability for environments to handle very complex programs, and to download these to inexpensive target machines will be essential.

There seems to be little incentive for any revolution in programming languages. Lisp and Prolog are already incomprehensible to ordinary folk, so there would be little benefit for users if these languages were to be replaced by technically superior but equally opaque alternatives. Government purchasing policy in the USA could ensure that the Common Lisp standard becomes accepted for use on workstations. This will have little impact outside highly technical groups. A trend which is already apparent is for software products to be coded in a conventional language (such as C or even Fortran) for portability and efficiency. This enables complex applications to be delivered on small computers.

Expert systems methods will be used to develop numerous computer systems which might otherwise have been developed by conventional methods. Many of these will be embedded within conventional applications and computer operating systems. Existing data processing staff see this as a natural use for expert systems — indeed they frequently see no other — and they can capitalise on the speed of development and ease of modification which are important benefits of the knowledge-based approach. In this context, expert system tools will be introduced as an extension to current methods of programming. We see this as a move in the direction of '4th generation' programming languages (see fig. 1.1).

The real impetus for software development will come from the demand for end-user software, i.e. expert systems which can be used by experts and users themselves. At present such ease of use is still quite rare. Even the best software packages benefit from a contribution by a computer professional, since they all require some element of programming to achieve satisfactory results. Doing away with professional help completely is an ambitious target. Users have a very simple specification for what they want their software to do, namely 'that which is obvious in this case'! Naturally, what is obvious is highly context dependent, and we humans tend to have little patience with a computer's ignorance. There will be movement towards software which is easier for lay people to use, but it will not be easy. 'Achieving simplicity is the peak of sophistication'.

16.5.2 Hardware

Computer hardware continues to develop at an unrelenting pace. We know of one normal-size office which contains as much computer power as existed in the whole of the UK in 1960. Furthermore, this is a working office containing people and desks, and is not just a computer room.

Personal computers are already the businessman's workhorse. This gives a powerful incentive for expert systems to be delivered via personal computers. The growth in computing power offered by personal computers means that it will shortly be possible to run even the largest of today's software systems on a desktop machine. Given that today's software technology is already ahead of industry's ability to exploit it, this means that processing power is no barrier.

Radically new hardware designs seem unlikely to make any general impact for several years at least. Some of the world's best computer designers are currently working on highly parallel architectures to achieve much higher processing speeds than are available today. (As a generalisation, current machines process all their data through a single path. The hope is to use many paths, possibly millions, all working together.) New materials and physical phenomena are also being explored, including optics and superconductivity. However, these will have to be developed to the point of being cost competitive against today's silicon-based products before they will make an impact on the business market. Their short- to medium-term role will be in specialist applications such as vision processing and military surveillance which currently require brute force techniques to make headway. If the US Strategic Defense Initiative goes ahead, then this will undoubtedly provide a major stimulus for both hardware and software development.

16.5.3   Knowledge engineering

At present there is a small cadre of experienced knowledge engineers, plus many more who are teaching themselves by doing projects. As the demand for knowledge engineering skills becomes more widespread, there is an obvious requirement for de-skilling, to reduce the demands on individual ability. After all, bright and able staff will always be in demand and cannot be reserved for knowledge engineering. To judge by the pattern of development of other professional skills, we can expect the current empirical approach to be gradually refined into widely agreed methods. This phase has just begun. However, we believe that those who advocate a pre-specified methodology commit the error of assuming that there is one, underlying form of knowledge. This is like suggesting that a lawyer should have one methodology for defending his client in a court of law. There are constant principles, certainly, but the lawyer's skill lies in tailoring his actions to the evidence at hand and the attitudes of the people involved. Therefore we prefer the view that knowledge engineers will require an armoury of different techniques, and the mental agility to apply whichever of them is relevant at the time. It seems unreasonable to assume that any one procedure will always lead to good results. This would be an attempt to substitute method for thinking.

The interpersonal element of knowledge engineering will always remain. We are sceptical of ever seeing fully effective automatic tools. Even the initial step of providing tools which interrogate the user to establish the cause of a wrong decision have been shown to be of limited use. The user has to identify each change in such pedestrian detail that the task is immensely tedious.

As a professional skill, knowledge engineering will remain apart from the main stream of data processing because of its different objectives and its different methods. The two could only merge if the basic axioms were to change.

16.5.4   Research

The contribution of research is the hardest to forecast, since who can foretell what has yet to be discovered? There are enormous opportunities, including learning, common sense, and reasoning. A formidable list!

The present state of these capabilities is bleak. Firstly, computers do not learn in the human sense at all (i.e. by abstracting new principles from experience). Secondly, no computer has common sense. An optimistic attempt is being made by a US team to implement the 'knowledge of the world' contained in an encyclopedia, but its eventual usefulness is unknown. Thirdly, the current reasoning methods used in expert systems are a poor substitute for human reasoning. Two marvels of human thought are reasoning by analogy, and the effortless ability to recall relevant know-how from among the countless items which must have been remembered. Neither of these are tractable by today's methods.

If research could make significant progress in any of these areas, and the advances could also be applied to real world systems, then business computing would never be the same again.

16.6   THE WAY FORWARD

16.6.1   Who should act

Exploiting expert systems is a priority for those organisations whose competitive edge is essential to their immediate survival. This means applying expert systems in areas which have direct leverage on profitability such as sales, marketing, customer support, professional activities, and in the products themselves. The benefits to be gained have already been described in chapter 4.

The second area of application is where expertise is at a premium. Common signs of stress in an organisation due to shortage of expertise include:

- business being lost because of an inability to respond,
- failure to innovate,
- dependence on a few, key individuals,
- high turnover of staff, and
- costs being incurred through human errors.

An organisation can survive with any or all of these, but only at a cost to its success. This is as much true of a charity or a government department as it is of a profit-motivated business. The expertise of the staff is the single greatest asset, and expert systems allow that asset to be much more effective.

The third area of importance is where expertise is already being sold, typified by the professions and consultancies. These organisations have successfully maintained high barriers against others entering their market-place, but that is now changing. Expert systems might provide good guidance for the majority of their clients, since most problems are dealt with using a small fraction of the total knowledge in the field. Two avenues are open: contribute to expert systems products and sell expertise in that form, or use expert systems to increase the added value of existing consultants. This latter is already happening, for example management consultants using expert systems to tackle specialist aspects of their work.

16.6.2 What to aim for

If the reader has examined the previous chapters of this book, then the type of applications to tackle with expert systems should be clear. The applications should have the following attributes:

- They should be modest in scope compared with what is expected of a human. The better defined the scope of an expert system, the more likely it is that the system will be able to provide good quality advice as well as guidance. If the scope is too wide, then the know-how will be very general and will require too much interpretation from the user.
- They must aim to improve the performance of the user, rather than attempt to replace one of his functions. This means supporting the user by providing help and guidance, so that he can interpret the advice and apply expertise himself.
- They must have the potential to further the aims of the organisation, whatever these may be (i.e. not necessarily financial). It would be a waste of valuable staff if the expert system did not address a business priority.
- They must fall within the scope of an expert who is confident in his own skill, recognised as being authoritative, willing to cooperate, and can devote sufficient time to the project.

16.6.3 How to start

If it has been established that an expert system can contribute to business success, the next question is how to begin. The key issues for success are to secure the *continuing* involvement of top management and of the users. Given that this will be achieved, the overall strategy is straightforward:

- Decide to walk before attempting to run. This means gaining experience with low-risk applications, and allowing the implementors leeway to make mistakes without being immediately penalised.
- Pick an application which is not strategically vital (since this would exert great pressure on the team), but one which should have the attention of top management.
- Define in advance how the system will be judged as being successful, in such a way that success can be measured (even if only subjectively). This is the best way of avoiding undue expectations.
- Make use of experienced help. An experienced knowledge engineer should be asked to review the choice of application and its objectives, ensure that the right experts have been recruited, and assist with the overall design and presentation of the system.
- Use an existing software tool which can run on a normal business computer. If the first application demands a knowledge engineering environment or a workstation then it is too complex for an inexperienced team.
- Direct the implementation team to deliver prototypes to users at an early stage. Nothing focuses the mind so much as having to produce a demonstrable product, and the feedback will be of inestimable value.

The message is that there is no substitute for experience. A successful first application will provide the incentive to apply that experience on a wider front, and to encourage management to recognise the value of using expert systems. In addition, it will introduce users to the possibility of sharing expert know-how, something which is difficult to appreciate without personal experience. The support of management and the demand from users are the driving forces which will allow expert systems to make a much wider contribution to business success.

References

References have deliberately been given sparingly, and have only been included where they are considered to make a definite contribution.

d'Agapeyeff, A. (1984) 'A short survey of expert systems in UK business' *Alvey News*, supplement to issue no. 4, April 1984.

Barr, A. and Feigenbaum, E. (1987) *The Handbook of Artificial Intelligence.* Addison Wesley.

Beerel, A. C. (1987) *Expert systems: strategic implications and applications.* Ellis Horwood, Chichester, England.

Bennett, J. S. and Engelmore, R. S. (1984) 'Experience using EMYCIN' in Buchanan, B. and Shortliffe, E. (eds) *Rule-Based Expert systems.* Addison Wesley, pp. 314–328.

Buzan, A. (1982) *Use your head.* BBC books (Ariel), London, England.

Erman, L. D. (1980) 'The HEARSAY-II speech understanding system: integrating knowledge to resolve uncertainties'. *Computing Surveys* **12** 2, pp. 213–253, June 1980.

Feigenbaum, E. A. and McCorduck, P. (1984) *The Fifth Generation.* Pan Books, London (also published in hardback by Addison Wesley, 1983).

Gammack, J. G. and Young, R. M. (1985) 'Psychological techniques for eliciting expert knowledge' in: Bramer, M. A. (ed.) *Research and Development in Expert Systems.* Cambridge University Press, Cambridge, England, pp. 105–112.

Haynes, C. (1986) Quoted in: *ICL Review*, April/May 1987, p. 21.

Hewitt, J. and Sasson, R. (1985) *Expert systems 1986: Volume 1 — USA and Canada.* Ovum Ltd, 44 Russell Square, London WC1B 4JP, England.

Hewitt, J., Timms, S. and d'Aumale, G. (1986) *Commercial expert systems in Europe.* Ovum Ltd, 44 Russell Square, London WC1B 4JP, England.

Johnson, P. E. (1983) 'What kind of expert should a system be' *The Journal of Medicine and Philosophy*, **8**, p. 77.

Lindsay, R. K., Buchanan, B. G., Feigenbaum, E. A. and Lederberg, J. (1980) *Applications of artifical intelligence for organic chemistry. The DENDRAL project.* McGraw-Hill.

McCorduck, P. (1979) *Machines who think.* W. H. Freeman & Co., San Fransisco.

McDermott, J. (1982) 'R1: a rule-based configurer of computer systems': *Artificial Intelligence*, **19**, 1, September 1982.

Moto-oka, T. (1982) *Fifth generation computer systems.* North Holland, Amsterdam and Elsevier, New York.

Sell, P. S. (1987) Response to a question at a meeting organised by the Mars company held in Henley, England.

Shortliffe, E. H. (1976) *Computer-based medical consultations: MYCIN.* Elsevier, New York.

Smith, R. G. and Baker, J. D. (1983) 'The DIPMETER advisor system'. *Proceedings IJCAI-83*, pp. 122–129.

Steels, L. (1987) 'Second generation expert systems' in: *Research and Development in Expert Systems III*, Bramer, M. A. (ed.). Cambridge Univerity Press, Cambridge, England, pp. 175–183.

Waterman, D. A. (1985) *A guide to expert systems.* Addison Wesley.

Wilmot, R. and Stanley, D. (1987) 'Organisational difficulties of expert system implementations'. Paper given at the annual meeting of the Xi User's Association, Coventry, England (unpublished).

Appendices

Appendix A — Glossary

AI programming language
  A computer programming language which is particularly suitable for artificial intelligence and expert systems work. Lisp and Prolog are the most important.

approximate reasoning
  A method of reasoning in which information can be true or false to any extent, usually represented by a number known as a certainty factor. (cf. 'crisp logic').

artificial intelligence ('AI')
  The attempt to develop machines which do things that, if done by a human, would be thought to require intelligence. For example: 'think', 'see', move about under their own control, or understand a conversation.

backward chaining
  Also known as 'goal directed reasoning' or 'conclusion driven reasoning'. An inferencing strategy whereby the expert system is given one or more possible solutions to explore (usually by the user), and goes back through a chain of rules to find out the questions which must be asked (cf. 'forward chaining').

Cobol
  The computer programming language in which most of the world's business systems are written.

causal model
  A model of decision making based on a theoretical description of the problem area, rather than on heuristics (q.v.).

crisp logic
  A method of reasoning in which information is treated as being true, false, or unknown. (cf. 'approximate reasoning', 'fuzzy logic').

database
   1 (data processing) An organised way of storing large amounts of data.
   2 (expert systems) The component of an expert system which is used by
   the inference engine (q.v.) as a 'notepad' to hold data, conclusions, and
   intermediate results.

decision tree
   A way of representing a series of choices, drawn like the branches of a
   tree.

decision support system
   A computer system which can present summarised data at a level which
   is convenient for decision making, e.g. market projections, aggregate
   sales and 'what if' projections.

declarative programming/knowledge
   Where the developer provides a statement of the problem, and the
   computer software works out a solution (c.f. 'procedural
   programming').

deep knowledge
   See 'formal knowledge'.

domain
   The area of expertise of an expert or an expert system.

expert system
   A computer system which contains the know-how of a human expert,
   and which can use this know-how to solve difficult problems.

expertise
   A deliberately general term meaning the knowledge, skill, or other
   abilities which distinguish an expert from non-experts.

external interface
   The component of an expert system which passes data between the
   inference engine and other programs, as opposed to the user (c.f. 'user
   interface').

fifth generation computer
   A term used by the Japanese in 1981 to describe their vision of a
   computer with advanced processing, storage, and communicating facilities (including speech and vision). It will not be technically feasible to
   start building such a machine until well into the 1990s.

formal knowledge
   A model, designed by knowledge engineers, of how the expert is

believed to think, with the intention of generalising what the expert says he does.

forward chaining
Also known as 'data driven reasoning'. An inferencing strategy whereby the expert system is given some data, and uses its rules to work out any new implications this might have (c.f. 'backward chaining').

frame
A method of representing knowledge as a data structure rather than in rules. For example, a frame representing a car might include colour, number of wheels, and how to start it. See also 'inheritance'.

fuzzy logic
A method of approximate reasoning in which truth values such as 'very true', 'fairly true', etc. are handled as possibility distributions. Hence a piece of information might be 'very true' to some extent, and also 'fairly true' to some different extent.

hardware
The pieces of a computer that you will have to find space for. As a minimum you can expect a box containing the processor, a TV-like screen with a keyboard, and a printer. (See also 'software').

heuristic
A rule of thumb; a piece of practical expertise which usually works in practice; a 'rule of good guessing'; a piece of 'compiled hindsight'. Expert systems are largely made up of heuristics.

induction
Finding the rules which seem to apply in a set of example decisions.

inferencing
A more accurate term than 'reasoning' used to describe the logical processes used by computers. Inferencing in expert systems is usually directed either towards specific conclusions (see 'backward chaining') or to find the implications of new data (see 'forward chaining').

inference engine
The 'reasoning' component of an expert system. That part which uses the rules and facts to work out conclusions.

inheritance
A feature of frame systems (q.v.) whereby if 'means of transport' has properties 'range' and 'cost', then because 'car' is also a 'means of transport' it automatically has properties 'range' and 'cost' too.

intelligent knowledge based system (IKBS)
A wishful name for knowledge based system (q.v.).

iteration
A problem solving technique whereby an approximate result is tested against what is wanted, and the discrepancies used to produce a better result. The process is then repeated many times, each cycle leading to a slightly improved result.

know-how
Practical expertise derived from experience. Typically found only in spoken advice.

knowledge based system (KBS)
A computer system in which the knowledge used is made explicit, and is separated from the computer programs which interpret and apply it. Expert systems are a particular type of knowledge based system.

knowledge engineering
The activity of building an expert system in cooperation with a subject expert.

knowledge engineering environment
An elaborate set of tools for building expert systems, hence also called a knowledge engineering 'toolkit'.

knowledge representation
Any of several ways of recording expertise for use in a computer. The best known are rules, networks, and frames.

Lisp
A programming language designed for LISt Processing, i.e. handling text in chained structures. Lisp is much favoured for artificial intelligence and expert systems work, particularly in the USA.

Lisp machine
A computer specially designed to run Lisp programs efficiently.

meta-rules (meta-knowledge)
Rules in the knowledge base which are not directly concerned with reaching conclusions, but which express an expert's knowledge of when to apply other rules. Know-how about using know-how.

natural language understanding
The ability to extract meaning from normal human conversation or from

documents. This has only been achieved on a computer for extremely restricted texts.

paradigm
A method of doing something.

parallel processing
Processing in many different places at once, rather than carrying out the same work on one processor, one step after another. This requires designs very different from today's computers (c.f. 'von Neumann computers').

procedural programming
The conventional way of programming computers, whereby the programmer has to specify every step which the program is to take (c.f. 'declarative programming').

Prolog
An AI programming language based on classical logic which encourages declarative programming (q.v.).

reasoning
The human process of interpreting data to produce new conclusions. Human reasoning is much more subtle than the inferencing procedures used in expert systems.

rule
A statement of expertise in the form:
IF these conditions are true
THEN these conclusions or actions follow.

semantic net (or network)
A way of representing knowledge as a network of concepts joined by lines showing the relationships between them.

shell
A software tool for building expert systems. A shell is an 'empty' system which contains no expert knowledge.

software
The (very complex) set of instructions which are necessary to make a computer work. A computer running an expert system will have an operating system ('DOS') plus additional software to run the expert system itself. You can think of the music on a cassette tape as being the 'software' in a taped music system: invisible, yet essential. (See also 'hardware').

symbolic reasoning
    Computing with ideas expressed in words. The words are 'symbols' standing for some idea which can be understood by people.

uncertain reasoning
    Computing with information which is labelled with a degree of uncertainty, e.g. with a certainty factor in the range 0 to 1.

user interface
    Either the appearance of the expert system as seen by its users, or the component of the expert system software which is responsible for handling the dialogue with the user (and hence controlling the appearance).

von Neumann computers
    The standard design of today's computers in which all of the instructions go through a single processor, one after the other. c.f. 'Parallel processing'.

workstation
    A powerful minicomputer, usually designed for a single user, with specialised facilities for expert systems development. Workstations are generally too expensive to be used for delivering expert systems to users.

Appendix B — Applications

B.1 HISTORIC APPLICATIONS

There are a few applications which have been quoted over many years. All are large, complex systems originating in the USA, and all aspire to be world class problem solvers. The fact that the same systems are quoted over and over again is indicative of the small number of applications which actually worked prior to about 1984.

The indisputable technical accomplishments of these systems usually take precedence over any discussion of their business success. X/CON's outstanding business success has already been described in section 4.6; it is the definitive example. Dendral has also been used in commercial laboratories. Elsewhere the position is less clear. For example, Mycin is undoubtedly a world-ranking consultant, but it is not used by physicians. The dialogue with the system takes up more time than the physicians are willing to give it. Mycin was used mainly by medical students, since it was a good source of knowledge, and endlessly patient. Similarly, it is not clear if Dipmeter Adviser has ever been commercially viable, although development work has continued over several years.

The moral is that just because an application is well known, it cannot be assumed to be a success in business terms.

Dendral
>   Dendral (Lindsay *et al.* 1980) was a pioneering system which proved to be extremely effective at deducing the structure of complex molecules from laboratory measurements (e.g. from a spectrometer). It is believed to be in use in many laboratories today. Meta-Dendral was an associated system which aimed to deduce good rules from sets of known results.

Dipmeter Advisor
>   Dipmeter Advisor (Smith and Baker, 1983) attempts to identify the geological structure around a borehole by analysing recordings ('logs') made by instruments lowered down the hole. If done manually, each log could take several hours for a skilled expert to analyse.

Hearsay-II
>   Hearsay-II (Erman, 1980) was an early attempt to interpret human

speech. It pioneered the 'blackboard' architecture now favoured for the very difficult area of real-time expert systems.

Mycin

Mycin (Shortliffe, 1976) is a medical system which diagnoses infections such as meningitis, and goes on to recommend appropriate drug treatment. It uses a knowledge of infecting organisms to interpret the patient's symptoms, history, and laboratory tests. Mycin must be the best known of all expert systems. Its famous achievement was in reaching, and sometimes surpassing, the diagnostic skills of the world's best physicians in this specialist area. It was also the first to have effective explanation.

Prospector

Using a variety of geological data about a given site, Prospector estimates the probability of finding minerals such as sulphur and zinc. It acts as a consultant for geologists, and has been credited with identifying a valuable molybdenum deposit which human geologists had passed over. Prospector's use of certainty factors is echoed in many present-day systems.

Sacon

An early success in building an expert system as a front end to a conventional computer program, in this case a forbiddingly complex engineering package known as MARC. Sacon (Bennett and Engelmore, 1984) guided engineers in formulating their problem and using MARC effectively.

X/CON (originally R1)

X/CON (McDermott, 1982) configures computers from DEC's VAX range. It is believed to be the world's most profitable expert system, and is in daily use at sites in the USA and Europe. X/CON has spawned associated systems X/SITE (computer room planning) and X/SEL (salesman's assistant).

B.2 CURRENT APPLICATIONS

These are all examples of applications in live use or under development. There is considerable difficulty in obtaining details about many of them for reasons of competitive advantage. This is particularly true for applications in finance or business management. The following examples are in the public domain.

Burner fault diagnosis and repair

This system, developed by BP, assists engineers with the specialist task of adjusting and repairing the burners used to heat crude oil when it is brought to the surface. By doing so it allows the flow of crude oil to be maintained at its maximum, a flow which can be worth £1 million a day. The system has been distributed to offshore sites around the world.

Clarifying employment law
Most of the UK law on employment is aimed at ensuring fair treatment for employees. Hasty, thoughtless, or unreasonable action by an employer can lead to substantial penalties as well as industrial unrest. This system helps employers to act fairly and wisely according to the law. It has also been used by employees to guide their negotiations with an employer!

Corporate evaluation
This system takes the user through an assessment of the creditworthiness of a potential borrower or investment target. Its philosophy is that financial measures cannot be interpreted without an understanding of the underlying business. Its main use is in providing an analysis method to those who make lending/investment decisions, or as a second opinion.

Engine test selection
Rolls Royce subject their aircraft engines to a continuous programme of tests. In the most extreme cases an engine valued at perhaps £100,000 will be deliberately destroyed. It is obviously important to set up every test to obtain the maximum benefit, and this calls for a rare level of experience and skill. A highly experienced engineer built this system largely by himself as an aide mémoire and as a guide for his colleagues.

Monitoring steam turbines
Westinghouse of the USA have an expert system which continuously monitors vibration measurements from electricity generators. The system gives early warning of problems, thereby avoiding potentially massive repair bills. It was justified on the basis of 1% improvement in availability, which is said to be worth $2.5 million per annum.

Organisational performance
The UK's Department of Health and Social Security is required to scrutinise the performance of its operating units on a regular basis. This is done by analysing routine statistical reports. The expert system takes over the tedious, but technical, task of calculating the 'performance indicators' and picking out those reports which warrant further investigation.

Recommending crop treatments
This system recommends the most cost-effective spraying programme for the wheat crop in a given field. It uses the past history of the field, the farmer's individual requirements, and a database of agricultural chemicals. Funded by ICI, it is available to farmers as a service from agrochemical suppliers.

Security export regulations

The security export regulations (commonly known as the COCOM agreement) prohibit the supply of advanced technology to Eastern bloc countries. The regulations are complex, interdependent, and technical. This system contains the know-how of key, Government specialists to help the responsible department interpret the regulations consistently and accurately.

Other applications include the following:

Management and sales

Assessment for promotion
Business 'health'
Claiming capital allowances
Contingency planning and incident recovery
Cross-selling to existing clients
Evaluating business decisions
Guide to new product proposals
Guide to proposals for capital expenditure
Guidelines for successful takeovers
How to be effective in retail buying
Identifying under performance in business units
Internal audit
Introducing computers to a business
Management consultancy
Negotiating multi-product deals with major customers
Personnel management
Pricing of customised products
Quality standards
Recruitment
Sales commission and bonus
Siting retail outlets

Computing

Advanced operating systems
Analysing crash dumps
Capacity planning
Configuring computer hardware
Disk-drive quality assurance
Fault diagnosis (several examples)
Front end to complex packages
Help desk assistant (several examples)
Interpreting performance statistics
Optimising database usage
Out-of-hours operator's assistant
Selecting data communications services
Selecting software to best meet given requirements
Self-help system for users with equipment problems

System set-up and tuning
Terminal user's assistant for communications problems

Finance and financial services

Administering insurance syndicates
Advice on letters of credit
Audit planning
Authorising credit card limits
Commodity buying
Compliance with statutory requirements
Credit evaluation of businesses and individuals
Electronic banking services
Forecasting exchange rate movements
Foreign exchange trading
Insurance underwriting
Investment planning
Legality of making takeover bids
Life insurance as security against loans
Managing stock portfolios
Monitoring market trends
Mortgage adviser
Personal tax assessment and planning
Processing loan applications
Repatriation of funds (tax treaties)
Risk assessment
Securities trading
Selecting financial instruments

Laws, procedures and administration

Clarifying the law on unfair dismissal
Company pension entitlement and benefits
Compulsory management reporting
Data Protection Act adviser
Documentation for public tenders
Eligibility for staff loans
Entitlement to, and processing of, welfare benefits
Export arrangements
Guide to fire safety for major stores
Guide to the law on maternity benefits and claims
Improving consistency between different administrative units
Operating internal procedures (many examples)
Staff relocation arrangements
Validating application forms

Manufacturing and Engineering

Alarm interpretation

Configuring complex equipment
Controlling process plant
Design and selection (many examples, e.g. new detergents, gas/oil separators, power generating systems, steel framed buildings)
Diagnosis and repair of telephone handsets
Evaluating actual and predicted corrosion problems
Equipment fault diagnosis (many examples, e.g. carburettors, process plant, electronic equipment)
Equipment tuning
Generating assembly plans
Guide to engineering standards and sources of information
Guide to machine shop organisation
Identifying machine and operator faults from packaging errors
Interpretation of helicopter vibration tests
Maintaining product quality
Maintenance of welding machines
Monitoring rotating machinery (several examples)
Parts list and specifications
Predicting fatigue cracking in steel structures
Production planning
Recognising, correcting and repairing faults in industrial furnaces
Recommending alloys for corrosive environments
Recording the know-how of a commissioning team
Selecting industrial insulation materials
Setting up aircraft engine tests
Troubleshooting

Others

Air crew scheduling
Careers advice
Crop management
First aid
Interpreting psychological tests
Minimising ship berthing charges
Risk of adverse drug reaction
Route planning
Schoolroom systems
Sports coach tutor
Treatment of crops

Appendix C — Sources of information

C.1 ORGANISATIONS

British Computer Society, Specialist Group on Expert Systems
> The only large grouping of expert systems people in the UK, and a useful source of contacts. Regular meetings are held in London and the North of England, and there is an annual conference (see section C.2). BCS membership is not required.
>
> Contact: Ms Judith Dennison, SGES Membership Officer, School of Cognitive Sciences, University of Sussex, Falmer, Brighton BN1 9QN.

American Association for Artificial Intelligence (AAAI)
> A very large, US organisation based in California. Worth joining for the AI Magazine alone (see section C.2).
>
> Contact: AAAI, 445 Burgess Drive, Menlo Park, CA 94025, USA.

C.2 CONFERENCES

Historically, the major international conferences have been heavily biased towards research, with stated aims such as to 'stress the computational principles underlying cognition and perception in man and machine'. The interests of academics are clearly different to those of industry. Some organisers have responded to the industrial emphasis on applications by splitting conferences into 'science' and 'engineering' themes. However, businessmen should still be selective about international conferences as the practical content may be small. All large conferences seeking a business audience now have an exhibition of hardware, software and service suppliers.

For management awareness, a number of commercial organisations run introductory courses on expert systems. These are widely advertised in the computer trade press and by mail-shots to training officers and others on their mailing lists. We recommend choosing a course which has at least two speakers from industry, preferably with differing experiences. Many professional associations also have an expert systems activity tailored specifically to their member's interests. Any manager involved with an expert systems project should have at least the level of awareness provided by an introductory seminar.

The comments made below are intended to give an indication of the past character of each event. Naturally, they may be superseded by changes in the organiser's intentions.

Avignon

An annual conference held in Avignon, France. This began as a highly academic event but has become more industry oriented. The majority of the contributions have been from France.

AAAI

Sponsored by the American Association for Artificial Intelligence, and a major annual event. This is the premier conference in the USA, and attracts well known names from research and industry all over the world. Contributions have become so numerous that up to five themes have been run in parallel during the week-long conference. The associated exhibition and supplier 'events' can be expected to include every significant US product and service, plus those organisations from overseas which are actively marketing in North America.

ECAI

The European Conference on Artificial Intelligence. A biannual event alternating with IJCAI. In the past this has favoured the more weighty theoretical contributions.

Expert Systems

Sponsored by the British Computer Society's Specialist Group on Expert Systems. This is an annual conference, lasting a week, and held in England. It is the principal technical conference for the UK, and also attracts interest from Europe. The focus is on expert systems rather than artificial intelligence, so topics such as machine vision and robotics are not usually discussed. There is a mixture of academically refereed papers and industrial contributions. The conference has previously included tutorials aimed at management and at intermediate-level expert systems builders, plus an interesting variety of fringe events. The exhibition usually includes most of the British product and service suppliers, plus the European distributors of US products such as workstations and knowledge engineering environments. Recommended.

IJCAI

Sponsored by International Joint Conferences on Artificial Intelligence Inc. A biannual conference which alternates between Europe and North America. Recently it has featured advanced tutorials and a substantial exhibition. This is the largest international event, comparable in size with the AAAI meetings in the USA. Past proceedings for both IJCAI and AAAI are available from Morgan Kaufmann Publishers Inc, PO Box 50490, Palo Alto, CA 94303, USA.

KBS
>   Organised by Online, a commercial conferencing company, KBS is a two
>   or three day conference held in London. The programme is more varied
>   than those organised by the professional associations, but the bias has
>   been towards applications rather than theories. The exhibition has
>   included all the leading UK suppliers.

The International Expert Systems Conference and Exhibition
>   Organised by publishers Learned Information, this is an annual event
>   lasting two days, held in London. The organisers have sought to combine
>   both research and practical contributions, and in the past there has been
>   a mini-exhibition.

C.3 PERIODICALS

Articles on expert systems have appeared in many professional journals as
well as those specialising in artificial intelligence or expert systems. Fortunately, much of the hyperbole surrounding 'thinking machines' has now
disappeared, and articles are generally of a more considered tone. However,
articles describing research work which are intended for a general readership sometimes express the excitement of the future vision without clarifying
the current position. This has the potential for considerable harm, as it
generates undue expectations among business managers who might sponsor
an expert system project.

Selected articles and books are given in the References section. Major
publishers such as Addison Wesley, Cambridge University Press, Ellis
Horwood, Morgan Kaufmann, and Wiley also have specialist AI/Expert
systems lists. Note that many of these books concentrate on technology
rather than profitable applications.

The following journals are all useful:

AI Magazine
>   Applications, methods, and research in progress are covered in substan-
>   tial but still highly readable articles. Recommended. Free to AAAI
>   members (see section C.1).

Artificial Intelligence Journal
>   A scholarly publication for academically refereed papers on artificial
>   intelligence. The *Nature* of the AI world. Published by Elsevier Science
>   Publishers Inc, Journal Information Center, 52 Vanderbilt Avenue,
>   New York, NY 10017, USA. Reduced rates for AAAI members.

BCS-SGES Newsletter
>   The organ of the British Computer Society's Specialist Group on Expert
>   Systems (see section C.2). Definitely a newsletter, with a mixed bag of
>   articles, comment, news, and reviews.

Expert Systems

A UK journal which publishes refereed papers mainly from academic sources, but which aims for a wider readership. Published by Learned Information Ltd, Hinksey Hill, Oxford OX1 5AU, England.

Expert Systems User

A 'chatty' journal which has published numerous descriptions of commercial applications, if not in any great depth. It also features product news and reviews, interview, conference dates, etc. Published by Learned Information Ltd, Hinksey Hill, Oxford OX1 5AU, England.

Knowledge Engineering Review

This journal encourages reviews of theory and techniques in knowledge engineering, with the aim of communicating these to system developers and teachers. It avoids descriptions of particular expert systems or specialised research papers. Published by Journals Department, Cambridge University Press, The Edinburgh Building, Shaftesbury Road, Cambridge CB2 2RU, England.

Appendix D — Example project costings

These examples of expenditure on actual projects should be treated purely as illustrations. They are intended to show the degree of variability involved.

Case 1
A system to handle a specialised aspect of government regulations. This was developed using an expert system shell running on a personal computer to the point of being suitable for use within the relevant government department. It was built by an experienced consultant, a knowledge engineer, a lead expert and two other experts, in an elapsed time of six weeks. The total budget was approximately £30,000, including knowledge engineering effort, expert time (estimated), and the purchase of a computer.

The key issue was to capture the unwritten know-how of the government experts. This amounted to detailed commentary and interpretation of the regulations themselves. Being intended for internal use meant that the users would be familiar with the jargon and concepts; a general audience would not, and would require a more explanatory system.

Case 2
A guide for small businesses when introducing their first business computer. It was developed using an expert system shell running on a personal computer, and was refined to the point of being ready for initial field use. It was built by a consultant, two knowledge engineers, a lead expert and four other experts over four months. The total budget was approximately £50,000 including expert time.

Building the first prototype required about 40% of the total budget. Reviewing the prototype with experts and potential users and the subsequent refinement accounted for the remaining 60%.

Case 3
A program to identify favoured routes for travelling by rail between thirteen cities. It was written in Prolog running on a minicomputer as a high quality demonstration of the potential for a full system. The total budget was approximately £200,000, although a substantial amount was spent on developing a user interface which used a light pen in place of a keyboard.

The type of application envisaged for a full system might be to route flights between several European cities, a considerably more complex task.

The crux of the problem was to search among the possible routes, using a few heuristics to guide the search. The system had only a small component of know-how. Scaling up from the 'toy' problem chosen for the pilot system to the complexities of (say) Europe or the USA was expected to pose a considerable challenge. An intermediate stage will be needed to verify that the techniques will indeed scale up to meet the full requirement.

Case 4

A system to advise risk assessors on the loading of insurance premiums for fire risks. This system was developed using a knowledge engineering environment, to the point of being a management demonstration. The total budget was approximately £250,000.

A formal knowledge approach was used. Substantial effort was devoted to devising a model of the reasoning process, a computer language in which to express it, and a method of describing the knowledge on paper so that it could be discussed with the experts.

Case 5

An automotive company is currently working on an expert system to diagnose faults in gearboxes. By seeking a generalised model of the expert's diagnostic skills, it is hoped to be able to diagnose faults which are new to the expert, and even hypothetical faults in designs which have yet to be manufactured. Seven knowledge engineers/AI programmers and an external consultant are involved, using workstations and a knowledge engineering environment. The projected cost is in the region of £500,000 over two years.

This is a clear example of the 'intelligent machine' approach. We wish them luck.

Index